Memory and Salvation

Memory and Salvation

CHARLES ELLIOTT

DARTON·LONGMAN+TODD

First published in 1995 by
Darton, Longman and Todd Ltd
1 Spencer Court
140–142 Wandsworth High Street
London SW18 4JJ

© 1995 Charles Elliott

The right of Charles Elliott to be identified as the Author of this work
has been asserted in accordance with the Copyright,
Designs and Patents Act 1988

ISBN 0–232–52141–7

A catalogue record for this book is available
from the British Library

Phototypeset by Intype, London
Printed and bound in Great Britain
by Page Bros, Norwich

Contents

Acknowledgements

This book started life as the Idreos Lectures given in 1991 at Manchester College, Oxford. I should like to thank the founder and the trustees of the lectures for inviting me to give them, and the President and Fellows of Manchester College for their warm welcome while I was delivering them.

In extending the material and preparing it for publication, I owe so many unpayable debts that I shrink from mentioning any individually. I have learnt much from Fr Gerry Hughes SJ and my other collaborators in the erstwhile Institute of Contemporary Spirituality, and it was their questions about the relationship between the outer world and the practices of spirituality that put me on the trail that led to this book.

Many academic friends have been amazingly generous with their time and care. Colleagues at Trinity Hall, especially Alison Liebling and Jonathan Steinberg, have sustained me when I was near giving up and they, as well as David Ford, Chris Rowland, Nick Adams, Frazer Watts and Walter Wink, read an early draft and made many valuable suggestions for its improvement. Helen Muller has taught me much in many areas, and in particular guided me through the literature on Melanie Klein.

My colleague William Clocksin was inexhaustibly patient with my incompetence in the face of modern technology and generous with time and equipment.

My biggest debt inevitably lies to my family who have endured a cuckoo in the nest for longer than any of us would have wished. They have been immensely tolerant and supportive.

CHARLES ELLIOTT
Trinity Hall, Cambridge
January 1995

PART ONE

1

Memory at Work

One of the basic arguments of this book is that we create our world in reaction to conscious and unconscious memories, and we shall examine the theoretical underpinnings and theological implications of this contention in subsequent chapters. Before we do so, however, here are four true stories that illustrate the part memory plays in creating the world. The first is about an individual, and the other three are about different kinds of social group. For memory belongs not just to the individual person, but to the group too, whether that be the family, the tribe or the nation.

The Individual

Roger was brought up by a father who, despite his many strengths and virtues, was cut off from his own emotions, with the result that, in Roger's eyes, he was a demanding tyrant who could rarely be satisfied by Roger's achievements and whose tongue lashed his young son as mercilessly as a whip.

When Roger married and started a family, it was unsurprising that many of the features of his own childhood were repeated in the next generation. Roger was a harsh, demanding father who expected of his children the same devotion to 'work' as he, workaholic as he was, brought to everything he did. His wife found this side of Roger's personality hard to tolerate and the tension in the marriage became increasingly hard for each of them to handle. The combination of marital discord and an emotionally absent though achievement-driven father brought their second child to near disaster. He failed key exams at school, started stealing, and was later discovered to be taking hard drugs.

It was only when a wise friend suggested that the whole family

1

go regularly to family counselling that Roger began to recognise how his conscious and unconscious memories of his own childhood were being replayed in his relationships with his own children. To some of those memories he had ready access and could make the connections between his own experiences as child and father quite readily. To others, especially those associated with conflict or psychic pain, the path was less direct and rapid: he needed time and an empathetic environment before he could recall even fragments. He began to realise how much material lay buried in his unconscious and to surmise that that too was being played out in his relationships with his family. Only long psychotherapy or psychoanalysis would enable him to recover more of it – and look afresh at his own behaviour in its light.

For reasons that need not detain us here, Roger declined further individual therapy. He and his wife Jane jointly decided that the dozen or so sessions with the whole family had given them sufficient to work on; and in the event, family relationships began to improve so dramatically that Roger lost the incentive to go further.

His later comment on the process was illuminating. 'I never even began to imagine', he said, 'how far I was the captive of my own past in the family situation. It is not just a question of role models, important thought that may have been. It was much more the memory of how I thought my father had "made" me what I am. I wanted to do that for my own sons, without ever stopping to ask if they could or should become what I wanted to "make" them – in memory of my own father. Now I think we are all shot of that and I am free to let them explore their own possibilities – and to share that exploration with Jane and me.'

The Group

The second story is less narrative than a picture of clip of film, a glimpse of a scene that, like a Surrealist painting, exposes the unconscious forces at work in a conventional environment.

The scene is Cardiff Arms Park in the closing minutes of a rugby international between England and Wales. Wales are three points down, after a dour game, played in mud with a heavy, greasy ball. Wales is given a scrum down, ten metres from the English line.

The crowd, mostly Welsh, goes mad. I watch the faces round me

2

– brown-eyed, weathered, almost square. Celts to a man. The intensity of feeling is palpable. The shouts, the catcalls at the English players, the abuse, the tense determination as each man around me *wills* the Welsh pack to drive over the English line – all assume a quality that belies the muttered comment ten minutes later when Wales have lost: 'It's only a game, for God's sake.'

It is not only a game – and the need for one Welshman to remind another of it is itself a symbol of the statement's mendaciousness. This is not a game: it is a re-presentation of an old rivalry, a bitter enmity that has been played out again and again since long before Tudor times. We are reliving resentments that have their roots deep in history, refreshed by the Merthyr Rising and by the Rebecca Riots; by the tragi-comic antics of the 'Scotch cattle'; by the unrelievedly tragic butchery of the mining industry; by every sleight, real or imagined, meted out by English arrogance on Welsh inferiority and kept alive by English (and in part Welsh) resistance to the rebirth of the Welsh language.

Such memories are not in the forefront of the minds of these disappointed Welsh rugby fans, as they mooch disconsolately to the car park, hardly able to bring themselves to discuss the game. Nor are they in a more abstract sense part of the *Zeitgeist*, the common web of assumptions and habits of thought common to everyone brought up in the Valleys. That is to eviscerate their power, reducing them to a shadow of their real potency. They are a folk memory – but more than a folk memory: a representation of what it means to be Welsh, a re-making-present of the fundamental delineaments of Welsh identity.

Accordingly, to suffer the humiliation of defeat on the rugby field at the hands of the quintessence of English arrogance and self-assured superiority is an outward sign, more than symbolic, of the continuity of the history of being on the underside – of defeat, of manipulation, of domination and oppression. Memories, whether conscious, half-remembered or temporarily lost in the unconscious, cohere with present experience. They are part of a continuing self-narrative.

Whatever else, it is not just a game.

The Nation

The third story hardly needs retelling in its narrative form, for the history of the Birmingham Six has become notorious, made the more so by film and memoir. What needs to be asked in our context, however, is how it came to happen: how successive waves of policemen, scientists, lawyers and judges came to behave how they did, with the result that in aggregate they brought British justice into worldwide disrepute. A number of memories may help us understand that.

The first is the all too conscious set of memories of the savagery of IRA mainland killing campaigns. Such memories ignite fear, crude, physical fear of tissue and blood, of physical destruction. The IRA mainland bombing campaign was at its height. People were being killed and maimed randomly, without reason or warning: in the South-east last month; in London last week; in the Midlands today. Where tomorrow? Who tomorrow?

The memory of what had happened was projected into what could happen. And in that atmosphere of tension – it actually stopped well short of panic – politicians demand action. The political memory is that the public display of incompetence or carelessness costs votes. Macmillan, Heath, Callaghan, all had seen public support ebb away once they were susceptible to the charge of complacency or ineffectiveness. So kick the police into action; *make* them deliver a culprit. For a culprit is a scapegoat – and a scapegoat will relieve tension, as, remember, it always has. And if the quality of the evidence against the culprit is not *quite* as good as the most pernickety lawyer would demand, well . . .

But that was not all. Another set of memories was at work, the memories of the tricky, feckless but unscrupulous Irish, the Irish of Captain Boycott, of mutilated cattle and burnt homes, of the Easter Rising and secret collusion with Hitler. The social memories that underlie prejudice are seldom re-examined with the detached eye of the scholarly historian. Steeped in their own ambiguous relationship to truth (and what in this context is truth?) they generate an assumption that Irish – working-class Catholic Irish, moreover – are not to be trusted. So here are six Irishmen, some of whom are known to be sympathetic to the IRA; all of whom left Birmingham for Ireland

4

shortly after the bombs went off. They deny that they are involved. But then they would, wouldn't they? They are Irish.

So far we have been dealing with individual or social memories that are either conscious or, at least in principle, available to the conscious memory. But there is more to it than that. As we shall see in a later chapter, some depth psychologists teach that we live in the fear of repressed memories of inner chaos and disintegration. These memories are not immediately available to us in adult life, but they are still powerfully at work in the unconscious, shaping the way we see and relate to the world around us.

I am not concerned here to establish the scientific basis of this approach; I ask the reader to grant it for the sake of argument. It relates to the case of the Birmingham Six in this way. If we are persecuted by memories of primal chaos, permanently terrified of the collapse of both inner and outer worlds, no wonder the Birmingham bomb triggered so unreflective a reaction. Take the judgment of Lord Denning. Read in its entirety, it is a masterpiece of legal reasoning and the careful weighing of evidence and precedent – until he has to contemplate the fact that allowing the appeal would be to admit that the whole legal system had made an error of historic proportions. To admit as much was to admit the powers of anarchy to the citadel of British justice. It was unthinkable that the British police force was corrupt, violent and untruthful; that Government forensic scientists could bend evidence to suit the police's case; that the jury system can be deeply flawed. And it was unthinkable not because the evidence was insubstantial; it was unthinkable in the more literal sense that to think it is to contemplate a kind of destructured chaos that is intensely frightening – because it chimes with unconscious fears that can never be stilled.

It is expedient that six are wrongfully incarcerated . . .

The Tribe

There is even less need to recount in detail the history of the massacres in Rwanda that made stark headlines first in 1959 and then, more horrendously, in May 1994. The scale, crude barbarity and thoroughness of the killings were – and remain on each rereading of eyewitness accounts – numbing. What was going on?

It is dangerous to give glib answers at this point. No *one* explanation fits perfectly such facts as we have. It will be years before enough research can carefully unfold the trauma of those weeks and what lay behind it. Political, economic, agrarian, social, ethnic, even personal factors all played a part – and the mix almost certainly varied from place to place and from group to group. But to students of the role that social memory plays in shaping the lives of people, the story, however retold, cannot escape an account of the relations between Tutsi and Hutu.

In pre-colonial days, the two peoples lived symbiotically, with the agricultural Hutu trading amicably with the pastoral Tutsi. But the Belgian colonisers considered the tall, fair-skinned Tutsi more advanced evolutionarily than the smaller, darker Hutu, and therefore poured the meagre resources of the colonial state into the advancement of the Tutsi to the neglect of the Hutu. Further, they co-opted the Tutsi into the lower rungs of the administration of the colonial state, with all that that meant in terms of the imposition of the hated corvée, the exaction of fines, the burning of recalcitrant villages.

In the final years of colonialism, however, the Belgians reversed their policy. The oppressed became the new oppressors. Tutsi fled, to return thirty years later as the Rwanda Patriotic Front, committed to the wholesale slaughter of their hard-line Hutu persecutors – a commitment matched by many of the Hutu, killing by killing, in the grisly arithmetic of genocide.

Of course, other factors played a part, not least of them the intense pressure on land and the grim calculation that it is wiser to kill one's neighbour of a different ethnic group and annexe his miserable acre of land than wait to be killed by him from the same motive. But behind even this rationale lurked a social memory of wrongs perpetrated and suffered; of injustices meted out and borne in silence at the end of the barrel of a colonial gun; of a deep-dyed longing that one day the score may be settled, the slate wiped clean – and the land rid of the Other.

No doubt these semi-conscious memories were more alive for some than for others; and no doubt propagandists on both sides played a dishonourable part in heightening a reconstructed and distorted memory for each group. It is therefore important to avoid an over-determinism that sees the memories of the group or the individual as the only spring of action. That would be absurd. Yet there is one sense of memory as a spur to action with which we shall be centrally concerned in the chapters that follow that does seem to have been operating in this context. It can be put like this: those Rwandans so caught up in their own understanding of their history that they had lost their freedom of action – for example, to denounce the killing or to refuse to take part in it – were the compulsive victims of their own memories. Like the representatives of the British legal system in the case of the Birmingham Six or the Welshmen longing for a victory over the English, they cannot (or cannot normally be expected to) flout their own history, their own memories of strata of inter-actions and relationships. The status of those memories – conscious or unconscious, individual or social – may be important at one level; at a more fundamental level, it is irrelevant. What matters is that individuals and groups are held in thrall by those memories. They become their more or less willing slaves.

The question then becomes: How may they be freed? It is to that question that we shall come later in the book.

First, however, there is much ground clearing and initial ploughing to be done. In the second part of this chapter I shall look at different types of memory and introduce, in very summary form, certain types of psychoanalytic thinking that illuminate the part they play in shaping the world in which we live and the way we react to it. The rest of Part 1 will look further at the role of memory in social life; Part 2 will then explore this role from the standpoint initially of the psychoanalytic tradition and then the more social psychological. The focus of each chapter will be the same: What account does this genre of theory give of the role of memory in shaping action, of both individuals and groups? Wherever appropriate, I shall give examples of the ways in which the theories might be thought to 'work' in practical terms.

By the end of Part 2 we shall be conscious of the scale of the challenge to Christian theology that this type of thinking represents. For we shall have seen that there are powerful reasons for acknowledg-ing that we are unfree over a substantial range of decisions we make both as individuals and as members of groups. In what sense, then, can we say that Christ has set us free? If we are constantly acting out inner material, how may it be said that, 'in Christ', we find a new freedom? This will be the focus of Part 3. It will involve us in looking again at theories of the Atonement, the locus of accounts of Christ's freeing action; and at our understanding of the nature of the Church, the company, supposedly, of those made free in Christ. We shall also have to look at the nature of the memories we have of Jesus himself, and how we read those memories. For we can see at once that the way we read them will be shaped by the other memories we already have. If 'the memory of me' is to have, as I shall argue it can and should have, a genuinely liberating effect on all our actions and the world we make through them, it is important to consider not only what constitutes that memory but how we appropriate it.

It is clear that the memories we looked at in the first part of this chapter are of very different kinds. Some are individual; some are collective or social. Some are, in some sense that will not always be easy to nail down, 'truer' than others. Some are conscious, at the forefront of people's minds; others are less conscious or even quite unconscious. When we talk about the power of memory to make and shape the world, then, we are clearly using that term as an umbrella. It covers a wide range of somewhat different phenomena. That implies that the first step in the argument must be to clarify the various senses that may be attached to the notion of memory. Inevitably, then, the flavour of the rest of this chapter is anticipatory, looking forward to more detailed treatment of memory-concepts in later chapters.

The grid below may help to elucidate immediately the various types of memory with which we shall be concerned. A glance at the grid shows that there are no less than ten different usages, all but one of which will at some point or another be important to this argument. Let us therefore go through them one by one, without anticipating the fuller discussion that the succeeding chapters contain, but making clear the precise meanings and differences between meanings, in order to minimise confusion hereafter.

To assist the reader to follow the inevitably compressed discussion that follows, I have indicated the sections in this chapter in which the various cells of the matrix are discussed. I have also put in parentheses further important distinctions which are introduced in those sections.

A Memory Matrix

	Individual		Collective
Conscious		2	(Collective/social 3)
Less than conscious		4	
Unconscious		5	
Repressed	6		7
Habit		8	(Learned/instinctual)

1 The Individual/Collective Distinction

At first sight this distinction between individual and collective looks commonsensical and unproblematic. There are many memories that are unique to me – my childhood, the memory of my feelings, significant milestones in my 'faith autobiography' – and there are plenty of memories that I share with the whole nation or with particular subsets of it. I remember VE Day and the great snow of 1947, both events that anyone alive in the UK in the 1940s is likely to share with me; and I remember Len Hutton batting magnificently for Yorkshire and the lamentable performance of my College football team when I was a member of it, memories that will be shared by cricketing Yorkshiremen and a somewhat smaller group of failed Oxonian footballers respectively.

It would be nice to think that that is all that can or need be said about it. But alas, it is not quite as easy as that. Maurice Halbwachs, one of the first modern philosophers to take memory seriously and still a potent voice in the field, points out that individual and social memory are umbilically linked in the sense that I can have very few memories, except perhaps of states of my own inner consciousness, that do not depend in some way upon my membership of a wider community.[1] This is a point that has been taken up and developed by those known now as social interactionists, who put much emphasis on the way we describe ourselves to ourselves; that is, the way we construct our own narratives. For example, the memories of my childhood are peopled by other actors – family, friends, chance encounters – and it is in remembering the way I interacted with them that I remember myself as a child. Indeed, it would be hard to give an account of my childhood without at the same time giving proper recognition to a large cast of people who impinged upon me

9

during that period. For I did not exist in a social vacuum: I knew myself largely in encounters with other people, a point to which we shall have to return in the next chapter when we look briefly at the relationship of memory and personal identity.

For the moment, notice only that my individual memories of my childhood are individual in two rather narrow senses of that term. First, they are individual in the sense that it is I that recall them; that it is I that hold, as it were, the camera that records the scene. And second, in so far as they have a particular emotional load – the devastation of my first day at boarding school, for example – it is my fears, anxieties, griefs and traumas that I recall. I cannot and do not recall anyone else's; and no one else can recall mine 'from the inside' because I alone experienced them.

2 Conscious Memories

Most of our memories most of the time are not fully in our consciousness: I do not walk about thinking of the memory of a childhood picnic, even though if challenged I can recall the occasion more or less easily and accurately to mind. Partly as an aid to memory, many memories are held in narrative form, and the content of those narratives – which may be more or less 'accurate', more or less schematised for the sake of making them easier to remember – can play a powerful part in shaping the world and the way people react to it. They may, for example, remember that things were a great deal better under a different political dispensation; or they may remember that they personally have always been inadequate, failures at all they have attempted. Clearly, each set of memories will trigger quite different behavioural reactions, and each set of reactions, repeated in a nation or a sub-group, will assume specific structural form. These are themes to which we shall return in Chapters 6, 7 and 8.

There is one important point that applies to conscious social memory, and that is the importance of ritual or ceremony in maintaining it. These may be national ceremonies like coronations, victory parades, Labour Days, commemorative holidays like Bastille Day or Thanksgiving Day; but they may also be much more local and community based, like Beating the Bounds or well-dressing. They may take a very free form with the naming of the particular day as the

10

central commemorative event (like Martin Luther Day or Guy Fawkes Day) or they may be rigorously choreographed like the Cenotaph ceremony or many liturgies. What is significant in each, however, is that they involve people, ideally the whole community, in the performance of a specific event of re-enactment, re-presentation – in other words, making present again, putting the remembered event back in the present tense. 'The Guy *is* burning,' the child squeaks as she watches the bonfire in the back garden.

3 Social and Collective Memories

Although I have so far used social and collective memory interchange-ably, there are two senses that need unravelling. There is first the memory of any collectivity – a village, a trade union, a school, a firm – of its own history, its own past, its what-makes-us-as-we-are. This is not to deny, of course, that different individuals in the collectivity would give different accounts with different emphases; nor that some will be fairly ignorant of any historical past. None the less, I want to argue that it makes sense to speak of collectives of people having a shared memory of their past, and of that memory being one of the things that gives any collectivity its sense of identity. Think, for instance, of the Roman Catholic Church in Poland or Muslims in Bosnia or, for that matter, of the Orange lodges in Northern Ireland.[2]

There is a different sense to be hung on the term 'social memory'. By that I mean the more or less deliberate attempt by a particular social group to give history its own stamp. The extreme example is a totalitarian regime that claims a monopoly of remembering, and seeks to encourage its people to forget by restricting consciousness to the present, to domestic trivia or to work for the State.[3] In this way, the State authorities may seek to limit or change the awareness of the people's own corporate or collective identity, a theme trenchantly analysed in the case of Czechoslovakia by the novelist Milan Kundera. He quotes his friend Milan Herbl's shocking aphorism: the first step in liquidating a people is to erase its memory.[4] As I shall use these terms, then, collective memory is a neutral term; social memory is the memory of history's winners.

As Fentress and Wickham have shown with reference to rural France and Sicily, the memories of the collective may be very different from those of the social winners. For example, they report Joutard's surprise at how little of the French Revolution and of the First World War peasants in the Cevennes now remember. They conclude like this: ' "Great Events" of the past are designated as such by people external to most local societies and certainly all peasant societies. . . . Just because historians regard Napoleon as worth remembering and discussing, other people are not required to think in the same way or indeed to commemorate any Great Event at all.'[5] More poignantly, they also show how the collective memory of the Rhondda strike of 1910 differs from the social memory of that event as presented by Winston Churchill. In this case, both are faulty, but the collective memory contains a core of truth denied by Churchill.[6]

Again, however, we are in danger of being misled by too-tight distinctions. For *collective* (and not only social) memory may itself be shaped by the winners. It is not necessarily an *imposed* memory or a memory of great events played by literate people. It may be the memory of a clan or group of people who are neither winners nor losers – yet. But their current self-understanding may be constructed by their relationships with others who *are* winners (or, less probably, losers) and their 'neutral' history will be influenced by this constructed self-understanding. Irish Catholic Nationalists, for example, tend to read their history against English hegemony. Their history is not written *for them* by the English, but their self-understanding and their interpretation of their history, from the Settlement to 1912 to 1968, are influenced, even defined, against the backdrop of their relations with the English.[7] We should therefore be cautious about seeing group memories as either neutral or 'written by the winners'. There is a third term between the two, and perhaps that is the most common form of group conscious memory of all. We shall see in Chapter 11 how significant this is when we read the 'history' of losers in the New Testament.

4 Less than Conscious Memories

I have distinguished in the matrix between conscious and 'less than conscious' memories. Although there are no deep analytical differences riding on this distinction, it is well to recognise from the outset that we are all familiar with types of memory that are 'just below the surface', 'not quite there', 'just beyond me'. Whether or not all our experiences are permanently recorded in our brains (and on that there is still scholarly dispute[8]), it is clear that some memories that we know we have in theory we do not have or cannot now recall in practice. Maybe they will come back. Maybe they will surface in dreams; for the moment we cannot now remember them.

The same is broadly true of groups or societies; social memory is not perfect and some things get forgotten. More especially, societies more than individuals may find that their social memory is deliberately 'rigged' by controlling groups so that certain events or personages are not consciously recalled. It was an offence to recall even to your nearest and dearest the Christian gospel in China during the Cultural Revolution and for far longer in Communist Albania. But that does not necessarily mean that those memories are totally lost for all time, as the astonishing growth of the Christian Church in post-Cultural Revolutionary China shows. The same is broadly true of society's memory of its own past. As we saw above, rulers or oligarchs may have an interest in suppressing parts of a group's history and may be partially successful for a time, despite the efforts of those whom Connerton has called 'relentless recorders' – Solzhenitsyn and Wiesel are his examples.[9] Yet the memory may still re-emerge. The social memory may be controlled: the collective memory cannot be.

5 Unconscious Memories

The third row of the matrix is labelled unconscious. Perhaps a less than happy label, it is designed to serve as a reminder of the whole Jungian tradition to which we shall have to turn in Chapter 4. Without anticipating the material explored in more detail there, I shall argue that the sense in which Jungian archetypes are 'memories' is very different from that of the repressed memories of the Freudian tradition, though Jung would claim they are no less carefully based on clinical practice and ultimately on biological mechanisms. To put it crudely and preliminarily, however, whereas Freud was clear that we all had to experience his developmental stages and accrue our own memories in the process, Jung believed that we *inherit* memories of the archetypes which, as we shall see, play such a crucial role in his understanding of both individual and social behaviour.

Precisely because archetypes are common to all humanity, they represent a common stock of psychological possibilities for both good and ill. A social structure that in some sense incarnates those possibilities thus has resonances for a large number of people. We shall explore this with respect to the military and militarism, following the work of Anthony Stevens, but we shall also look at the power of the anima in such patterns of behaviour as romantic love, marriage and divorce − a topic that feminist writers remind us could have been mirrored by a discussion of animus.

In the 'collective unconscious' cell of the matrix also belongs exactly that Jungian term (the collective unconscious), foreshadowed by the poet W.B. Yeats as 'a [the?] Great Memory passing on from generation to generation'.[10] We shall need to explore the collective unconscious and its social manifestations at some length, but, as ever, there is a danger of allowing these distinctions to lead us by the nose.

For example, collective memory in the normal, non-technical, non-Jungian sense of the *conscious* memory of a group may well be influenced by *unconscious* processes and, through a process of schematising, may be influenced by mythological figures which have the character of archetypes. So here we have a hybrid. Peter Burke has given a nice example that traces the historiography of the Second World War through the First, back to *The Pilgrim's Progress* (via allusions to the Slough of Despond and Valley of the Shadow of Death) to St Paul in the Acts of the Apostles (whose conversion forms a model for Bunyan's account of his own). And with the voice from Heaven one is clearly in the language of myth − and possibly nearing the archetypal material of a God who addresses the individual directly. If Burke is right, then, here we have an example of the collective unconscious actually forming the social memory.[11] This phenomenon, which may well be less uncommon than at first sight appears, will not be discussed further here. I mention it only to point out that the rigid demarcations imposed by the matrix above (and the fuller treatment of the cells of that matrix hereafter) must always be set against the interpenetrations and influences that are the stuff of reality − and the curse of the systematiser!

6 Individual Repressed Memories

In the individual repressed box of the matrix I shall be concerned to explore the thinking of Melanie Klein and the Object Relations school of psychoanalytic thinkers, whose memories, Klein claimed, are of the primitive fears and anxieties that all children experience at the *pre*-Oedipal stage and which are then likely to be acted out in later life either by the individual or, as Bion emphasised, in the group. These memories are for the most part quite unrecognised, unconscious and supposedly beyond recall. But that does not impugn their status as memories in this sense; they are living realities in the unconscious of material that once was not only conscious to the child or baby but which the infant experienced, terrifyingly, as about to consume him or her.

Although these memories are individual — that is, they are experienced by the individual irrespective of social setting and at a time when the individual is not even aware of social settings beyond the crucially important relationship with the primary carer — I shall argue that, in later manifestations, they have particular social *outcomes*. I shall want to show that these individual memories predispose groups to adopt structures or institutions or ways of behaving that defend them against the primitive fears contained in these memories. We can then put Klein in the repressed/individual box of the matrix, but only if we remember that the importance I shall attach to her work lies less in its clinical than in its social application.

7 Collective Repressed Memories

The reverse is true of the work we could, at a pinch, put in the collective-repressed box of the matrix. Under that rubric I shall consider work that depends centrally upon Freud's Oedipal theory, but which uses that theory to explain social phenomena, namely racism in a number of its forms. Joel Kovel, whose work will be the focus of this box, argues that the repressed memories of the developmental stages, through which all infants pass according to Freud, are structured and reinforced in a social setting, giving enormous power and coherence to a social institution that serves the needs incorporated in the memory. Whatever its methodological difficulties (and they are not to be lightly sloughed off), this genre of theory has the great benefit of relating the memories of childhood development directly to a particular social institution – of which the injustice and oppression needs no demonstration. If Christ has set us free, as Christians claim, how has he set us free of this mess?

8 Habit Memory

I want now to turn finally to the poor relation of the philosophy of memory, namely habit. I shall have little to say in this book about individual habit memory, at least explicitly. It could be argued, of course, that every acting-out of unconscious material is, at least in part, habit memory. When in Chapter 7 I treat narcissism, for example, I put much emphasis on the relationship between the narcissistic personality and consumption, especially kinds of consumption that give oral satisfaction: of cigarettes, sweets, cakes, chewing gum. Now clearly these forms of consumption get set in habitual modes: they are in two senses addictive. I 'get into the habit' of smoking as a way of acting out the lack of a good object that I unconsciously remember from my childhood: and that habit is then reinforced by advertising and all the subtle (and not so subtle) pressures of the tobacco companies.

This is a particularly clear example of a more general phenomenon and one that is not necessarily confined to the Freudian tradition. Behaviour that responds to deep psychological 'drives' (to use a term with a long and confused history in the literature) quickly becomes habitual: indeed, if it is compulsive, it is *bound* to become habitual. A non-habitual compulsion is a contradiction in terms.

I am less interested in the individual manifestation of these compulsive habits than I am in their social expression, and here we need to make an important distinction between learned habits and instinctual habits. In dealing again with narcissism, I shall have much to say about the way in which individual narcissistic patterns of behaviour seem to become incorporated into social habit, from educational practice to popular culture. And in that chapter I shall argue that, perhaps precisely through the mechanisms of habit, societies tend to select for particular forms of behaviour and organisation which, becoming habitual, are hard to change. The portrayal of violence in films may, as I shall argue, satisfy the repressed anger in the narcissistic personality: but it becomes first a fashion and then a habit in the film industry. Cinema-goers become habituated, possibly even addicted, to violence on the screen, which means that they are likely to give a lowly rating to a film that dispenses with it, or minimises its portrayal. *Mutatis mutandis*, the same argument could be made for sexual activity. Competition becomes centred not on finding alternative narrative themes but on the daringness and explicitness with which violence and sex are represented.

But what of instinctual habit memory? To give an example of instinctual habit memory at work, we need to recognise the debate within the discipline of linguistics between Chomsky and his critics.[12] Chomsky argues that language rules are biologically (or instinctually) based; that there is, to use a different vocabulary, an instinctual memory of the basic rules of grammar that make it easy for human beings quickly to become adept at language skills.[13] Indeed, this very rapidity of acquiring *creative* skills is one of Chomsky's arguments. Another is the facility with which small children come to use language, and a third is the way in which neurological damage seems to affect only specific language functions. None of these arguments convinces his critics, and clearly the implications of his view run counter to much modern thinking in philosophy and the empirical biological and behavioural sciences.[14] Perhaps more seriously, linguists have attacked him for over-reducing the complexity and specificity of language rules. It is not my intention to enter this debate, but merely to add three comments to it.

First, if (and we acknowledge that is a big if) Chomsky is right, then we have here an example of a crucial form of social organisation being directly dependent upon inherited memory. I shall touch on this again in the next chapter.

Second, Chomsky's position is surprisingly close to that of Jung and the alleged inheritance of archetypal material, the motor of social behaviour in Jung's paradigm. As we shall see in Chapter 4, Jung was derided for his belief that cognitive and/or unconscious material could be transmitted biologically, and again the implications of his view are very far-ranging.

Third, and perhaps most interesting in this context, Lawson and McCauley have recently floated the tentative idea that awareness of and/or responsiveness to religious symbolic systems might be inherited in much the same way as Chomsky believes knowledge of the rules of grammar are inherited (oddly, they do not mention Jung). 'The competence approach to theorizing in linguistics [i.e., Chomsky's] is appropriate for inspiration not only because of the analogies between linguistic and religious phenomena, but also because (contra Chomsky) it offers some promise of *connecting* the cultural and the cognitive.'[15] Clearly, there is a great deal of work to be done before this tentative rapprochement with a style of thinking that contrasts so markedly with present scientism can be trusted. But it is a straw in the wind that ensures that we do not allow habit memory, in this instinctual sense, to become a poor relation of the other types of memory we have reviewed above.

For the ramifications could be vast. If Lawson and McCauley prove to be right, then the 'grapple with the text' which we shall come to in the last chapters of this book is not, as it were, an imposed cognitive task, but a pre-programmed capacity to rediscover religious truth, an instinctual reaching out to the transcendent. The healing of memory, in the senses to be analysed here, is on this account already built into the system. Like building a family (another example of habit memory to which we shall refer in Chapter 3), religious knowing, the 'stuff' of healing, is thus a natural process. Some may be more sucessful than others. But it is as natural a human inclination, *essential to the survival of the species*, as sex or eating. To repeat, it is too early to regard such an account as established; but the very fact that social scientists can now think in these terms puts a quite different spin on the subject of this book than would have been possible five years ago. I hope that will become clearer in the closing chapters.

We have much to do before we get there. In the next chapter I want to look more closely at questions that surround the reliability of memory, and in the last chapter of this Part to examine more closely ways in which some of the types of memory we have been examining form or help to form social structures and institutions. That will then have set the stage for Part 2, where we shall look at a range of psychoanalytical models to see what account they can give of the relationship between memory and the way we make the world. Our task will be analytical and critical, within the various paradigms we discuss. It is not our object to choose between the paradigms, even less to try to synthesise them into some kind of meta-theory. The subject has been ill served by such attempts in the past. Rather, we shall seek to understand each approach in its own terms and be content to hold each tradition 'in the air', as one partial and imperfect way of approaching a deeper truth. That will lead us to look in Part 3 at how the memories that these models explore, and the world they create, may be redeemed.

2

The Trickiness of Memory

From this brief prospectus of the different types of memory with which we shall be concerned in Part 2 of this book, it is already clear that we have to treat it with a good deal of caution. This raises a key question which is best faced now. It can be put like this: if memory is *un*reliable, are not its effects on the way we make the world (and ourselves) dangerous? And if the argument is that the memories of the Gospels can heal our own memories, is not this to confound confusion by replacing one inaccurate set of memories with another? I shall have more to say about the reliability of the Gospel memories later; here I want to raise some questions about the reliability of memory in general.

That memory is often incapable of verification is clear. As Philip Roth has put it, 'memories of the past are not memories of the facts but memories of your imaginings of the facts'.[1] How do we differentiate between genuine memory – memory of real, objective fact – and pseudo-memory, memory contaminated by either error or 'normal' mnemonic tricks like patterning, simplifying or over-interpreting; or, more relevant to subsequent chapters, unconscious processes of projection, scapegoating or primitive anxiety? For, as Theo Platinga has put it, 'our memories are not inert but undergo a process of editing, whereby they are regularized, rendered more retainable and reshaped with an eye to *subsequent* circumstances and events'.[2] Pseudo-memory can play havoc with both the individual psyche and *a fortiori* with the social structures that the psyches of a whole community create and maintain. We shall have to return to this many times, not least when we come towards the end of the book to consider the nature of memories preserved in the Christian Gospels. For the moment, however, I want to make three basic points that will recur throughout the book.

The first is about 'distance' – that is, time that has elapsed between the event and the recall of that event in memory. Thus Elizabeth Loftus: 'During the time between an event and a witness's recollection of that event . . . the bits and pieces of information that were acquired through perception do not passively reside in memory waiting to be pulled out like fish from water. Rather, they are subject to numerous influences. External information . . . can intrude into the witness's memory, as can his own thoughts, and both can cause dramatic change in his recollection.'[3] It is thus a commonplace that there is no definitive relationship between the clarity of recall and time elapsed since the event: I remember some scenes from my childhood better than I remember some events that occurred last week. But of course that cannot be taken to be true in every case, any more than can the reverse. What is clear, however, is that the longer the memory has been with me, the more it is likely to be reconstructed, in I.M.L. Hunter's phrase,[4] that is, the more time both conscious and unconscious processes have had to work upon it. By conscious processes I mean later experience that I read back into the memory: for example, I may have had a close friendship with Martin. I then discover that he has been cheating me over a number of years. I am then inclined to remember my earlier friendship with him not as I actually experienced it, but in the light of the later discovery of this betrayal of me.

By unconscious processes in the same context, I mean much more than what Nietzsche described as the 'existential necessity' of sifting and focusing. For example, I may unconsciously project on to figures in my memory in much the same way as I do on to figures in my present environment. If I am frightened of the 'little Hitler' inside me, I may project that back on to my father, making him in memory much more authoritarian a figure than he actually was. Or I may come to blame my failure to relate adequately to women on poor parenting by my mother and then erect her into a travesty of motherhood, ignoring the love, comfort and emotional support she was in fact able to give me whatever her (perfectly ordinary) shortcomings might have been. More generally, there is plenty of evidence that 'schema' or 'prototypes' or stereotypes in general unconsciously distort memory so that the memory fits the expectation. And this may

21

be true not just of memories of others, but also of memories of the self.[5]

Secondly, the great difficulty with all this is that we have no means of telling which is true memory and which is false. Of course, we can ask witnesses, and of course, on questions of straight fact – were my mother's eyes blue or brown? – they will be able to help and we may be ready to trust their recall if we are in a generally trusting relationship with them. But in general those kinds of questions are not the important ones. If the pseudo-memory was as easily corrected as that – either because it was a 'simple matter of fact' (though matters of fact are rarely simple) or because there was a large and credible body of opinion that was ready and eager to see the pseudo-memory corrected – then it would not survive for very long and would certainly not assume the awesome power that we shall meet in later pages. Neither of those conditions of ready correctability often exist. Either at the individual level or the social level, the pseudo-memory is typically much more complex than the colour of my mother's eyes, and is deprived of 'memory supports'. Its content may take the form of a vague generalisation (all Jews are mean; all Blacks are promiscuous; all Communists are evil) that is, of course, open to counter-examples but for which some, however little, circumstantial evidence may be adduced. Further, as we shall see, pseudo-memory tends to be incorporated either in ideology or in self-image (a kind of inner ideology) which effectively limits the number of people who are ready or able to correct it.

Thirdly (and this argument applies particularly to repressed unconscious and less than conscious memory but can also apply, *mutatis mutandis*, to conscious memory), much of what we remember and misremember is not in principle open to correction or verification. That does not, of course, impugn its perceived reality. We may not *know* the past is real; but it may still feel real.[6] Ben Lukacher has argued this with respect to the 'memories' that analysis (whether Freudian, Jungian or eclectic) deals with.[7] Analyst and analysand together reconstruct a prior experience, perhaps in the light of a dream reported by the analysand. The analysand can tell the analyst that the reconstruction 'feels right' or that it leaves her cold. She cannot tell him that it *is* right, because by definition she cannot recall the event or series of events in question. To put it more strongly, she, with her analyst, can only reconstruct the past in the light of the present. Her report that a specific reconstruction 'feels right' is as much a statement about her present as it is a statement about the verisimilitude of the reconstruction.

Without prejudging that debate, I want to argue that my conscious memories about my feelings are unverifiable by anyone else, and yet it is the feeling quality of memories that are likely to be much more important in the creation and maintenance of social structure than cold facts. To go back to an example which appears in Chapter 8 but that I have already touched upon, if I remember the past with affection and a sense of security – as a 'good time' both personally and nationally, as a time when my family, friends and I felt at one with each other and with the world – it is that emotionally loaded memory of the past that I shall compare unfavourably with the (possibly no less emotionally loaded) experience of the present, with its slump, its inflation, its unemployment, its feckless politicians and its rising crime rates. The fact that I argued then as I do now with my family and friends, that I worried then as I do now about our financial security, that I despised then as I do now the lack of vision and idealism among our politicians – all that is forgotten, and the pseudo-memory of the 'feel-good' emotional quality of the past becomes engrained in the present. And it cannot be challenged. Friends may say, 'You were as cantankerous and argumentative then as you are now, and looking at you we would say you are neither happier nor unhappier now than you were then,' and there is nothing I nor they can say or do to resolve the argument. My memories of my past emotional states are mine – to remember right or wrong.

What I have said about the verifiability of individual memory can be applied with some modification to social memory. In so far as social memory is about fact – that Guy Fawkes attempted to blow up the Houses of Parliament; that the fall of the Bastille marked a turning-point in the French Revolution – then it is the task of the historians to check the historicity of those facts. But of course that is by no means all there is to it. For historians do not deal with facts: they deal with interpretations, reconstructions of casual chains. As we have already seen, there is an important sense in which they 'make' history and in which they make social memory – either formally, in the sense of professional historians writing academic history which eventually percolates through to the student population and, in a literate community, to the wider circle; or informally in the sense of the grandmother telling the family history ('We Elliotts were sheepstealers on the Borders and there's a bit of us that is always agin the law'), or the village elder (a role not yet quite extinct, at least in this sense, in Europe) summarising village gossip: 'You can't trust a man from the other side of the hill: they always were a bit rum from that way.'

Both individual and social memory are conditioned not only by questions of what we might call internal accuracy – did it *really* happen quite that way? – but also by the fact that remembering itself is, as it were, fortuitous. We remember some things and we forget others. What can we make of that?

Leaving aside both Freudian repression of the memory of individual trauma and the political manipulation of social memory to which I have already referred, let us note first the necessity of forgetting. As Nietzsche put it, 'All acting requires forgetting, as not only light but also darkness is required for life by all organisms.'[8] Nietzsche may have had a particular ideological case to argue, but his plea for not being bound by history and story still needs to be heard, as the histories of Ireland, the former Yugoslavia, Rwanda and El Salvador constantly remind us.[9]

But that raises a more mundane question: How far is forgetting a conscious decision? We might note that linguistically we do use phrases that suggest that forgetting is indeed something we can and do decide to do: 'Try to forget all about it, dear'; 'It's time to forgive and forget'; 'I choose to forget the whole incident'. This evidence suggests that at the conscious level there is at least a measure of control over what we 'choose' to forget and what we do not. The critical question then becomes what precisely we do choose to forget, what we choose to remember, and to what we are indifferent. There is a huge agenda here, and we shall only nibble at the edges of it: suffice it to say for the moment that there are likely to turn out to be unconscious processes at work which operate alongside the conscious decisions. We may think that we are in control of what we remember and what we forget (as opposed to repress). Almost certainly we are not.

And that adds a further layer of indeterminancy to memory. Not only do we not know the truth value of our memories, especially our more emotionally charged memories: we do not know how what we have remembered relates to what we have forgotten. To put it another way, all our narratives are partial, but we do not know which parts are missing and why.

That means that as we put together any kind of narrative – about ourselves or our colleagues or our nation – there is a process of interpretation: of selecting some facts and ignoring others, of privileging one theme and neglecting another. The memory is being manufactured: it will emerge as an artefact. In an open society, with properly funded research facilities, the memory created by academic history will be open to challenge; others can develop competing artefacts. In the informal sector, the same is roughly true. Granny can be challenged; the village elder can be mocked or ignored. The question then arises: Which interpretation do we trust? How do we know that the view that Guy Fawkes was seeking to re-establish the Roman Catholic Church in England is to be preferred to the view that he was acting virtually alone for his own non-political motives? How do we know that Granny's explanation of the bloody-mindedness of the Elliott clan has any value? These are, of course, familiar questions to historians, theologians and philosophers – indeed, to anyone concerned with hermeneutics. All I seek to establish at this point is that, just as the analysand can never be sure that the analyst's reconstruction of her experience is 'accurate', so the community of interpretation (the nation, the village, the family in the examples I have explored; the Church in an example I shall explore later) can never be sure that the interpretations of their histories are 'accurate'. That means that in so far as memory, in this case particularly collective and social memory, emerges as narrative, there has to be a degree of openness, of scepticism, of uncertainty. We can never know for sure how accurate the narrative really is. And that means that trust is all.

Now that may be thought deeply embarrassing for my central argument which will emerge in the succeeding chapters: that the memories of Jesus Christ have a unique salvific value, challenging and 'replacing' the harmful memories of the past. For it will immediately be asked: If all memory is artefact, how can we trust the particularly odd memories of Jesus? I shall want to return to this in

25

Chapter 11, but for the moment I make briefly some quick counter-points.

First, as Wolfhart Pannenberg has shown more persuasively than anyone, Christian theology can live comfortably with the openness of memory, not in the sense of being careless of truth but in the more Hegelian sense of recognising the role of traditions of interpretation. The question of 'Is A true?' cannot be finally resolved into 'Do we now think A is true and if so why?', but by asking the second question we recognise that truth is historically determined. Or as Tupper has put it, 'events only become events with meaning as they enter the stream of a tradition and are made intelligible thereby'.[10] The parallel with Lukacher is striking. It is important to emphasise this in a supposedly post-modern age, when subjectivity and relativity are thought to be the only criteria of truth — or of 'truth'. There is a danger that, in emphasising the subjectivity of both memory and the hermeneutics of memory, we lose sight of the objectivity which we accord to the vast majority of the memories with and by which we live. As we shall see below, we may have little intellectual reason for doing so, but the fact is that we come to trust a great deal of memory as though it were reliable. We may be in a vortex of subjectivity in the study; but we live our lives as though there is at least a core of objectivity available to us. And that means, as we shall see in the last chapters, that we can live our faith-lives not in benign neglect of the provisionality of memory, but with that provisionality bounced off the hardness of the text — and vice versa. And that raises a related point.

For, second, such openness to the construction of memory does not absolve us from probing the memory in theology any more than it does in psychology. The facticities of the memory-event, be they never so interlinked with interpretation, affect and error, are there for the digging. Subjectivity voyages in the expectation of encountering fragments of objectivity. The disciplines of biblical criticism, from philology to reader-response criticism, are made the more relevant rather than the reverse.

But lastly, with Pannenberg, Moltmann and Kung, we need to insist, again like most schools of psychoanalysis, that the point of 'memory-work' lies in the future, not the past. For theology, the 'fact' of Jesus Christ, unknowable as 'hard fact history' as it may (perhaps) turn out to be, none the less generates a hermeneutic of the future as well as of the past. Indeed, there is an important sense, for theology as for psychology, in which *the point of interpreting the past is precisely to gain a key to the future.* For all modern theologians with an interest in eschatology or, more simply, in 'hope', the Christ-event and our reaction to it holds open the possibilities of the future. 'The essential nature of the future lies in the unpredictable new thing that is hidden in the womb of the past.'[11] And that, as Pannenberg emphasises in many of his treatments of the theology of history, is as true of the understandings of the past as it is of the actual events of the future: we cannot know today how we shall interpret the past tomorrow any more than we can know what 'new thing' God is going to make tomorrow. In both senses the future is radically open. We stand, in a word, uncertain as to past and as to future, and that uncertainty is as rooted in theology as it is in psychology.

We are, then, in a state of considerable epistemic confusion. We do not know the real reliability of the memories we have. We do not know what we have forgotten or why. We do not know how we shall reinterpret our memories at some point of the future. And all of that is equally true of our psychological memories and our faith memories. This means that we cannot be confident of any of the narratives we construct out of memory material. So how do we know, for example, who we are?

Since David Hume, a crude equation of memory and personal identity has been hard to maintain, yet accounts by neurophysicians and psychologists of people who have lost their memories, especially though Korsakoff's syndrome, stress how the 'chaotic confabulations' of their patients demonstrate a literal sense of not knowing who they are. They dart from one 'persona' to another, seeking an identity in which they feel connected to a past. None fits – and so the pathetic search continues.[12]

Those patients are looking for memories, as it were, within themselves. But the memories they are looking for are, at least in part, of themselves interacting with others. This has led scholars like Rom Harré and Alistair McFadyen to see social interaction – its present fact and our past memories of it – as the essential definition of our identity.[13] The memories we have of others relating to us and of our relating to them construct our knowledge of who we are. Those memories may not, however, be precise: indeed, there is some evidence that we select memories that fit an existing model we have already developed of a particular relationship or set of relationships.[14] To say, as I shall in many contexts in the rest of this book, that we make reality in response to our memories of others has to take account of this degree of plasticity in our interactional memories.

A more philosophical interpretation (or reinterpretation) of social interactionism comes from scholars of linguistics, like Lyons and Beneveniste, who take one step further Descartes's original siting of identity in the capacity to think. For *cogito ergo sum*, they read *loquor ergo sum* – or, better, *loquimur ergo sumus*.[15] It is in the process of spoken interaction with others and the subsequent memories of it that I discover who I am, where this ego is situated. And, linguists would add, there is something about the way grammar functions – an instinctual memory, if Chomsky is right, as we saw in the last chapter – that helps me work that out. Self-expression, says Lyons, has to be taken seriously – and literally.

One particular form of social interaction that determines identity and certainly shapes personality (and one that has been highlighted in the theological literature) is that between mother and child, or, better, primary carer and child.[16] We shall, of course, have much more to say about this relationship in later chapters, but it is important to note here that Kung and Pannenberg, coming from very different theological perspectives, both see the establishment of 'basic trust' between mother and child as fundamental for the child's subsequent sense of its own identity. They have a particular apologetic agenda to pursue in so privileging both that relationship and the acquisition of basic trust as a precondition of successful human development, but for our purposes we can note it as a special case of the wider point made by social interactionism – that our knowledge of ourselves as individuals is based on the memory of our relationships with others. 'The self is made up of reflected appraisals,' as Harry Stack Sullivan put it.[17] In that sense we are dependent upon others, especially but not uniquely close others, for who we are – and others are dependent upon us. But that dependence will not operate in a memoryless world.

So far I have put this relationship primarily in terms of identity, the ego's knowledge of itself. But what of personality, the chain of predispositions in our responses to events and other people? What role does memory play there? The general position of this book is that much of our behaviour, whether as individuals or in groups, is a species of acting out memory material, whether we are conscious of it or not. We shall review that from a number of paradigmatic perspectives in Part 2, but we shall have to leave open the question of why does A react to her memories like this and B react to the same – or nearly the same – memories in a quite different way. Those questions are still largely unanswerable; so we shall confine ourselves to the more modest task of showing how memory disposes many people to act in certain ways – first as individuals and then, perhaps more importantly, in groups.

Just as individuals discover and become who they are through the memory of social interactions, so do groups. The community exists only in the context and experience of the interactions that go on between its members and the rest of the world. We are all, in MacIntyre's phrase, co-authors of our own and the community's narratives.[18] These narratives in turn form the structures of power and influence in the community, as Karen Brison, for example, has recently demonstrated in her brilliant study of village gossip in Eastern Sepik[19] or Fentress and Wickham found in the French Pyrenees.[20] If those seem remote or exotic examples, a moment's reflection of 'office politics' will bring the point to earth. There memory, gossip and speculation create not just atmosphere but, within the micro-environment of the office, determine who has access, influence and even power.

Memory, in short, is powerful stuff – a paradox in view of its fragility and indeterminacy. Yet it is no exaggeration to say that it helps make us. It helps make our communities. It affects the way we create, adapt and handle reality.

And it is that which makes the notion of the healing of memory so significant, not only, *pace* the trade in psychotherapeutics, for the compulsive, acting-out individual, but for the whole of human society. Healed memories help to create a less destructive world. Christians therefore privilege the memories of Jesus because they think that those memories have a particular role to play in that healing process. In that sense, they bring the past into contact with the future – and, more subtly perhaps, allow the present to remake the past.

Before we come on to see how that works, we have first, in the rest of this Part, to relate memory to social structure more precisely than we have done in this chapter; and in Part 2, to look more closely at some classic accounts of the relationship between memory, the individual and society as we explore in greater detail the cells of the matrix that we explored in the last chapter. That will enable us, in Part 3, to return to the central question: In what sense has Christ made us free if we are too often the captives of our memories, both individual and social?

3

Memory and Structure

In the last chapters, we looked at types of memory and forgetting, anticipating more thorough discussion of the ways in which various schools of psychology have conceived the role memory plays in forming persons, communities and relationships. In this chapter, we shall also be engaged in a type of ground-clearing. As I want to argue that the interface between theology and psychology has important things to say about the way we conceive of our faith and our world, I need at this early stage to explicate those features of 'our world' which memory plays a major part in forming.

To keep this chapter within reasonable bounds of length and complexity, I shall limit the discussion to three areas: institutions, ideology and language. I have chosen these because they constitute the major part of the skeleton of any account of how society functions, but I shall introduce other significant parts of the skeleton in the course of the discussion of these three.

Institutions

I begin with institutions, by which I mean all forms of social structure which have an explicit or implicit objective; explicit or implicit 'rules of membership'; and of which it makes sense to say that people are members whether or not they are themselves conscious of their membership. In this usage, institutions include groups as diverse as the family, the military, systems of government, corporations, churches, interest groups and nations.

Immediately, I want to make a distinction between the formal structure of such institutions and what I shall call the quality of life. I shall relate memory to each of these in turn.

One way of looking at the way in which memory helps determine the way institutions are structured is to recognise that the institution, or key people within it, have learnt by experience that this 'shape' of structure performs better than another. In that sense, shape is an embodiment of collective memory. Institutions learn, and in that learning process they are as heavily dependent upon memory as are individuals.[1] An institution that has lost its memory would be as confused and directionless as any memoryless individual. There is a process of memory-based learning going on in most institutions most of the time that allows them to adapt and change, to develop out of their past.[2] It is no accident that those most self-conscious institutions, large industrial corporations, institutionalise their own strategies of corporate learning in which corporate memory plays a key role.

Memories, then, help constitute institutions; but what kinds of memories are these? They may be conscious memories that pertain to particular events in the life of the institution – an institutional crisis, perhaps, or a time of great success and creativity. But even those memories are likely to be distorted, to be simplified, to be, even, manipulated by powerful people within the organisation for their own or institutional ends. The collective memory thus becomes a social memory, serving the ends of particular power groups. Further, the memories of the past of the institution are more than the aggregation of the memories of the individuals.

The memories at work, however, may not be conscious in the normal sense at all. They may be a variety of habit memory. If, for example, we think of the family as an institution or structure, and ask what memory is at work there, we shall find at least three different types of answer, two of which depend upon a form of habit memory and one of which depends upon an implicitly more conscious memory. The first two derive from theoretical approaches that are respectively Freudian and sociobiological. We shall examine each in turn.

In a hypothesis he sometimes confused with pre-historical 'fact', Freud based his theory of family formation on the 'primal struggle' between a dominant male, the original father, and his sons, triggered by the father's possession of all the nubile women. In the struggle the father was killed and all the women were divided between the sons. For Freud, the guilt that this induced in the sons explains the internalisation of the authority of the father figure, now manifested as the socially conforming super-ego. In so far as the primal struggle was encoded in the unconscious of each man in his instincts, the super-ego reinforced his 'drive' to conform to the pattern dictated by the instincts. Thus, for Freud, patriarchy was an inevitable form of family organisation because it is instinctual as a result of the (mythical) primal struggle; and because it is held in place by the male super-ego. In our terms, the 'memory', albeit unconscious, of the primal struggle thus underlies the structure of patriarchal families.[3]

The 'myth' of the primal struggle, however, is just that: a myth. As such it will not bear the weight that Freud seeks to put upon it, and it certainly will not 'explain' in any significant sense why families in some parts of the world are patriarchal and in others they are matriarchal. What may be rescuable from the wreckage is the role of the super-ego in males maintaining a particular social form, even when it comes under personal and social criticism. The role of memory in super-ego formation is, however, a more disputed area, with only orthodox Freudians wishing to maintain a direct link between the unconscious memory of the Oedipal conflict and the development of the super-ego. That is an area to which we shall have to return in a slightly different context.

For the moment, I want to turn from Freudian theories of the relation between (one form of) social structure and memory to another that is very different in intellectual provenance. Sociobiology is no less controversial than some elements of Freudian thought, but it shares with the latter an interest in instinct, the most basic form of habit memory. Largely as a result of the work of the mathematical geneticist William Hamilton in the 1960s,[4] sociobiologists concluded that patterns of altruistic behaviour in animals are explicable in terms of the survival of genetic material common to the altruist and his (or her) beneficiary. Hence the origins of theories of inclusive fitness. So far from evolution and the processes of natural selection encouraging a self-regarding strategy, an interest in the survival of one's genes ensures an interest in the survival of one's kin.

This observation gives a theoretical explanation of a wide range of social behaviours, from parental care to clan formation and group defence to complex forms of mutual support among genetically linked subjects. In the hands of Crook, it can also be used to explain both polygamy and polygyny, as well as what Crook has felicitously called 'male sexual obsessions'.[5] For example, female chastity at marriage has in very many cultures traditionally been at more of a premium than male chastity. The explanantion of sociobiology of that phenomenon is that males wish to invest care, time and resources in the nurturing of their own progeny – i.e., a generation carrying their own genes – and only female virginity at marriage will ensure that. Other phenomena of polygynous societies are open to the same type of explanation: for example, the contrast between the tendency of women to collaborate and men to compete (though there is some interesting counter-evidence that suggests that the degree of female collaboration is strictly limited[6]); the tendency for men to be older than women on marriage; the tendency for men to be possessive and dominating towards females in their household; the much greater odium that tends to attach to female adultery than to male; and the way in which women are (or were) used as barter items in kinship systems.[7]

Perhaps most interesting in this account is the way in which Crook has demonstrated that polygyny gives way to polyandry in resource conditions that would not withstand high population growth rates often associated with polygynous households. Indeed, the polygynous male seeks to inseminate as many women as possible in order to maximise the chances of his genes (or genomes) surviving; but in a household located in an extremely resource-constrained environment, such a strategy would have the reverse effect. A Malthusian check – that is, widespread famine and high mortality – would be inevitable. In these conditions, the best survival strategy is for a band of brothers to 'marry' one woman and for all the brothers and their progeny to live as one economic unit. This is the family structure in parts of rural Tibet.

Does it work? When the Crooks resurveyed the families originally studied in the 1970s by Aziz and Goldstein,[8] they found that completed family size in a polyandrous family is significantly higher (at the 5 per cent level of probability) than in a monogamous family in the same environment. They conclude thus: 'A parent with a marriageable daughter interested in her reproductive success should seek to place her in a khang-chen (roughly, household) wherein a polyandrous association with a band of brothers would be quite acceptable.'[9]

This seems an altogether more promising line of enquiry into the instinctual origins of family structure. It turns out not to be instinctual in a mechanistic way, but to depend upon a form of learning and adaptation which then becomes habitual. The degree to which this is conscious at any point is open to debate, though the Crook data do suggest that Tibetans make very conscious choices about what form of family structure to adopt – for example, they switch very quickly from polyandry to monogamy as soon as they move from the extreme poverty of the remoter rural areas to a modest economic security in the towns.

This might suggest an objection: that what the sociobiolgists teach us is that family structure adapts to the environment; that, as Dickeman has put it, the ecosystem determines social structure.[10] According to this view, it is not the memory of a particular event or series of events that effects outcomes: it is the process of adaptation to changes in the environment that selects out the best adapted and allows it to thrive. It is no part of my intention to deny that interpretation, but the process of adaptation itself implies that the outcome is dependent upon the collective memory of what has succeeded and what has failed. That does not imply that each unit in the adaptive process consciously remembers each mutation. That is absurd. It is to insist that, according to this model, which some will find objectionably reductionist even in this restated form, the social structure that emerges *collectively* from the process constitutes the 'species memory' or the unconscious collective memory of all that has gone before.

The third model of institution mutation that I want to touch upon briefly deals neither with the deep unconscious that is Freud's concern, nor with the ecosystem and remembered responses to it that is central to the sociobiologists. It deals with the function of a particular social structure, and argues that structures change in accordance with changes in function or in the technology that allows that function to be discharged. Although structural functionalism, as this approach is generically called, has been heavily criticised by recent social theorists,[11] its value lies in directing attention at the way in which structures and institutions have a teleological expectation built in. If they do not perform, sooner or later some of them wither and perhaps die.

They (or particular power groups within them) therefore have an institutional interest in making sure that they adapt in such a way as enables them best to achieve their overt (and perhaps covert) functions. To apply that very crudely to the family, it is evident that the functions of the family are currently being reassessed and renegotiated. While it was – or was thought to be – to provide men with a comfortable environment, sexual satisfaction and a home for their offspring, it is now likely to give much greater prominence to the possibilities of providing a rewarding environment for the exerise of all the talents the woman brings to the partnership. While sociobiology has little to say about this most modern development of the family, structural functionalism can at least point to the changes in the expectations that women bring to the experience of marriage.

Now if those expectations and functions are what determines the way institutions are structured, what account can we give of memory? Structural functionalism implies memory in a roughly analogous way to sociobiological theories of inclusive fitness: that is to say, in so far as they demand some form of learned response to given events, the process of learning predicates a memory of the past. Concretely, women are demanding a restructuring of the family – with more parenting by the father, more equal opportunities to follow a career, more equal access to family financial resources – because they remember, either personally or through some form of formal or informal, written or oral history, that the 'traditional' form of family was deeply demeaning and unjust to many women. It may well be true (though some in the feminist movement would deny this) that they do not remember a 'time' when things were better; a time when women and men shared more or less equally in child rearing and career development; and to that extent the role of memory is repulsive, steering them away from what is objectionable, rather than attractive, drawing them towards something that promises to be better. But an attractive memory is easily included in a structural-functionalist approach: consider the role of the memory of the early Church as presented in Acts on many brands of Christian radicalism.[12]

These three models of the origin of family structure have, I hope, gone far enough to establish that memory and structure are inevitably linked, though the nature of the memory concerned and the type of the link may well vary from one theoretical perspective to another.

Before I leave this topic, I want to anticipate material we shall look at in more detail in a later chapter, and acknowledge that the 'memory' at work in an institution may be neither the conscious, quasi-historical variety associated with structural functionalism, nor the instinctual associated with Freud and, in a different way, with sociobiology. The memories may be unconscious or repressed, lying hidden behind the epiphenomena of normal institutional life. According to one post-Freudian tradition of psychoanalytical theory, the group is exposed unconsciously to the terror of annihilation and destruction, with the implication that there is in the group unconscious a 'memory' of that primal terror. At its worst, the group can become almost literally possessed by unconscious fears, anxieties and anger which relate less to the actuality than to unconscious memory material in each participant, triggered and perhaps exaggerated by the group.

Given this terror of annihilation, what holds the group together, and/or the people in the group? It is easier to see that intuitively for the individual than for the group. For Bick, for example, the infant's experience of dis-integration, of literally falling apart, is countered first 'by the skin functioning as a boundary'[13] and then by the holding-together of the embrace of the primary carer. As Paul Hoggett has put it,

> the nurturing embrace constitutes the first experience of secure boundedness, an experience which, upon incorporation, finds representation in the idea of one's own skin functioning as a boundary – Freud's corporeal ego. The body of the subject is therefore itself a representation of the embrace of the one who cares (in religious terms, the body of Christ).[14]

The question then becomes, what performs the same essential task for the group or institution; what holds it together against the primitive fear of disintegration? For Hoggett it is the 'primary task'; the explicit, objective function of the group that achieves this. We are (almost) back with a reinterpretation of structural functionalism. We may wonder if that is not too glib, too simple. Many groups and even institutions have only a very vague idea of what their primary task is; or may encompass many different accounts of what the primary task is; or may have a variety of tasks, none of which is in any significant sense primary but all of which swim into pre-eminence from time to time. Some may think that the Church, for example, shares this confusion about what its primary task really is.

It is beyond the scope of this chapter to enter this debate in any detail, but it is relevant to our purpose to note that *one* source of integration, of holding-embrace, that is common in many kinds of non-commercial institutions is precisely the shared memory of the institution. Tradition, in the many senses and representations of that word, often plays a major role in holding the institution together, and thus, in Bion's terms, defending it against primitive anxiety that it is about to fall apart. In this context, it may be significant how quick institutions are to generate 'traditions' or perhaps to co-opt the traditions of others; and how frequently institutions that have been through a period of crisis and trauma, when they may well have been faced at the unconscious (or even conscious) level with the possibility of disintegration, move to re-establish their overt traditions, to remind themselves of their history. Regimental traditions are an obvious case in point.

I want now to turn from formal organisation and unconscious anxieties on the one hand to what I term the quality of life of institutions on the other. The distinction I wish to draw is between the formal hierarchical structure of an organisation and the 'ways of going about things', roughly equivalent to what Benson has called 'rules of structure formation', analogous to Chomsky's generative rules of grammar.[15] What is the relation between the grammar of an institution and its memory? I think we get an insight into this when we relate to the grammar Walter Wink's term, 'the spirituality of institutions'.[16] They are not identical, since the grammar is about the norms which surround the way things shall be done; the way in which sub-groups will relate; the way in which power shall be used and constrained, and Wink's 'spirituality' is more about the way in which people react to these dispositions. But both Wink and Benson are inviting us to look at the normative context within which life in the institution is lived; and more particularly at the ways in which power within the institution and of the institution is used. In this sense we are back to the last two stories of Chapter 1.

There is more at issue here than the memory associated with the learnt rules, especially of the learnt rules of power-plays (though those should not be underestimated). Much more, there is the memory base of the norms within which the institution and the power brokers within it operate. These norms define the moral commitment of the group and therefore the cathexis that, on Etzioni's account, holds it together.[17] We shall have more to say about the relationship between memory and norms in the next section, for we may regard norms in this sense as part of the ideology of the group; at present, I want to develop the argument in a rather different direction.

One of the features of the life of members of institutions, and perhaps especially the institutions of economic life (*pace* Hoggett, I take the issue to be far wider than capitalist institutions), is their capacity to 'split off' their loyalty to the institution from their loyalty to patterns of normative behaviour they follow elsewhere. This is the classic case of the concentration camp guard who murdered Jews by the thousand during the day and went home to read Grimm to his children and sing lieder with his wife. What role, if any, does memory play in enabling and sustaining this splitting process?

One way of looking at this is to see the participant in any organisation using the life of the organisation as a defence against inner pain of all kinds – from wholly unconscious phantasies of attack and potential destruction (much analysed by Melanie Klein: see Chapter 6) to the pain of a row with his wife this morning and the self-blame that afflicts him as he reviews his ineffectiveness as bread-winner, father, lover, husband, workmate (see Chapter 8).

On this account, then, the normative splitting occurs because the worker or participant wishes to 'lose' himself in the secure bosom of the institution.[18] The security of knowing your place; of knowing what to do; of knowing where you stand; of knowing how well or badly you are performing – all that security which operates at many psychic and existential levels means that 'people literally lose their minds within the impersonal order of things'.[19] For to challenge the prevailing 'spirituality' is to surrender the security that is so valuable, not only in itself, but as a defence against all the other threats that life outside the organisation holds. It is the memory, conscious and unconscious, and probably semi-conscious too, of those threats that allows, indeed compels, the worker to split off his normative judgements from his loyalty to the institution.

There is, of course, much more that could be said on this theme of the role of memory in institution formation and maintenance. I have sought to show only that we can make little sense of the nature and dynamics of the institutional life with which we are caught up without reference to the role of memory. I shall argue later that the way in which our memories are formed and distorted has its own impact on our institutional life; and that that life will be 'healthy' only to the extent that our memories which help form it are themselves healed of traumatic and distortive material.

I turn now to the second of the structural components of social life that I wish to review from this perspective.

Ideology

I shall limit the discussion here to a short consideration of three components of ideology: explanation, values and technique.

Explanation

Explanation is usually a central concern of ideology. It needs to be able to explain, for instance, why the present is so much less satisfactory than the past; or why this group (e.g., men) have come to dominate that group (e.g., women). While it is usually the case that the objective of ideology is not only to understand the world but to change it, it is aided in that task of changing the world if it can give a satisfactory explanation of the way things are and of the way in which suggested changes would actually deliver what is promised.

Explanation depends upon establishing patterns of causality, usually through inferential or analogical reasoning.[20] These are by their nature memory based. In the more extended use to which explanation is put in ideology (consider the ideology of the IRA or of the Verkramptes), inferences and analogies are woven into a substantial narrative that seeks to 'explain' how the Ulster Unionists have no moral right to control the Six Counties or how the Bantu have no moral right to majority rule in South Africa. We have explored some features of the collective and social memories involved in this process of narrative formation already; now I want to emphasise the role of memory in giving and maintaining an *explanatory* mode to those recollections. The most obvious case is that of analogy – always a powerful rhetorical tool in the hands of the political ideologue. 'Remember what the Bantu have made of "independence" in Zambia, Uganda, Tanzania and Zaire. Then think of what mayhem they will cause here now that our fellow countrymen have been so foolish as to give them majority rule . . .' Or, to change sides in our Ulster example: 'Just reflect on the grip the Roman Catholic Church has established on the everyday lives of ordinary people in the Irish Republic. If the Catholics held power in Ulster, the Roman Catholic Church would soon be in as dominant a position here as it is south of the border . . .'

In the same way, inferential reasoning draws upon memories of both established patterns and assumed facts. Thus: 'All black leaders have proved corrupt and incompetent. Now we have majority rule, we have a black leader. Therefore we are led by someone who is corrupt and incompetent.' The premise, 'all black leaders have proved corrupt and incompetent', invites the hearer to assent to a presumed collective memory of the political fitness of black leaders. Or to give another example that is slightly less loaded: 'All nationalised industries are inefficient. Railways are nationalised. By privatising railways, we shall improve efficiency.' I am less concerned with the logical structure of this inference than with both its superficial plausibility – so that it can be made to function as an explanation – and its implicit appeal to memory. 'You remember how inefficient were the steel industry, British Airways, the old Gas Boards. Why, you waited in days for the gas man – and then he always brought the wrong part and you had to wait all over again . . .'

It is not wholly coincidental that in the examples I have chosen the memory content of explanation is a form of playing upon fear. Corrupt black leaders. Interfering Roman priests. Hopeless inefficiency that messes you around and puts up taxes. Or, to refer to a more serious ideology, the rising level of exploitation of the workers as Marx and Engels thought they observed in nineteenth-century England. Now, if some of the schools of psychoanalytic thinking that I shall explore in the later chapters of this book are right in suggesting that at the unconscious level we are usually locked in a sense of anxiety and fear of attack – what Melanie Klein, for instance, calls the paranoid-schizoid position – we can see how these supposed memories of earlier social traumas feed into and feed upon the unconscious 'memories' we have of impending disaster. To this extent, the memory base of ideological explanation is not just of supposed history: it is of unconscious fears that get touched, 'activated', by the rehearsal of the ideology and its explicit prognostications of external collapse – to mirror the dreaded state of internal collapse.

Values

I turn now to a consideration of the way in which memory shapes values. By that I mean more than that values are (often but certainly not always) inherited from the past – the Decalogue, the Sermon on the Mount, the school rules, the often unspoken codes inculcated in the home. That function of memory is not trivial, but it is not central to my argument, not least because many people, especially young people, consciously refuse to adopt value systems from the past (as they suppose). More germane to my argument is the way in which memory serves to link moral cause with moral effect. To say that does not imply that I believe that everyone operates some form of moral consequentialism, justifying their acts only in terms of its perceptible consequences. But it does imply that a major determinant of our moral codes is what we remember feeling about the outturn of particular moral decisions. They may have had a disagreeable result for me, but I might still feel that 'it was the right thing to do', and that I would, however reluctantly, do the same thing again in equivalent circumstances. If, on the contrary, I made a decision that I felt was right at the time, but which subsequent events showed had baneful unanticipated consequences or which I later saw was motivated by selfish considerations that I had managed to repress while making the decision, I might very well not make the same decision in analogous circumstances – or have to modify my basic moral ground rules quite explicitly to make doing something for selfish reasons accepted as 'right'. What this amounts to, then, is the beginnings of a theory of moral learning, not unlike that of Laurence Kohlberg.[21]

In that process of moral learning, as with the process of furnishing an explanation, as we saw above, the telling of a narrative is often central. Now the narrative may have explicit moral intent – as the various Covenant narratives in the Old Testament – but more often it will be narrative that is told in the community and thus forms part of the collective memory; or it may be internal narrative and thus form part of the inner narrative which subtends my identity. The narratives of mining communities since the strike of 1984 include bitter references to scab lorry drivers and unco-operative railwaymen and go far to reinforce traditional myths of the ethical demand for working-class solidarity. The memories of Welsh nationalism include the attempt by 'the English' to stamp out the Welsh language by forbidding its use in school and public employment, and therefore reinforce a socio-ethical demand that Welsh people emphasise their Welsh identity by speaking the Welsh language. It is, in this remembered historical context, the *duty* of 'real' Welsh people to speak the language. The memory forms, or helps form, the obligation. That this can lead to a communal ethic that is no longer relevant to the present, and indeed is a hindrance to the present, is tragically illustrated in much of the 'memories' that underlie moral codes in the two communities in Northern Ireland. The 'duty' to humiliate the Catholics, in Orange Marches, for example, is unhelpful to those trying to build bridges between the communities.

Technique
The last of the three components of ideology that I isolated for brief consideration from the standpoint of memory is that of technique. It is a significant variable in this context, because ideology that does not 'seek to change the world' is politically neutered; and one that does seek to change the world needs to be able to say, in however broad terms, how it is proposed to move from the present to the envisioned future. And there is here an element of techne: the 'how' of social and political relations. This, too, can be the subject of learning from experience, and will involve inferential and analogical reasoning. But the point I want to make in this connection is slightly different. The relationship between memory and imagination has exercised philosophers and psychologists at least since Hume – and arguably since Augustine.[22] That we sometimes confuse imagination and memory, even though memory tends to be less coloured than imagination,[23] merely serves to underline how closely they are linked as mental processes. Hume thought that we reconstitute units of memory to create 'imagined' things and events – so that famously the unicorn is a fanciful amalgam of a horse and a rhinoceros. While

we may be reluctant to tie imagination *that* tightly to memory, the power of analogical reasoning in imagination and related technical innovation is clear enough: 'If A does that to B in conditions C (a remembered relationship), then I imagine that P will do this to Q in conditions R' is a perfectly natural linguistic statement of the relationship.

Technical relationships in ideology, however, are seldom as colourless as that. Or, to put it another way, the choice of analogy which is used in deciding technical priorities and relationships is itself ideologically loaded (usually by some a-prioristic value judgement.) Thus 'reducing the burden of income tax is the way to increase the productive effort of managers and entrepreneurs' is based on a (faulty) analogy with countries that have lower levels of taxation than the UK and higher rates of economic growth. The fact that academic research shows very little correlation between levels of income tax and managerial entrepreneurial input is thus ignored, and the analogy that supposedly supports the ideological position, already established, is wheeled out to buttress it.[24] This is not false or distorted *memory*, as such. It is, rather, an abuse of remembered data (that some countries do have higher rates of growth and lower tax rates than the UK) to justify a technical choice (the reduction of income tax) which the value system of the ideology has already indicated as desirable.

If we put together the role of memory in explanation, values and technique, we see how crucially dependent upon memory ideology is. And that makes it the more important to ask about the nature of memory, its reliability, its independence of other influences, its robustness when shared among individuals and transmogrified from individual memory to group memory to collective memory. Above all, the way in which unconscious memory – perhaps of childhood traumas; perhaps of childhood phantasy (not to be confused with fantasy, a distinction to which we shall return); perhaps of unhealed relationships in the more recent past – plays upon, filters out, puts a particular spin upon, reconstitutes conscious memory means that, in looking at ideology, we are dealing not with one-dimensional memory but with the deepest parts of the human psyche. As we shall see, ideology can reflect powers and principalities buried deep in us all.

Language

'The human consciousness which experiences is in the first instance a capacity to express something that we experience. This expression of reality takes place in language, supported by images and concepts, connotations and emotions which already have a long history and thus are also already given in the socio-historical group in which we live.'[25] We do not come, then, to language in a memory vacuum, for the language already has a history in the community in which we learn it and has already taken on, as it were, the ideological colouring of that community – as the scholars of sexism and racism so amply testify when analysing the ideological content of everyday language in our own contemporary society.[26]

But we do not deal with one language, with one common store of shared meanings, any more than most of us live exclusively in one community. One thing that social theorists have taught us is precisely that part of social reality is the meanings that are acquired by language in different social settings with different social actors. A 'fair wage' is a classic example. To a personnel manager meeting the chairman of her board it means one thing: to a branch official addressing a union meeting it means something quite different: and the difference lies not just in the amount of the wage, but in the emotional load attached to the phrase and the ideological and significative power determined by each community – in this case, management and workers.

That example is apposite in the context of a wider point. Those who seek to live by the Christian gospel are apt to use 'justice' language in their religio-political witness. They demand a 'fair price' for Third World exports; a 'fair wage' for workers; 'human rights' for those imprisoned without trial; 'non-violent solutions' to international tensions; 'equity' or 'fairness' in the allocation of land; and the 'proper sharing of burdens'. I am not concerned here to analyse those concepts, many of which are essentially rhetorical rather than substantive or analytical. My interest lies more in the memory-load associated with that type of language. There are two rather different points here.

The first raises questions about the possibility of real dialogue which trades in shared meanings across different language communities. Or, to put it another way, can 'fair' mean the same thing to a radical

Christian and the chairman of a multinational corporation when talking about, for example, the price Ghana receives for hardwood? And if not, are there means by which these two language communities can be enabled to communicate in a way that makes it possible for both sides to move forward, ethically and politically? Or are we so caught by our language that we are for ever condemned to trench warfare? This is so significant a question that we shall return to it in Chapter 10.

It is raised to a higher significance by the second point. Language draws upon the memory of the community that uses it: but we all also individually bring our own memory to the way in which we use and react to language. 'Justice' language is often the site in which more or less repressed memories of experienced injustice re-present themselves. The issue is, of course, wider than language alone – it may come to include ethical and political commitment – but it is language which, as it were, often acts as a lightning-conductor, transferring the psychic energy that attaches to a particular group of memories to the communicative community in which justice language is in use. The woman who has been raped as a young girl brings to language about 'women's rights' an intensity of purpose that someone who has not had the same experience, or a man, will find hard to relate to. Someone who lived through the Holocaust uses language about forgiveness with an existential *angst* that most of us will never know. In each case, the memory of the experience of injustice colours and conditions the sufferer's values, and that is reflected in the way she uses terms that others see as less charged.

That is clear. But what about those of us who have deeply repressed memories of injustice – of which we might have been the object *or the subject*? As we shall see when we look more closely at the ideas of Melanie Klein, it may well be that we are so haunted by guilt that we could not adequately repair our relations with an external object. And if we are haunted by guilt, even at this unconscious level, what will that do to the way in which we use language – especially language relating to rights, to duties, to altruism? In short, we bring to the language communities of which we are part our own memories, conscious and unconscious. And we learn the rules of the language community, and therefore tap into its own memories and its own ideologies. It is the interplay between our memory and the memory of the community that will help determine how we play the language games of our community.

I have sought in this chapter to show how memory, in many of the senses analysed in Chapter 1, is at work 'behind' three of the key structural forms of our world. This is important for the wider argument of the book as a whole because I shall want to argue in later chapters that the role of faith, as developed by theology, is to heal the destructive memories that are incorporated or instantiated in the oppressive structures of our world. We have, however, much ground to cover before we can explore that idea more creatively. In Part 2, then, I shall review the account that five different theoretical approaches have given of the way memory affects not just the individual psyche, but the society as a whole, usually through one or more of the structural components reviewed above. That will prepare the way, in Part 3, for a more direct assault on our main task: considering the way in which the Christian gospel may be thought to be redemptive by establishing counter-memories that can free both our selves from our compulsions and our structures from their oppressiveness.

PART TWO

4

Jung: Psyche, Archetype and Memory

A good place to start a more detailed exploration of the way in which unhealed memory holds us captive both in the way our structures develop and in the way in which we relate to them is with Jung. Of all leading writers on the unconscious, he has proved the least threatening to Christians. The Christian literature on Jung and Jung-derived ideas is huge and growing fast, in marked contrast to that on some of the no less relevant thinkers we shall be exploring in subsequent chapters.[1] So let us start on well-mapped territory and ask of Jung what account he can give of our trappedness, and what meaning he might ascribe to the claim that Christ has set us free.

In the University Library in Cambridge there is one copy of Ira Progoff's *Jung's Psychology and its Social Meaning*.[2] Published in England in 1953, it has been borrowed twice, an average of once every nineteen years. Breaking one of the cardinal rules of the library, a scholarly hand has written on page 250: 'This book is about everything but what the title suggests.'

The frustration is understandable. For all his great significance and the rising tide of interest in his ideas, Jung was primarily interested in the psyche of the individual – its development, its healing, its painful striving to reach its full potential. And yet one of his key analytical ideas is so pregnant with 'social meaning', in Progoff's well-chosen phrase, that no account of the relationship between memory and social structure can comfortably ignore it. As Jung's later apologists have frequently insisted, however, his clinical practice and his commitment to it meant that he did not himself adequately explore this level of implication of his ideas. They therefore remain abstract, sometimes seeming even ethereal and speculative, always hard to nail down in a scientifically satisfying way. Poetic, suggestive, teasing, challenging, they call us forward down a path that is as ill defined as it is dangerous.

It is well to acknowledge that much at the start, for Jung, ahead of his time, was himself impatient of many aspects of contemporary scientific thinking (as he was of many aspects of religious thinking), regarding the analytical, disaggregative approach of Cartesian method as likely to obscure elements of truth as to reveal them. Thus he could write: 'It is the function of Eros to unite what Logos has sundered,'[3] and, of course, for him the balancing of Eros and Logos was a key component of healthy psychic development. Given this determination to treat psychological and social ideas as wholes rather than as parts of a whole that may eventually be aggregated, we look in vain for a hard-edged, linear link between Jung's explorations of the psyche and the formation of social structure. What we find rather is a way of looking at ourselves and our world that is hugely suggestive and which can help to explain the nature of history and culture rather than a more tightly drawn structural manifestation of either. Accordingly, the following chapter inevitably distorts Jung's thought by forcing it into a specificity, almost a concreteness, that Jung's own writing seldom shows.

We shall first outline Jung's notion of the self and then look in more detail at two central ideas: archetypes and the collective unconscious. We shall then be in a position to summarise the role of memory in Jungian theory, before applying it to two specific issues: the myth of salvation through romance, and the role of ritual. These applications will encourage us to look at heterodox developments of Jungian theory, especially on the way in which the collective unconscious is modified, and, again, on ritual. We shall then look at another key Jungian idea – the shadow – and apply that in the context of aggression and conflict. The chapter closes with a short summary that draws some of the leading themes together. I have tried to write the chapter in a way that will be accessible to readers who have only the haziest idea of what Jung wrote while maintaining the interest of readers who are familiar with the non-specialist literature in the field.

Jung's Theory of the Self

Jung shared with Freud the notion of the 'ego' as the centre of immediate consciousness, the 'locus' where the inner reality of 'me' becomes aware of the outer world. Each ego is, of course, different: some are more introverted, others more extroverted; some more aware of the data collected by their senses, others more aware of their emotional responses to those data. To that extent, the ego determines the way a person relates to the world: what she perceives; what sense she makes of it; how she reacts; how she feels about herself and her relationships.

The ego does not, however, exist independently. As Freud operated with a trinity of ego, superego and id, so Jung conceived of the ego as part of a wider process. Both holding that process together and lying at its very heart is the self, a key concept for Jung. The self, the totality of consciousness and unconsciousness, relates to the world through the ego – and yet contains the ego. If this sounds paradoxical and even inconsistent, that is because the insight Jung was trying to express does not easily fit into scientific language patterns with their exclusive dualities. He wanted to insist that the self cannot be conceived apart from the ego; nor the ego apart from the self. He wrote that the ego revolves round the self 'very much as the earth rotates round the sun'.[4] This dethronement of the ego – in contrast, for instance, to Freudian theories – led to Jung's disciples hailing him as a latter-day Copernicus, shifting the centre of the psyche from the superficially apparent to the deeper reality. More mundanely, we can make the functional distinction between the processes whereby we relate to the outer world and the inner processing of that experience.

Central to that 'inner processing' are two more basic Jungian ideas: the personal unconscious and the collective unconscious. As a first approximation to ideas that in the end turn out to interpenetrate each other, we may think of the personal unconscious as the material of which I have at some stage been aware (that is, conscious) but have now 'forgotten'. In terms of the matrix that we examined in Chapter 1, it includes all the material in the 'Individual' column, though Jung would not have used the Freudian term 'repressed' in quite the same way as Freud without, of course, denying that some 'forgotten' material may prove exceedingly hard to recall. For Jung, this material is personal in that it has been mediated by my ego, but it is unconscious in that I am not now thinking about it – and perhaps never did think about it. Maybe it was a bit of data picked up by my senses and then stored, without my noticing it consciously at all, in my unconscious where it remains accessible in principle to my conscious thoughts at a later date. As he put it in a relatively late work, the personal unconscious is composed of 'fantasies (including dreams) of a personal character which go back unquestionably to personal experiences, things forgotten or repressed'.[5]

There is, however, a further twist to Jung's account of the personal consciousness. He wrote, in a way that echoes Hegel and anticipates Pannenberg: 'all the *future* things which are taking shape in me and will sometime come to consciousness; all this (i.e., as well as past memories and sensations) is the content of the unconscious'[6] (my emphasis). How, we may well wonder, can it be said that the future 'things . . . taking shape within' is part of the unconscious?

This can be approached at two levels. First, the personal unconscious has its own potential, its own dynamic. For Jung, the personal unconscious is composed of complexes, a term he used without the pathological overtones that have passed from Freud's usage to common parlance. These complexes are groups of 'ideas' (to be understood in a wider sense than merely items of cognition or intellectual associations, so that, for example, elements of value and will are included) which constellate around a nucleus.[7] Jung became convinced from his clinical experience that these complexes are autonomous in the sense that they have a life of their own that is beyond the control of the will power of even healthy, well-adjusted people. They 'take over' the person and 'make' him or her act in ways that are unpredictable on the basis of the past. We shall examine this in more detail in a later section of this chapter with reference to the animus/anima complex, but for the moment the key point is that this autonomy of the complex is part of what Jung meant by 'the future, things which are taking shape in me' being located in the personal unconscious. I am, in a nutshell, capable of more than I know – for good and ill. That is a potentially chilling idea, which we shall encounter in a later and more sombre context.

The Collective Unconscious

The second sense in which the personal unconscious contains the future is more complicated. Jung believed that the nucleus of the complexes of the personal unconscious are related to the archetypes of the collective unconscious. That is, my personal unconscious is not only mine in an exclusive sense: it draws on material that is common to all in my culture, without my being consciously aware of the process.

Anthony Stevens illustrates the relationship between personal and collective unconscious with reference to the mother complex:

> The complex is formed and becomes active as a consequence of the child's living in close contiguity to a woman (usually the mother) whose behaviour is similar to the child's built-in anticipation of maternity [the mother archetype, drawn from the collective unconscious]. In the absence of the personal mother, the archetype can be activated by any other female who is consistently in loco parentis – an aunt, grandmother, nanny or older sister. Later in life the same complex can be projected on to other older women or on to institutions or public figures which perform the maternal role – the Church, the Queen, the University or even the Army. The religious manifestations of the archetype are legion – the earth goddesses of the Mediterranean region, for example, culminating in the Holy Virgin, Mother of God – all of whom could activate the mother complex and release powerful feelings of devotion in believers.[8]

Note how, on this account, the archetypes, rooted in the collective unconscious, 'activate' the complexes of the personal unconscious. Stevens is faithful to Jung when he writes that this process 'releases powerful feelings'. Like Freud, Jung used metaphors (which he sometimes seems to forget are metaphors) drawn from hydraulics or mechanical engineering to describe the 'psychic energy' or libido that is released by the archetype. He even uses an analogy with a steam engine which converts 'heat into the pressure of steam and then into the energy of motion'. In much the same way, 'human energy, as a natural product of differentiation, is a machine; first of all a technical

53

one that uses natural conditions for the transformation of physical and chemical energy, but also a mental machine using mental conditions for the transformation of libido'.[9]

We need not follow Jung into this dangerous and potentially misleading analogy to grasp his point: that the interaction between the archetypes of the collective unconscious and the complexes of the personal unconscious is attended by the release of energy – psychic, emotional, spiritual and/or even physical. This energy is the locus of the Self and is manifested in the 'new birth' or deep transformation of the personality which is the outcome of individuation. The source of the energy may be the archetypes; but in the individuated personality, it will reside in the Self. It is from this interaction that Jung's theory of the Self gains its dynamism; and it is the origins of that dynamic, the archetypes, that therefore assume such cardinal importance.[10] We must now therefore turn to a closer examination of the archetypes.

The Archetypes

Jung's revolutionary hypothesis was that we 'inherit' the archetypes of the collective unconscious at birth. They are not learnt, as are the ideas that cluster round the nuclei of the complexes of the personal unconscious: they are 'there' at birth. Often accused in his own lifetime and since of a pre-Darwinian belief that learnt characteristics can be inherited (an idea itself now less ridiculed than it was in the heyday of Darwinianism), Jung insisted that the term archetype

> is not meant to denote an inherited idea, but rather an inherited mode of functioning, corresponding to the inborn way in which the chick emerges from the egg, the bird builds its nest, a certain type of wasp stings the motor ganglion of the caterpillar and eels find their way to the Bermudas.[11]

It is thus close to the kind of habit memory we explored in Chapter 1 with respect to polyandry in Nepal, in so far as it is, in Jung's phrase, 'a pattern of behaviour'.[12] 'This aspect of the archetype, the purely biological one, is the proper concern of scientific enquiry.'[13]

Suddenly and perhaps unexpectedly, then, we find ourselves in the intellectual climate of Chapter 1, with the ethologists and social biologists. Jung would regard such company as perfectly appropriate.[14] As animals have learnt, by trial, error, mutation and adaptation, to cope with their natural and social surroundings, so we, Jung would argue, have by a parallel process learnt to adapt our psychic and social life by equipping ourselves with an array of archetypes that can deliver health, energy and psychic wholeness in the environment in which we find ourselves. In this sense archetypes bestow a potential, which it is the task of the maturing individual to realise.[15] No wonder Jung sometimes referred to archetypes as 'dominants' and even, in perhaps an unconscious echo of Pauline cosmology, as 'ruling powers'.[16] Their role in the psychic life of the individual and in the social life of the community is as necessary – and as potentially positive – as the sex drive in Freud or the need to preserve one's genetic pool in the post-Darwinians. 'Knowing' the archetypes, however, can be problematic, since 'archetypal content expresses itself first and foremost in metaphors'.[17]

Like the peacock's tail or the red spot on the beak of the herring-gull, however, archetypes have emerged from a long process of adaptation.[18] Jung refers to them as having 'crystallized out in the course of time' so they are thus 'primordial', a phrase Jung used long before he settled (in self-defence against those who misunderstood the earlier term) on 'archetype'. One of the problems that attend Jung's frequent reference to biological analogies is that they tend to obscure the part that memory plays in the formation of archetypes. Though they may function and be encoded in much the same way as release mechanisms, they are ritualised and committed to social memory in myth, religion, symbol and legend. That is one of their key features which helps to answer the question of the origins of and nature of our knowledge of the archetypes. We are back to social and collective memory, both conscious and unconscious.

For Jung believed that we have essentially two sources of knowledge of them: in dreams and in myths. In dreams the defences of the psyche are lowered so that archetypal material can, as it were, break through into consciousness, to be recognised by the skilled analyst for what they are. And in myths, particularly the classical myths of ancient cultures, we encounter a remarkable consistency of images and motifs that speak of archetypes in narrative or dramatic settings:

wise old man, wicked witch, beautiful princess, snake, wild beast, divine light and so on. Later Jungians have split on the real value of myth and fairy tale as evidence of archetypal structure. There are now (at least) two schools of thought, one pointing out that such material can only tell us about content, the other maintaining that the regularities observable in such material can offer a base for inference about structure.[19] Thus Hillman: 'myths ... describe the behaviour of the archetypes; they are dramatic descriptions in personified language of psychic processes'.[20] Most modern Jungians have abandoned the attempt to produce a list of archetypal images as ill conceived (even though Jung gave his blessing and name to such a venture). They would rather insist on the emotional response of the person dreaming or imagining the images.

We have now reviewed the three sets of concepts out of which Jung constructs his theory of the Self – the ego, the complexes and the archetypes. We have seen how the interaction between these, and especially between the last two, is attended by releases of energy and how hard to control this energy can be. In Jung's schema, the Self is what holds these three 'components' together – or which, in cases of mental illness, fails to hold them together. Its function, however, is not only integrative: it is also purposive. It seeks to move the whole structure of the psyche, with itself at its heart, to higher levels of integration. As a river finds its way, albeit with meanders, deep sluggish pools and chaotic waterfalls, to the sea, so the Self has within it a power or force that moves the psyche to a new quality of life. This process Jung called individuation, the struggle (and Jung never minimised the pain, conflict and confusion that individuation costs) to reach the highest possible degree of self-realisation or Self-fulfilment.[21] In this struggle the actualisation of the archetypes in the life of the person is so significant that, in a phrase that is more poetic than scientific, Jung could call the Self the archetype of the archetypes. Jung's expectation was that, as more and more people strove for individuation, social, political and cultural life would be transformed. For the archetypes which are the main motors of that process are themselves not only shared cross-culturally (thus suggesting a potential inner harmony for the whole of humanity), but also are symbols of social relationships. They speak of relatedness to others, not merely private wholeness.

And that takes us to the final point that needs to be made in this sketch of Jung's understanding of the nature of the person. The Self, in its drive to individuation and self-realisation, is in search of finality, Omega – God. He is the ultimate possibility of individuation, or, to adapt a phrase of R.S. Lee, the envelope of the parameters of the Self.[22] Thus God and Self share some of the deepest symbols: the mandala, for example, with its circles and squares (or crosses which share with the square four points, the image of completeness) and (usually) heavily emphasised centre is an almost universal symbol of deity and the (whole) Self. As we shall see, this transcendent element in Jung's thought, distrusted by scientists, critical theorists and Christians alike, led Jung to see the social forms of religion – ritual, worship, symbolism – as crucially important not only for the individual but for the whole of human society.

Memory in Jungian Theory

We must now leave Jung's basic theoretical approach and, subject to the caveats with which this chapter opened, see how far his ideas will go to explain the links between memory and social structure. Memory for Jung is clearly of the utmost importance. The personal unconscious is composed of complexes in the formation of which memories of the past, whether repressed or simply forgotten, mingle with more abstract ideas to constellate around a nucleus. More significantly, that nucleus itself is derived from or related to archetypal material from the collective unconscious and in its very nature is sedimented primordial or archaic memory. Archetypes do not arise out of thin air. Though they may be adapted and even embroidered by the imagination, they incorporate significant elements of the lived experiences of aeons of time. As I have already stressed, in so far as they are re-presented[23] in myth and dream and symbol, the memory of them and of their power is kept alive. Indeed, for Jung this process of the re-presentation of archetypes in the consciousness of individuals and communities is the essence of the drive towards wholeness. To 'forget' (in the sense of ignore or cease to be interested in and moved by) the archetypes is to court inner and outer disaster. Only when individuals and societies are alive to that part of their hidden collective memories represented by their archetypes, as made manifest in their myths and symbols (usually religious or quasi-religious), are they in touch with the source of that psychic energy they need to bring them through the dangers of development and change. Proper in-touchedness with that material will allow them to adapt successfully to the new situations.

Jungian Theory Applied: Romantic Love and the Family

If memory is critical, what about social structure? Can Jungian thinking relate memory to structure or at least to semi-structured patterns of behaviour? In this rather weaker form of the hypothesis, the possibilities look more promising. Let us start with a theme close to that which we examined in Chapter 3, family structure. Here our interest is less in the family as a reproductive system than in the nature of (Western) courtship and the notion of romantic love. Two phenomena are immediately striking. The first is the hold on, one might even say the fascination for, our culture exerted by romantic love. It is enshrined in popular songs, in films, in novels, in fashion, in behaviour patterns, in language – and, of course, in ritual and symbol.

The second striking phenomenon is, as it were, the mirror image of this emphasis on (or over-investment in) romantic love: namely, high and rising divorce rates. Having sunk all our emotional capital in romantic love we discover its dividend is ephemeral – but intoxicating. We are no longer 'in love' with our partner: so we 'fall in love' (itself a most interesting and telling phrase) with someone else and divorce our first partner.

It is unprofitable to debate whether this twin phenomenon (which reduces to an almost insatiable craving for the heightened quality of life that 'being in love' produces) is or is not a structure in formal terms. For our purposes the pattern of behaviour I have sketched, even burlesqued, is now so endemic in Western countries (and those bits of the rest of the world that ape our culture) that it has the stability and power to generate expectations that justify our inclusion of it in this study. The question then becomes: Does Jungian understanding of the nature of the unconscious throw light on this behaviour? And does memory play a part in that?

Two of the best-known complexes in the personal unconscious are the animus and the anima – the inner male in the woman, and the inner female in the man. These archetypal structures

> represent an innate aspect of men and women – that aspect of them which is somehow different to how they function consciously; something other, strange, perhaps mysterious but certainly full of possibilities and potentials . . . a man will, quite naturally, image what is 'other' to him in the symbolic form of a woman – a being with an-other anatomy. A woman will symbolise what is foreign or mysterious to her in terms of the kind of body she does not herself have.[24]

The extent to which parents help to form this image – and especially mother anima – is much debated: Jung himself was careful to distinguish between mother (and the mother complex) and anima.[25] These complexes are projected on to people who can contain them: 'since this image [animus, anima] is unconscious, it is always projected upon the person of the beloved, and is one of the chief reasons for passionate attraction or aversion'.[26] So what is happening when people are 'in love' is that they are held, almost controlled, by the amazing psychic power of projection of the animus/anima, with the result that they are in danger of relating, not to the real flesh-and-blood, pig-and-angel creature that is Joe or Jill, but to an idealised creation of their own – whom they erect into an idol. And they worship the idol. Such language needs to be taken seriously, for, as is repeated in our popular songs and soap operas again and again, marriage is invested with a salvation mystique. As the 'natural' consummation of romantic love, it can save us – from all that threatens us and especially from ourselves.[27] When the projection is withdrawn, as sooner or later it will almost certainly have to be, the 'real' Joe and Jill can emerge, as it were, from behind the projection.

Now this is an exceedingly dangerous period for the survival of the relationship, and that for three reasons. First, the heightened ecstatic quality of life, the glorious technicolour of perception that stems from the psychic power of the complex, disappears. Life in black and white seems drab after full colour. Second, the real person is not ideal. He or she has faults, failings, irritating habits and inconsistencies. They were always there, but now that the projection is withdrawn they stand fully revealed to the ego-consciousness of the partner. Third, at this stage one or other partner may project his or her shadow via the animus/a on to the other. Since the shadow constitutes the unacceptable parts of the self (see below for a fuller treatment), it follows that its projection makes the partner appear most unattractive – or, worse, frightening and/or contemptible. Under such circumstances, of course, a relationship becomes intolerable to both parties. The partnership can then only survive if the owner of the projected complex can 'put it' somewhere safe. If he or she immediately seeks another person of the opposite sex to carry it for him or her, romantic love will follow and the original partnership come under impossible strain.

Jung has been assailed recently by writers of a feminist perspective because he concentrated mostly on the anima and tended to be somewhat negative about the animus.[28] Despite a placatory note, Johnson might be thought to fall under the same condemnation.[29] It is, however, a serious debate whether there is a perfect symmetry between men/anima and women/animus. Goldberg, for example, has argued that Jung's thinking on the animus is sketchy, late, and seemingly artificial, and that women can live with animus more easily than men with anima. There are theoretical reasons why that may be so, but clinical evidence suggests that some women, at least, need help in integrating their animus in much the same way as (perhaps more than) men do.[30]

According to Jungian psychology, then, a significant part of the pathology of our culture and of our sexual relationships can be 'explained' by our failure properly to integrate powerful complexes, located in the personal unconscious but drawing upon archetypal material from the collective unconscious.[31] As Robert Johnson has demonstrated very successfully in a series of best-selling books, these archetypes are predictably present as recurrent motifs in our literature, folk tales and myths. As he points out, the classic tale of romantic love, Tristan and Isolde, appears very soon after the emergence of medieval notions of courtly love and contains, in mythological form, a penetrating analysis of the problems and potentialities of anima and her projections. Writing of Tristan sipping the wine of herbs, he says:

The meaning of the love potion is that the supernatural world suddenly invades the natural world through romantic love. The fire descends from heaven! The world of soul and spirit, the over-whelming power of the religious potentiality in the psyche, sud-denly invades the ordinary world of human relationships. What we had always longed for, a vision of ultimate meaning and unity, is suddenly revealed to us in the form of another human being.[32]

The real tragedy, of course, is that as long as we are controlled by anima (or animus), real relatedness to real people is impossible. As Hillman has put it,

> It seems odd that anima could ever have been considered as a help in human relationships. In each of her classical shapes she is a non-human or half-human creature and her effects led us away from the individually human situation. She makes moods, distortions, illusions which serve human relatedness only where the persons concerned share the same mood or fantasy. If we want 'to relate', then anima begone![33]

In each of her 'classical shapes', then, anima warns us of the two phenomena with which this section started: the seductive irresistibility of the transforming power of romantic love, and its brittleness and final destructiveness.

To conclude this illustration, it is important to recall the role of memory in the process I have described. In so far as the archetype of animus/a is sedimented archaic memory, it is the motor that drives the whole convoy of emotions, relationships and structures – to healthy, whole-making relatedness or to destruction. A theology that ignores it or that merely preaches a sexual or family morality that fails to take account of its power is not only intellectually deficient, it is pastorally irresponsible. We shall have to return to this theme in the closing chapters of the book.

Jungian Theory Applied: Symbol and Ritual

For the moment that leads to the next structural form that Jung's thought emphasises – ritual and religion in general. Jung believed that humankind needs to be as in touch as possible with the unconscious

complexes and archetypes, though the very fact that they are unconscious makes this a difficult and demanding task. The penalty for
failing to integrate this unconscious material is that we become its
slave: hence Jung's famous aphorism about thinking we have complexes, whereas 'in reality they have us' – as anima 'has' a large part
of our contemporary male culture. To avoid paying this potentially
destructive penalty, the process of integration of archetypal material
into consciousness has to be attempted – and that is where Jung
thought religion and its rituals have a major role to play.

Central to that role is the power of symbol. Jung thought that
'archaic' symbols reflect some archetypes and thereby mediate their
power from the (collective) unconscious to the consciousness of
thought. Such symbols would include the mandala described above;
the cross; the lignum and its many variants; water, especially in the
context of ritual purification through immersion; sun; moon; mother;
many kinds of animals; fire; and the child. Through re-presenting
the archetypes, the symbol is, according to Jung, able to activate the
complexes in the personal unconscious and thus 'bring to mind'
the deepest parts of the self in the process of individuation.

If that is the case at the level of the individual, however, Jung
believed that it is *a fortiori* important and health-promoting for the
whole of the community. He recognised that religious ritual is in
essence a social activity: one cannot (usually) enact a ritual (i.e., represent the archetype through symbolic 'play') in isolation. As we
saw in Chapter 1, there is an important sense in which ritual *is* the
social memory of the community. This is consistent with Jung's
conviction that the whole community's capacity to rediscover
together at the conscious level what they share, in the collective
unconscious, at a far deeper and usually impenetrable level, is what
enables the community to survive as a community – that is, as a
group of people sharing sufficient values, memories, expectations,
hopes and fears to perceive themselves as 'belonging to' each other.
This prevents the community from dis-integrating in response to the
fissiparous tendencies of the ego and the complexes of the personal
unconscious, raised to a higher power, of course, as the egos are
multiplied in the community. To that extent the observance of
religious ritual is an essential precondition of the survival of the
community.

Clearly Jung had in mind a wider canvas than exclusively Christian ritual, but he was faithful to the deepest sense of the religious as being that which ties together the immanent and the transcendent. By locating the transcendent in the archetypes – or, to put the same thought in a more orthodox way, by insisting that the transcendent is revealed through the archetypes – he made it the business of religious practice to make immanent, and thus available to consciousness, what of the transcendent is *potentially* available and accessible in the unconscious. The touchstone for Jung was therefore not dogmatic orthodoxy, of which he was critical and impatient, but the effectiveness with which this 'tying together' of immanent and transcendent actually happens in ritual or liturgical acts. In so far as religious ritual portrayed symbols that really did re-present the archetypes of a culture and thus allowed individuals to 'own' them, it was religiously 'true'. If it obscured such symbols or misrepresented them or abused their power (for example, by hijacking it for narrow institutional ends), then it was false and destructive.

Jung believed, however, that humanity has a natural, innate craving for 'true' religion in this sense, an idea we have already encountered in a somewhat different form in Chapter 1. Just as the individual has an innate longing for the wholeness of individuation, so the community has an innate need to be connected with its common archetypal heritage. In this sense humankind is, for Jung, naturally religious; and that implies that religious ideas and practices are a 'natural' form of social life – the absence or enfeeblement of which represents a severe potential threat to the health of the community or even species.

For the need for the numinous, for the holy, can be met by many religious forms: from priestly theatre to popular dance; from the most rigorous ascesis to the celebration of the materiality (and sexuality) of creation; from the focus on the particular shrine to celebration of 'God in all things'. But what is common to all these varieties of religious expression is precisely that they are religious; they are attempts, in Jung's terminology, to symbolise the wisdom that is held in the collective unconscious. Just as the language of myth varies from culture to culture, though displaying a remarkable inner coherence and consistency of content cross-culturally, so religious practice does (and, as Jung's analysis implies, should) assume different forms, according to the culture which fashions the relevant rituals. But at

least the inner processes at work are identical: and the criteria by
which their integrity may be judged are invariant.

That is not, of course, to deny that at some periods a culture may
be more (or less) aware of its need for a 'valid' religion than at others.
Indeed, as many Christian commentators on Jung have emphasised,
he was deeply exercised by the hollowness of contemporary Christianity and its academic dogfights over doctrinal orthodoxy, which
tended to obscure the real needs that people have for a proper
connection with the deepest wisdoms. Thus Jung observed a connection between the rise of Nazism – a false religion that, as Jung held,
did at least activate archetypal material of German nationalism – and
the failure of European Christianity which had allowed itself and its
adherents to substitute a sterile intellectualism for a living re-presentation of the stuff of the collective unconscious. If Christianity had
been alive with the symbols that could activate the healing power of
the collective unconscious, then, Jung implies, Nazism would never
have taken the terrible form that could actualise such destructive
force. One shudders to think how Jung would have viewed the
current state of mainline Christian denominations in the West as they
collude with a triumphant individualised materialism and an associated trivialisation of meaning. In the last chapters of this book we
shall look at ways in which we can use Jung's insights in a more
coherent theological setting.

For this reason it is important to be aware of the way memory
lurks beneath the surface of this analysis. It is when human society
allows itself to be cut off from the memories incorporated in the
archetypes that the symbolic (and religious) life of the community
dies – and we are back with the sense of void and desperation voiced
by Wallace Stevens, T.S. Eliot, R.S. Thomas, George Steiner and a
thousand other philosophers, poets and cultural critics who see our
civilisation wasting away for lack of a link to the transcendent.

At this point in the argument, I shall leave Jung and see how far
we can use his approach to illuminate a further aspect of the main
argument – that memory is at work shaping us and our world.

Heterodox Questions about the Collective Unconscious

I want to raise one difficulty and point to one potential solution that is not to be found in Jung, but which is, I believe, consistent with his general approach.

The difficulty can be put like this: when Jung talks of the collective unconscious, whose is it? How collective is collective? Is it a universal unconscious that is common to Inuit, Bushmen and Bengalis? Or is it a collective unconscious that is unique to a particular community, though perhaps having some elements that are shared across a broader spectrum? There can be little doubt that Jung himself, with his intellectual eye always glancing over his psychologist's shoulder towards biology and theories of evolution, would have answered in universalistic terms: the collective unconscious contains primordial material that pre-dates ethnic divisions, and dates back to the emergence of *Homo sapiens* as a distinct species. Consistent with this, of course, he would recognise that it could acquire particular cultural or ethnic features – as *Homo sapiens* has acquired blue eyes in Scandinavia and curly hair in Africa. Or, to draw a parallel we have already observed, symbols and myths vary from culture to culture – but they point to a common underlying reality.

Once one agrees that the collective unconscious is culturally conditioned, even if retaining the same essential material, the way is open to see how symbols and even archetypes themselves may change in response to cultural pressures. No one who has worked from a Jungian perspective with clients' dreams can but be struck how 'modern' are many potent images – cars, lorries, aeroplanes, bombs, guns, concrete, trams, dams, bandages . . . the list of modern images that have great symbolic power is nearly endless. (In my own work, I have been astonished how Mrs Thatcher has acquired a quasi-archetypal character in people's dreams. She may, of course, represent only the anima, but the dynamic of many of the dreams suggest that she has other connotations, of which non-sexual manic power is the most obvious.) Jung may say that they point to or symbolise archetypes with which he was familiar, but there is no reason to suppose that these modern images do not have, in their own way, the inner resonance of more classical archetypes such as the lignum, sun or fire. These classic examples are themselves culturally determined: fire is, after all, in its domesticated form a fairly modern invention.[34]

From this there flows a conclusion of the greatest importance to which we shall have to return later. For if a culture affects the collective unconscious, it affects its resources for its own inner healing. Far from there being a linear progression from collective unconscious through the personal unconscious to the ego and the individuation of the Self, we may posit a closed circle: the Self (more or less individuated according to its own inner development) allies with other Selves in the culture and generates symbols certainly, and archetypes possibly, that are then available (if not immediately then at some point in the future) as nuclei in the complexes of the personal unconscious; and as archetypal material around which social forms of the future may be moulded.

To put the same point in a slightly different way, Jung usually writes as if I am the object of the sedimented, remembered archetypal material of the primordial past. What I am now suggesting is that I also add my own (no doubt infinitesimally tiny) deposit to that sediment, which, especially if it is repeated by many others and/or given great intensity in a series of group experiences, will be incorporated in the collective unconscious for future use. In this sense, collective memory as we encountered it in Chapter 1 is the first step towards re-creating archetypal material that will affect both the individual functioning and the social performance of later generations.[35]

Now, this line of thinking suggests a major departure from Jung. As we have already seen, for him the collective unconscious was a storehouse of materials for healing. If, however, we are adding our own deposits to the collective unconscious, can we be sure that that material is so unambiguously benign? To however small a degree, each of us plays our part in the survival of the human race. The more we 'deposit' material that releases psychic energy of destructive or hateful power into the consciousness of future generations, the more likely we make it that those generations will behave in destructive and hate-filled ways. With the growing and increasingly dominant technology of death, that can have only one conclusion.

For example, a cataclysmic event and the associated memories and fantasies (such as the atomic bombing of Nagasaki and Hiroshima in

1945) may be 'deposited' in the collective unconscious, an idea narratively explored by J.G. Ballard in *Empire of the Sun* and *The Kindness of Women*[36] and by Edith Sitwell in *Dirge for the New Sunrise*,[37] as well, of course, as by many writers on the Holocaust, Primo Levi pre-eminent among them. Indeed, if the 'purpose' of the collective unconscious is to enable the species to survive psychically and physically, one might suppose that there has to be a reflection in its material of major changes in technology, and perhaps especially of destructive technology.

Heterodox Questions about Religion, Ritual and Transformation

With the help of post-Jungians we can take that thought substantially further. If religion is a special case of mythology – i.e., it puts us more or less directly in touch with fundamental psychological processes – then we need to enlarge the canvas and examine not just religion (in a sense that almost predicates Judaeo-Christian traditions) but the whole of mythology as having the same liberating effect as Jung ascribed to a 'live' religion. Hence the interest of 'archetypal psychologists' such as Hillman and Miller in polytheistic mythology (supremely of classical Greek provenance) and their hostility to monotheism as presented by the Judaeo-Christian tradition. For they see monotheism as a kind of meta-metaphor for an overly narrow, enclosed view of human possibilities. Hillman, for example, sees Jung's concentration on the Self, a monad, as contrived and unnecessary. He wants to recognise anima(us) and a wide range of other images as at least as important in freeing the imagination, the developmental paths, the possibilities of what it means to be fully human and fully alive. And to do that he needs to rebel against a Self/God identity with its explicit monotheism and reinstate a pantheon.

In doing so, he and Miller have a social perspective in mind. They see the Self/monotheistic God agenda of Jung as reflected in the lack of variety and plurality in Western culture and politics. They trace a direct line between it and totalitarianism or its democratically garbed proxies. Going even further, they see the standardisation of culture; the dominance of a mass-production-based technology; the lack of creativity and originality in politics, art and relationships as derived from a fixation with the One, the centre, the Omega – the monad in all its guises, religious or cultural. By contrast, Miller, in terms consistent with the approach of Derrida, Foucault and the deconstructionists, longs for a polytheism that allows individuals freedom to make (or choose) their own images, their own symbols, and thus discover their true selves for themselves by breaking open the 'givenness' of the text of monotheism – an idea we shall explore again in Chapter 12. Although such a line of thought sounds shocking to those of us immersed in Judaic monotheism, it is not logically committed to the abandonment of morality. It is committed to an 'open' morality rather than a system of rules, but Miller would be quick to point out that the Greek pantheon had its own, pluralistic, morality.[38]

What is valuable in such an approach is surely that it reminds us that there is indeed a connection between culture (with its obvious memory content) and politics on the one hand and unconscious psychological processes (including, again, its memory content) on the other. Yet we may feel (as at times Jung himself seems to[39]) that the object should not be to preserve social structures or merely chart their origins in psychological processes, but to transform them. Does a Jungian perspective, with its emphasis on ritual, symbol and archetype, help us to see how that might happen? How, in a word, may memory be transformed?

Despite those who dismiss such an approach as speculative,[40] let us follow one recent author who has analysed the ritual content of the 1985 Live Aid rock concert (and, by association, its successors). As it was presented originally, this analysis belongs more in the tradition of Victor Turner with his Freudian roots rather than to Jung, but it does little violence to the analysis to present it in its own terms and then reflect upon it from the perspective we have developed above.[41]

Reich is primarily concerned to ask the question, against the positivists and the structural functionalists of the Durkheim tradition: Under what circumstances can ritual be genuinely transformative in a moral sense? In asking that very question, he is at least open to a Jungian possibility: that ritual, collective sedimented memory, can change the way people behave, both individually and collectively. Drawing heavily on Wolfgang Jetter, Reich emphasises the four modes of symbolic communication: immediacy; multivalency (in the sense that 'persons may bring into the symbol the entire world, general and personal history, birth and death'); comprehensiveness (because symbols can express so much) and directiveness, 'in so far as it invites one to cooperate in the realisation of the world view expressed by the symbol'. Thus, through the polyvalent form of memory, symbols speak powerfully to people, both, as it were, from 'outside' and from their own inner experience. Reich implies (though he nowhere states in so many words) that when these two 'messages' cohere, the emotional and normative force of the ritual can be powerful indeed. And in so far as the ritual is re-enacted (as was the case with the Live Aid concert) it becomes in its own terms a part of collective memory, frequently re-presented to different audiences.

This is not the place to present Reich's argument extensively, but it is worth a small digression to sketch out the main lines of his analysis as an illustration of how the various types of personal and collective memory interact in symbol formation and value change.

He shows how the Live Aid rock marathon presented symbols that had many of the features listed above. The music, and especially the theme 'We are the world', had its own symbolic references; but so too did the technology (with huge audiences hooked up across the world); the dialetic between the performers and the audience; and perhaps above all the visible co-operation of normally highly competitive rock groups appearing on stage together and, uniquely symbolic in Reich's view, passing the microphone (that most prized phallic symbol of power) from one to another in an act of fraternity and co-operation. In symbolic form here is a statement of an ideal, a vision of how the world can be: co-operation replacing competitiveness; as the theme song put it, almost over-consciously: 'There is a choice we're making; we're saving our own lives (sic). It's true, we make a better day, just you and me'. But it is not a vision unrooted in reality. The programme allowed for hard-hitting interviews with victims and aid workers, but more than that, the logistics of watering and draining so huge a crowd over so long a period maintained what Reich calls a factuality, a link with the common-sense world that stands in opposition to Utopian idealism.

As Reich pointed out, however, in whatever way we may read the symbols *post facto*, the truth is that different people (whether participating 'live' in the events in Philadelphia or London, or through the medium of television worldwide) reacted in a variety of ways. Some value systems and ultimately lives were changed; at the other end of the spectrum, others remained cynical or dismissive. If 'people' had, in Jung's terms, been in the presence of symbols of archetypal material, they had reacted to it in very different ways. This is not, of course, impossible to reconcile with Jungian thinking: for the archetypal material has to be mediated through the complexes of the personal unconscious – and, by definition, personal unconsciousnesses are personal and unique. In this sense, however, Jungian thinking (as other paradigms) leaves many loose ends. But that would hardly have surprised Jung, the constant critic of over-determination.

There is, then, no need for embarrassment at that level. I take this to be an apposite illustration of the way in which a Jungian (or post-Jungian) approach can demonstrate the power of memory to generate, mediate and concretise personal and social shifts in consciousness – and changes in action. The processes and relationships are complex and uncertain, but that does not mean they are not real or can be ignored by a theology that wishes to speak of the possibility of change, of liberation from destructive impulses. If memory is so powerful a part of our mental equipment, we need to treat it with all the care we can bring to bear. Before we let the argument move on and begin to see how other paradigms treat memory, and then how this impacts on theology, we need to return to the Jungian mainstream for a final, and chilling, demonstration of the relationship between memory and reality.

Back to Orthodoxy: the Shadow

Jung recounts an encounter with a highly gifted, creative, artistic patient. The patient brought a 'typical tetradic mandala', a symbol of wholeness, either achieved or potential. But on the other side of the board, the same patient had produced a circular form of representations of sexual perversions and obscenities of the most violent and crude variety. This is a precise representation of the Shadow, an archetype that embraces all that a person (and by extension a culture) finds unacceptable in her/himself. Thus the sexual confusion and fantasy that the artistic patient did not wish to acknowledge or own is portrayed on the reverse side of the board which carries (and, as it were, presents to the world) the calm and beautiful mandala. It is the latter which Jung called the persona, the mask that we all try to present to the world and which we quickly replace if it should slip. Thus Jung would recognise the truth of the poem of a philosopher who much influenced him – Nietzsche:

'Wanderer, who are thou. . . . What will serve to refresh thee? Only name it, whatever I have, I offer thee!'
'To refresh me? To refresh me? Oh, thou prying one, what sayest thou? But give me, I prithee . . .'
'What? What? Speak out!'
'Another mask! A second mask!'[42]

On the shadow, the reverse of the mask, it is important to echo two emphases of Jung's. First, there is nothing evil or sinful in the shadow *per se*. Jung usually associated the shadow, at least in part, with instinctuality, and recognised that its symbols can often be animals displaying great strength or vigour. What is evil is not the intrinsic energy of this instinctuality, but the refusal of the individual to recognise it and give it proper play in his/her conscious life.

Second, Jung used the word Shadow precisely to emphasise the solidity of what constitutes a block to light. No block, no shadow. Hence, to unwind the metaphor, the more differentiated the ego, the more removed from consciousness the shadow. And the more removed from consciousness, the more likely that the shadow will operate autonomously. 'Closer examination of the dark characteristics – that is, the inferiorities constituting the shadow – reveals that they have an emotional nature, a kind of autonomy, and accordingly an obsessive, or, better, possessive quality.'[43] One way in which it might so operate is by projection: that is, the familiar process whereby I 'see' (or more usually imagine or greatly exaggerate) in others what I most fear and dislike in myself. As with animus/a, Jung insisted that 'one reacts with projections; one does not awake them': that is, one is the victim of something in the unconscious over which one has no control. Immediately the source of shadow and projection is the personal unconscious, 'but when it [i.e., the shadow] appears as an archetype . . . a man [may] recognise the relative evil of his nature,

71

but it is a rare and shattering experience for him to gaze into the face of absolute evil'.[44]

To risk irritating by repetition, the Shadow archetype is collective memory. We cannot drive a logical or analytical wedge between the effects of the shadow – social and personal – and the effects of memory. It is worth pausing for a moment, then, to see what the effects of the projection of the shadow might be.

This projection of the shadow can operate at both the individual and the community level. As the individual refuses to recognise his own shadow, so the community can unconsciously collude in not acknowledging its own 'failings' – but detecting them in exaggerated ways in others, especially, as we shall see in more detail in later chapters, on 'outsiders'. For Jung this seemed an almost universal phenomenon. Of projections he writes:

> our ordinary life still swarms with them. You can find them spread out in the newspapers, in books, rumours and ordinary social gossip. All gaps in our actual knowledge are still filled out with projections. We are still so sure we know what other people think or what their true character is. We are convinced that certain people have all the bad qualities we do not know in ourselves or that they practice all those vices which could, of course, never be our own.[45]

Thus Jung can give a convincing account of scapegoating, a process which notoriously inflicts the scapegoat with characteristics that do not belong to her or him. As we shall see when we review the work of René Girard in Chapter 9, she or he becomes the bearer of our sins in a quite literal sense: but they are 'sins' which become so only because we fail to acknowledge them as the 'down side' of ourselves.

On whom can I attach this projection? Two criteria seem essential. First, the projected shadow needs to find some resonance with actuality in those who will carry it. Notice I say 'some resonance with actuality'. That resonance may have been created by deliberate ideological manipulation; by distorted history; by manipulated 'social' memory; by isolated incidents unjustifiably generalised. For example, Nazis were able to project on to Jews their own unacknowledged love of money only because many Jews were already successful commercially (and that in large part, as Staub and others have argued (see Chapter 8), because other areas of economic and social advancement were blocked to them).

Second, the victims of the projection must be prepared to carry that projection. That is not to say, to refer to two examples we shall explore at more length in later chapters, that Jews willingly became Nazi scapegoats or blacks the bearers of the sexual fears of whites; it is rather that at the unconscious level – that is, at the level of their own shadow – they 'recognise' the caricature their detractors are dumping on them. What is tragic in this situation is that both sides share the same fears and horrors, but one projects it on to the other and is in a socially dominant position to make that projection 'stick' in terms of public utterance.

We shall see later that the social implications of scapegoating are very far-reaching indeed, running from ethnic intolerance to war to genocide. More generally, the projection of the shadow is one of the key psychological explanations of ingroup/outgroup dichotomies that acquire structural form in a huge range of social relationships, from the family to first world/third world global arrangements.

Given its great importance, one might wish that Jung had given a more coherent account of the psychological processes by which whole communities do this. We need a more differentiated and precise account, for example, of the relationship between the collective unconscious, the corporate shadow and collective projection. And we need to recognise that even when a whole community may be said to be projecting on to its scapegoats the features it does not accept for itself – as Nazis on Jews; whites on blacks; Christians on Muslims – even then there is a range of degrees to which individuals are or are not caught up in that process. Further, it is clear that not every society projects its shadow(s) on to minorities; and that some which did eventually cease to do so. Jung can help us little with either of these problems. But in recognising that, we can simultaneously recognise the value of the notion of the shadow; of the power of its projection on others; and the far-reaching structural implications of this idea.

Shadow and the Archetypes of War

One way of seeing how the theoretical material of the last section relates very precisely to the central concerns of this book is to see how well they explain human tendencies to violence, and especially the organised (and therefore symbol- and ritual-rich) violence of war. Anthony Stevens has explored this with great insight that combines loyalty to Jung's model with perceptive application of it to one of the major presenting symptoms of our age.[46]

Stevens starts with Bowlby's work on the nature of the child's tie to its mother, demonstrating that this is an essentially biological attachment but one largely independent of physiological need. This attachment is one of many 'specific built-in response patterns which promote social interaction between intimate members of the species and withdrawal from those who are strange and potentially hostile'. Stevens thus reformulates Jung's hypothesis of the mother and shadow archetypes, showing that the primal relationship between mother and child on the one hand and the non-relationship between child and stranger on the other is genetically programmed. 'Becoming friendly to some and hostile to others is the natural realization of our genetic endowment.'[47]

But what is the nature of this hostility? Classically, the flight/fight choice is basic. Stevens argues that it is a response no less genetically programmed than the relationship to mother or sexual partner; and that it is located in an 'older' part of the brain. 'Those who have persisted in seeing human aggressiveness as a rational problem susceptible to rational solutions forget in their optimism that reason is a purely cortical function and that only cortical functions are accessible to educative persuasion.' In extreme conditions, the flight/fight response 'takes over' from rationality and determines behaviour.[48]

If that sounds bleak news for advocates of a 'third way' of non-violent resistance to aggression (in which Walter Wink would certainly include Jesus[49]), ethologists argue that it has been an indispensable mechanism for the spread of species. As species have spread, however, so intergroup rivalry developed, in turn leading to a process of natural selection, especially among leader groups, for aggression and physical strength. Whereas most animals have an innate braking

74

mechanism that prevents them from killing rivals, perhaps activated by well-defined submission signals, humans have no such mechanism.

Biologically, then, human beings are 'bred to fight'. It is but a short step from that observation to see aggressiveness or war as a Jungian archetype. Stevens quotes Lionel Tiger's work on male bonding,[50] a direct cause of aggression since it contributes directly to ingroup/outgroup identifications. Tiger claims that such bonding is an 'underlying, biologically transmitted propensity with roots in human evolutionary history' – almost a classic definition of an archetype comparable to Tinbergen's innate releasing mechanisms, Ernest Mayer's 'open programmes' and Wolfgang Kohler's isomorphs.[51]

Stevens identifies three sets of archetypes as involved in human aggression. The first is the shadow and its projection to the outgroup, already discussed above. The second is the 'mobilisation of aggression against the outgroup . . .; archetypes of this category mediate power-seeking, dominance striving, the maintenance of social hierarchies in the interests of group cohesiveness'. And the third is the mobilisation of aggression for the purposes of group defence. In what sounds like biological fatalism (though he disavows that label), Stevens writes:

These fundamental archetypal complexes exist a priori as accessible potential in the collective unconscious of each member of every human community. They can be activated either individually or collectively by any environmental changes which are construed by individuals or their leaders as constituting a threat to the group, to its security or to its vital interest. When this happens, the way is open to war.[52]

If this sounds over-biologistic (and exaggerated, since conflicts do not in practice necessarily lead to war or even violence) it is to some degree corrected by emphasis on the power of symbols. Whereas some scholars such as Ruth Harriet Jacobs have argued that modern soldiers are not the subjects of aggressive impulses since they are 'only' rationally operating high-tech weaponry, Stevens argues that the symbols of war 'convert' technology to aggression. He sees symbols as the bridge across which aggressive energy can flow between the archetypal programme of war and the situation which seems to require it. Neither the distance from the enemy nor the sanitised sophistication of modern warfare deliver us from our biological programmes, from, that is, the power of our memories.

Stevens reinforces this argument by analysing the process whereby recruits are socialised into military life. Analytically, the question is how the individual soldier can 'tap into' the aggressive impulses of the collective unconscious. Jung answered this general question by formulating the law of association: that is, the expectation that an archetype is activated when an individual finds himself in a situation which bears clear 'markers' which correspond to the archetype in question. Once activated, the archetype becomes functional in the individual consciousness as a complex with both ideational and emotional content. Military training can thus be seen as the process whereby collective archetypes are converted into complexes.

That is, however, to make the process sound too mechanistic. While Wallace has drawn attention to relaxed and mobilised states in animal populations,[53] Stevens detects an equivalent psychic change with what he calls archetypal possession which leads to radical changes in the collective and personal consciousness. This archetypal possession (well recognised, as we have already seen, in the literature on Jungian accounts of romantic love) comes to be triggered by 'releasing stimuli', such as aggressive speeches, bugles, drums, military music, declarations of threats to the homeland, rumours of women about to be raped or of intense suffering inflicted on compatriots, all stimuli well explored in novels about England in the early years of the Great War. Once this archetypal possession is released, there is a kind of qualitative shift in behaviour, reason and perceptions of reality. The Ukrainian proverb quoted by Lorenz catches it: When the banner is unfurled, all reason is in the trumpet.

By now the significance of Stevens' analysis (whether or not one accepts every detail) should be clear. It can be put simply like this: through our conscious and unconscious memories, we are biologically and psychologically programmed for war, and many of our social arrangements and our symbols both reflect that programme and enable us to obey it. We have already seen how they get ritualised into our collective memory, keeping us in touch with the archetypal material behind them – the Cenotaph, the Military Tatoo, the Changing of the Guard, Fly-pasts and Navy Days are some obvious British examples.

With modern technology that makes us an exceedingly dangerous species, whose only hope of survival is to recognise the compulsions under which we labour and to construct immensely robust counter-institutions as a kind of military chastity belt. To deny or repress those compulsions, however robust the institutional counterweights, could be fatal. For it is to leave us

> blind and unconscious of what denial and dissociation, repression and projection would have us be. Disguised as defenders of our egos and protectors of our peace of mind, these discrete flunkies are really secret agents in the service of the archetype of war. . . . And they are diligently at work in each and every one of us. . . . In the struggle to preserve our planet from destruction, we are ourselves the source of the evil against which we fight.[54]

What we need, on the contrary, is to recognise the archaic memories distilled in the archetypes and their power; and then to fashion strategies by which we may transcend them by putting them in the context of healthier archetypes that speak of unity, of wholeness and of integration. For Jung, the archetype of God and/or Christ had this function. Either we rediscover it, despite its overlay of tired doctrine, tedious institutionalisation in its 'gilded hearse' and pointless ritual; or we find a substitute of equivalent power (the agenda of some of the so-called 'new social movements' to which we shall come presently); or we blow the whole earth to bits.

Conclusion

So what have we got here that throws light on the central thesis of this book? I want to highlight six themes that have emerged from the discussion.

First, Jungian theory invites us to see that we are not always in control of ourselves, the events around us or the social forms and structures that we create and/or maintain. We are, as it were, acting out inner dramas, responding to unconscious memories, even though we might be quite unaware of them. As the Stevens material shows, we might thus be literally incapable of reason even in matters of life and death. And we are often incapable of reason in matters of romance and the choice of a life (or too often much-less-than-life) partner.

Second, archetypes are a particular form of memory resource. They are primordial, instinctual, encoded – but accessible even though not directly experienced. In the Jungian scheme, then, memory, in this admittedly slightly odd sense, plays a central, pivotal role in determining both the potential of the individual and of the community for inner and outer change and healing.

Third, both individual and community need to get in touch with the memories incorporated in the archetypes. Communities do this through various forms of social remembering, some of which we explored in Chapter 1, and others of which emerged in this chapter. Individuals do it in all kinds of ways, paramount among which, in Jung's thinking, are symbol-play or 'religious' ritual. The forms of social life that hold these symbols and rituals in place (ritual arks, if you will) are thus privileged in Jung's thinking, but by no means guaranteed attention or even preservation. The implications of that for ecclesiology will form the subject of Chapter 11.

Fourth, Jung's thinking is essentially optimistic – as the metaphor of the river was meant to convey. I had the temerity to question that optimism by suggesting that in so far as the archetypes in the collective unconscious are malleable, modifiable by the experience of present generations, both conscious and unconscious, it is possible that the range or power of negative archetypes is reinforced by our own negative experience – or the unconscious way we deal with them and the memory of them. In this sense we jeopardise both our own healing and that of subsequent generations. And in that case we are trapped indeed.

Fifth, this raised questions about transformation. In quoting Reich's controversial work on the Live Aid concert, I was suggesting that in so far as ritualised memories put us in touch with archetypal material, they may be transformative in a direct political and ideological sense. I deliberately chose a non-Christian example of that process at work, but in the last chapters of this book I shall want to return to ask under what conditions Christian ritual could be transformative in the same sense.

Lastly, we saw that the Shadow and its unconscious projection on to others is always a source of emotional difficulty, and can be deadly for communities as well as for individuals. The need to project may be, in some ultimate sense, a form of immaturity, especially if one is aware of what is going on. I shall argue in Chapter 11, however, that it is a natural psychic process which, when handled aright, can bring the memories of Jesus's life and death into transformative contact with the unhealed memories that too readily hold us captive.

Before we come to that, however, we need to look at work arising from a quite different theoretical background – but with the same questions in mind. How does memory hold us captive in our selves and in our structures? 'And how, oh how, may we be free?'

5

Oedipus and Race

As is well known, Jung broke with Freud because he could not accept the emphasis Freud wanted to place on the formative impact of infantile sexuality in the development of the personality. There is little doubt that popular perceptions of his overemphasis on sex and its influence on the psyche have led Christians to be even more wary of Freud than they have been of Jung. Allied to that anxiety have been two other sources of concern apart from the publication of *Moses and Monotheism*: Freud's lack of sympathy with religious belief, which he tended to dismiss as infantile or neurotic; and the work of some of his followers, perhaps especially Herbert Marcuse, who, by seeking to integrate Freud and Marx, have seemed to offer prescriptions for anarchy and sexual licence on a scale that even sexually well-adjusted Christians have found incompatible with any notion of freedom-in-Christian-community.

While, then, there is a discernible (even strong in North America) rapprochement with Jung, Christian appreciation of Freud remains cautious and uncertain. That is a pity, for Freud still has much to teach us and, as we shall see, his approach can illuminate the connection between memory, the unconscious and social structure with a precision (some would say an over-precision) that we do not easily find in Jung. At the risk of presenting a grotesquely foreshortened account of Freud's ideas, to some of which we shall have to return in the next chapters, I shall concentrate on only one central Freudian contribution and demonstrate how it has been used in the contested context of psychohistory to 'explain' the persistence of one form of social structure: I refer to the Oedipus complex and to white racism in the southern United States. In this chapter I shall start by giving an outline of Freudian developmental theory as it illuminates the idea of the Oedipus complex; show how it has been used to cast light on white racism; criticise some aspects of theory and application; and then look at another, more recent, example of the same approach. That will lead me to some more general criticisms, and to some overall conclusions about what this type of theory has to offer those interested in the theological significance of memory. For again, the main interest of this chapter is to explicate the role memory (in this case repressed memory) plays in influencing individual and social behaviour.

Developmental Theory

Freud believed that the baby organises his or her libido or sexual energy around three erogenous zones: the mouth, the anus and the genitalia. It is easy but misleading to see these as successive stages of development – hence loose talk of the 'anal stage' and so on. While some degree of succession is not ruled out, in reality the baby or child will find satisfaction and anxiety in each orifice. The mouth will suck the mother's breast and, if all goes well, the baby will experience the pleasure of an instant flow of warm, nourishing milk. More or less simultaneously, the mouth becomes the centre of exploratory probes of the reality of the baby's world. Fingers, toys, buttons, literally anything that comes to hand are searched, chewed, tasted – sometimes with delight, sometimes with distaste. Thus the mouth both enlarges the baby's world of sensation but also plays a unique role in allying it with mother and affording both baby and mother deep pleasure and satisfaction.

Almost inevitably somewhat later, the baby becomes aware of its anus and faeces. These too are sources of delight, satisfaction – and distaste. The delight of expelling waste and the sense of well-being that follows such delight are mirrored by the anguish of hard, uncomfortable stools or pains that presage a difficult motion. Once passed, the faeces are material for exploration; and very special material since they are part of the baby's own body, almost, one might say, of his or her own very self. But the faeces taste and smell unpleasing and the reaction of the mother or other carers to them – and especially to them in the mouth – reinforce the notion that here is something that is of the self, but yet innately unpleasant and disagreeable. A paradox, then: a pleasant sensation followed by the production of something intrinsically (and parentally reinforcedly) disgusting.

These two areas of exploration, the mouth and the anus, occupy much of the baby's attention in the early months of life. They become foci of the baby's relations with the mother: first through the delight (or frustration) of the nipple; then through the conflict over potty-training. One does not, except in the most superficial sense, succeed the other: both are areas of the body and areas of activity around which the desires of the child are concentrated and organised. Experience of each may play a part in forming the personality which will endure to adulthood.

The same is true of the third phase, the phallic. Sometimes criticised by modern feminists for doing so, Freud tended to regard the boy's penis and the girl's clitoris as equivalent: at one level appendages of skin and gristle; at another the focus of yet more delight. Freud was well aware of infantile masturbation – the deliberate pursuit of pleasure little different from the pleasure of sucking or defecating.

It was the phantasies that such pleasure released that became one of Freud's central concerns. In sucking the breast, the baby wants to possess the mother, to eat her, in a way somewhat analogous to the way lovers declare they want to eat each other: that is, to possess wholly, physically and, as it were, spiritually to ingest the other to achieve a perfect union. Freud believed that the baby wants to possess his mother sexually in the same way. (The switch to the masculine gender is deliberate. Although he later tried to extend it to girls, most of Freud's work on the Oedipus complex is based on boys.) The erect phallus becomes an instrument through which he can achieve his object – to possess and achieve union with the other, that is, mother.

He is, however, inhibited in this desire by father. Mother 'belongs' sexually to father and so the boy's desire for sexual union with mother brings him directly into conflict with a jealous, powerful father. How can he cope with this rivalry? This anxiety is raised to a higher power, Freud believed, by the boy's fear that the way his father will cope with the competition is by castrating his son. It is a one-way street: the little boy has no power to issue such a threat to the father. He cannot win. Therefore, Freud believed, the boy does not give up his desire for sexual union with his mother: he represses both the desire and the anxiety. He enters childhood in a state of sexual hibernation until at puberty he is able to switch his desire from mother, no longer a powerful sexual attractant, to other women. He may be more or less successful in repressing his sense of competition with and fear of his father. Or he may displace that competition and/or fear on to the other males, especially if they are emotionally close to mother.

In 'normal', 'healthy' development, the boy will in fact identify with the father (or father substitute), making him into an ideal – to be emulated when the time is ripe. In Freud's thinking, this process of 'dealing with' the Oedipal conflict is crucial for the child's development. The idealisation of father and the internalisation of that ideal can play a central role in generating the child's sense of identity or ego-strength. Similarly, the father's supposed threat of castration is internalised and the child capitulates to the threat and the power to carry it out. In the process, his capacity for 'moral' control is established: that is, his super-ego (or, a better translation of Freud's German, the 'over I') is developed to control his instinctual impulses (or the 'id', the it).

Thus in Freud's theory of the development of the psyche, the Oedipal phase is not just a passing twinge of infantile sexuality: it is central in shaping the key components of personality, the ego and the super-ego.

Oedipal theory has been heavily criticised by feminist writers, not least because Freud sometimes writes as though he believes women, lacking a penis and the associated capacity to enter their partner, are generally inferior to men. However sexist Freud may have been and however inadequate his account of female sexuality, with its heavy emphasis on penis envy, it would surely be a mistake to ignore the two central features of psychological development that Freud (basing his theory, it is worth recalling, on much clinical experience) wished to highlight in his work on the Oedipal 'stage': first, the early stirrings of physical desire for the body of the mother (representing the female in general); and second, the fear associated with that desire, leading to its vigorous repression. From these two ideas a complex social pattern can be derived.

In much of the literature on the Oedipal stage, and especially that written from a feminist perspective, the argument progresses from

Oedipus to patriarchy, male dominance and the inequitable distribution of power and function between the sexes. While I do not wish to impugn the importance of that debate, I wish in what follows to, as it were, take it in the flank. By concentrating on a somewhat different development of Oedipal-type theory, I shall ultimately show that its significance goes wider than relations between the sexes.

Kovel's Development of Oedipal Theory

The line of thinking I want to sketch is contained in Joel Kovel's 'psychohistory' of white racism in the southern states of the USA.[2] It will be helpful to pick up the four 'stages' of the development of the psyche I outlined above and see how Kovel uses them in accounting for the particular features, above all the psychic features, of white racism. We may begin with the oral phase.

In phantasy the child is ingesting the mother, the source of comfort and nourishment. In this sense, the child is experiencing an unfillable desire to eat the mother; to be a cannibal. It is a desire that has to be repressed (like the desire to possess the mother sexually), but it remains in the unconscious as a possibility, however surrounded by fear and guilt.

Kovel sees this repressed unconscious desire as something that is later, perhaps in late childhood, then projected on to others, and because it is a black deed, on to black men. He writes, 'scarcely anyone grows up without exposure to the myth of African Cannibalism: grinning black devils with bones through their noses dancing about the simmering pot containing the hapless missionary. What child has not contemplated this scene in one form or another?'[3] But why the prevalence and power of this myth? For Kovel, three things are coming together: a core of anthropological truth that some aboriginal groups have no taboos about eating human flesh; the repressed desire to eat the mother; and the fact 'that the culture of the West is representing by projection what it has done to the culture and peoples of Africa, namely eaten them up'. And he goes on:

> It is doubtful that such representation would have attained nearly the degree of forcefulness it has if the West had not committed upon the black people, in a mass historical form, precisely what it

accuses the blacks of having perpetrated in their savage state – and which foible is moreover one of the repertoire of rationalisations for the white man's burden.[4]

Illustration, hyperbole or explanation? We shall have to look more carefully at the logical status of this kind of analysis later, but for the moment it is important to establish the main line of the argument. At the risk of crudity, it can be put simply like this: most (all?) children experience a desire to eat 'the good mother'; the memory of that desire is repressed; but it is then recalled *in a projected form* by encountering the myth of African cannibalism – and is thus rendered safe from the standpoint of the (white) child. He (she) does not want to eat anyone – especially mother. It is they – the strange, black Others – who do it to us (or our symbolically pure and innocent representatives). Hence the anxiety about my (repressed) wish to eat someone can be relieved and transformed into anger/fear/distrust at/ of a particular, and easily identified, group of strangers. The myth thus serves a useful (even healthful) purpose in white, middle-class society by relieving an anxiety that is encountered very early in the child's development and which surfaces frequently when desire is centred on oral eroticism.

But at what a cost! And that is Kovel's point. The release of anxiety about infantile desire is achieved by projecting that anxiety on to another group – which, of course, attracts it by the unhappy circumstance of a collective memory that *some* dark-skinned peoples are known to have no taboos against eating human flesh. But that is enough. Black is black. 'One looks much like another and you cannot trust any of them.' The seeds of fear and distrust are not only sown early and deep; they are, by the strange processes of projection and inversion, sown in the rich soil of self-justification. I know I am right to distrust them because I know, unconsciously, the power of the desire that makes them do this. No wonder Kovel calls this myth 'obscene'.

Now suppose Inuit or Frenchmen had abandoned the same taboos. Would our fear and distrust be directed at them? In other words, is it the oral connection alone that focuses so much venom on the black man? A key distinction in Kovel's treatment is that between the *aversive* racist and the *dominative* racist. Crudely, this is the distinc-

85

tion between the anal stage and the Oedipal stage. It is the former, the anal, that finally pins the venom on the black, making irrelevant the question about French cannibals.

The blackness and smelliness of faeces are the source of both fascination and distaste, and it is a simple transition to associate those characteristics, whenever encountered, with a primitive response to the early exploration of faeces. 'Shit' becomes a term of abuse not only because it is short and sibillant-percussive: it carries with it a power derived from early experience. And that becomes attached *to a people*, partly because they are Other, strange, not-us; and partly because their immediately presenting characteristics – blackness and a different scent – resonate with repressed memories of that early experience.

Aversive Racism

There is, however, a further twist. I was at pains to emphasise that the 'stages' of development in Freudian theory overlie each other, rather than running in discrete sequence. The child wants to explore the product of anal satisfaction, the faeces, orally. S/he wants to eat it. When s/he does so, the experience is unpleasant and is likely to evoke consternation or worse from the mother. Hence blackness and food become mutually incompatible in the memory and mind of the aversive racist – and more generally in an anxiety that food handled by black people is somehow contaminated, unclean. One of my sons has a nice illustration of this: he went to Shepherd Market in London to buy some grapes for a sick friend. As the stall-holder was weighing them, he thought to ask if they were of South African origin. She confirmed that they were. Doing his bit for the sanctions campaign then at its height, he told her he would not have them. He was dismayed by her response: 'Don't blame you,' she replied blandly. 'Couldn't fancy them myself, with those black hands all over them.' In the common, if sometimes disguised or even repressed, anxiety about food handled by black people, we are not up against simple (or even compound) ignorance: we are up against something primitive, in the sense of a residue of early psychic development.

For Kovel, the anal 'stage' is the origin of the reactions of the aversive racist. S/he is aversive precisely in that s/he wishes to avoid

86

contact with her own faeces. The characteristic stance *vis-à-vis* black people is therefore that of distance: to avoid contact, to withdraw from any kind of intimacy with black people. This is not inconsistent with liberal political positions or even charitable donations and action: just so long as there is no question of real equality, actual (physical) mixing. By contrast with the dominative racist, to whom we shall turn in a moment, the personality structure of the aversive racist may be relatively well integrated: s/he has none of the terrible conflicts between id and super-ego which make life for the dominative racist and those around her so conflictual. And in a way, that is exactly the problem. By keeping her distance, even appearing liberal and, within limits, generous, she masquerades (almost literally) as someone who is free of racial prejudice.

When we lived in Zambia, we knew just such a person, a fine, young Rhodesian (as it then was) woman who was bitterly opposed to the overtly racist Smith regime. Her outspoken condemnations of the Rhodesian government had obliged her to flee north, to Zambia, where she took digs with some European friends while she continued her political work against the Smith government. One weekend she was out of town and her hosts, receiving an unexpected visit from a black Rhodesian friend, offered him Carol's bedroom in her absence. By the time Carol returned, the black Rhodesian had departed but her hosts explained what had happened. They were taken aback by Carol's reaction – anger, deep distress, tears, terrible anguish. The thought that a black man – someone she knew slightly and had no reason to dislike – had slept in her bed felt to her like rape. Acknowledging the irrationality and even injustice of her reaction, she could not deny the power of her feelings.

Now clearly the sexual symbolism – a black in the bed – takes us further than anal aversion; it takes us into territory which we shall have to explore below. But the point of Carol's story is less the sense of sexual violation than the co-existence of 'progressive' political attitudes and a (hitherto unacknowledged) wish to maintain distance between herself and black people.

The Dominative Racist

The wish of the dominative racist is not to maintain distance: it is to exercise power over. The repressed memories involved are thus quite different, and so are the political and social ramifications. In describing the dominative racist, Kovel draws on Adorno's analysis of the authoritarian personality, and clearly there is a close similarity of purpose. Adorno and his collaborators sought to explain the rise of Nazism by showing that German social conditions had produced, by the 1930s, a preponderance of a particular personality type, essentially one fascinated by the exercise of authority, both as a subject and object.[5] Kovel's project is parallel. He wants to show that white racism was given its particular character and its political endurance by the emergence in the South of a set of social conditions which reproduced personalities with repressed memories that *needed* the structures of racism and which had the power to enforce them.

Note the logic. Neither Adorno nor Kovel argue that the particular psychological types that they describe emerge out of nothing or randomly. The psychological is thus not offered as a first cause. The relationship is, rather, dialectical. The social (which includes a large number of variables from the family to the economic and political) produces an environment in which, through the particular operation of a set of repressed memories, a personality type becomes preponderant – which then, acting socially and politically, reinforces the social forces already at work. The psychological both strengthens and changes the nature of the social. For Adorno, the authoritarian personality issues in the particular structures of totalitarian Nazism and its willing acceptance by the great majority of the German people. For Kovel the personality of the dominative racist emerges from the cultural, social, economic and political milieu of the slave-owning South and culminates in the Ku-Klux-Klan and the Night Riders – and the widespread tacit support such groups enjoyed in the South, at least until the 1960s. It is, then, a mistake to see Kovel's approach as psychological reductionism: it owes much to a Marxian materialism.[6] For both Adorno and Kovel, there is a form of psychological reproduction: the kind of society the authoritarian or dominative personality produces generates both conscious and unconscious memories which together reproduce more authoritarian or dominative personalities; these then become even more intolerant of other forms of social organisation. We shall see more precisely how this operates below when we return to the Oedipal stage, but before we do that it will be helpful to explore a little further what Kovel means by the dominative racist.

The key characteristic of the dominative racist or bigot, as Kovel often calls him, is a harsh super-ego. Drawing on Bird's famous essay 'Etiology of Prejudice', Kovel argues that an overdeveloped but rigid super-ego ensures that the bigot cannot act out his fantasies, but needs to find substitutes to enable him to express the aggressiveness he feels when confronted with both a superior class of well-established (white) oligarchs (whom he would like to join but cannot) and an inferior group of blacks, on whom he can release his aggression and frustration without fear of retribution. The super-ego ensures a rigid morality. The bigot is the model employee; the firm (possibly harsh) father; the regular churchgoer; the upholder of law and order. He is deeply offended by (and unconsciously no less threatened by) change in the established order of things. He is not just conservative in politics, religion and morality. He is reacting to what he sees as abandonment of a golden age. Romantic in his attachment to a highly distorted understanding of the past, he greets any deviation from the established pattern as further evidence of decline. Frightened and threatened by such evidence and wholly unable to adapt to change, he is, at one level, the pathetic victim of his own psyche. Dominated by the repressed memories that generate his super-ego, he lacks the ego strength to assess change rationally and objectively and see in it both good and bad, opportunity and closure. He is literally unable to adapt: his only response is to lash out in anger and frustration – at those who are culturally sanctioned as the legitimate objects of his emotions.

It is when that cultural sanction is challenged, or when, to be more specific, blacks refuse to accept their culturally determined role as the emotional dustbins of bigots, that the bigot is moved to the most violent demonstration of his attitudes. The one safety-valve of his pent-up aggression is to be blocked. Where can he put all the violence he feels inside? He answers that by bitter resistance to change and by simultaneously re-enacting in ever more lucid terms his hatred of the 'inferior' group. The AWB in South Africa and the UDR in

Brazil follow this pattern with unnerving accuracy. Neo-Fascism in Europe may develop in such a direction.

Three additional features need emphasis. The first is that it follows from the story so far that the bigot *needs* his victim. The victim plays a crucial role in the inner drama of the bigot's psyche; and the delineaments of that role are determined by the bigot. The black needs to be dependent, senile, stupid, lazy, feckless . . . only so can the bigot cope. This implies, as anyone who has lived in a racist society knows from a thousand incidents, that *however* the black does in fact behave, the bigot will put upon that behaviour an interpretation that confirms his needed stereotype. It is hard indeed for the black to break out.

Second, both Kovel and Bird emphasise (though Kovel is less precise about) the role of guilt in the psychological make-up of the bigot. A harsh super-ego, of course, already implies excessive guilt feelings, and in this context they may focus in either or both of two directions. The bigot may feel guilty that he cannot join the upper class, the oligarchy, the landed gentry. He cannot achieve that social pre-eminence that might enable him to feel more secure, more powerful. In Freudian terms, he has repressed the memory of the unconscious aspiration to take the position of father and the acknowledgement that he cannot do so. He feels guilty at thus hating his father for his superior power but can express neither the guilt nor the hatred to 'the father', since it is the fathers' power that guarantees the security he craves. Hence his need of a scapegoat.

He may also, however, feel guilty at the memory of the violence of his own aggression towards the scapegoat. It represents a lack of control: the super-ego cannot control the violent impulses of the id. The 'it' takes over. 'It' is in control. The super-ego reacts in guilt, generating feelings of self-loathing, self-disgust. One way out of that is to make the bigot even more conformist to the 'higher' powers – a better employee, more ardent churchgoer, more forceful in his demands for 'proper' law enforcement. It will not necessarily, however, prevent him in the future from joining a lynch mob or assaulting a black, whether verbally or physically.

Third, and at last we can return more or less directly to Oedipus, the bigot is plagued by sexual fantasies about his victims. He is obsessed by myths of black sexual prowess; of the size of the black male genitalia; of the sexual abandonment of black women. Kovel writes of 'a preoccupation with, a deadly curiosity about, the sexual excesses of the hated group, etched in the imagination by the acid of a harsh moralism'.[8] This 'preoccupation' contrasts, as we shall see in a moment, with the Puritan restraint, the joylessness and routine constraint, of the sexual activity in the bigot's own life. Thus to guilt and hatred are added envy and excitement. For the latter-day bigot, the physical exploration of black sexuality may be forbidden: the super-ego may remain in control. Then the envy and sexual titillation turn to moralistic disgust, and the maintenance of myths and stereo-types. 'They breed like rabbits.' 'They are incapable of restraint.' 'Of course he raped her: he wouldn't know how not to.' From such seeds of stereotyping we shall see bitter fruits grow in a later chapter.

The Sexual Politics of Racism

This latter-day bigotry, and the sexual phantasies associated with it, compare with the grace, sophistication and gentility of *antebellum* Southern racism. Then the slave-owning oligarchs were able to main-tain a social system which offered them complete security; and, more important for our purposes, which offered bigots a resolution of the Oedipal conflicts which they could otherwise, in the absence of such a system, resolve only with hatred and violence.

To see this, we need to go back to white fascination with black sexuality, and the way this fascination was worked out in slave society – by the men. They neatly divided the sexual roles: black women gave them the passion they sought, white women became idealised beauties, marmoreal symbols of a sanitised femininity. Deprived of husband's sexual pleasure and play, and then deprived even of the delight of nursing their own children (who were customarily given to black wet-nurses) they were left, chaste, pure, boring and bored, on their gilded pedestals.

But see that process from the side of the child. Nursed by a black woman, all his primitive eroticism – of mouth and penis – is focused on black flesh. In the context of the Oedipal structure, it is the black 'father' he wishes to displace – and at whose hand he fears castration. And it is the black woman he desires. Later in life, goaded by these repressed memories, he can achieve both desires. He can subjugate the black man, and even castrate him as the final revenge. It is not for nothing that he calls him 'boy'.

And he can have his pleasure with black women of his choice, while guarding the honour of his idealised wife from the alleged sexual prowess of black men. Thus the celebrated rape fantasy of the South can be seen as a projection of Oedipal incest. The white man, as child, desired the body of the black mother. Therefore (by the inverted logic of projection) the black child desired − and black adult man now desires − the body of the white woman. By thus seeing the black man as the destructive aspect of the Oedipal child, the white man fantasises that every white woman is the potential victim of rape by the black man. The three features of the sexual psychology of white racism thus become structured in the Southern states: the idealisation of white women; the brutal treatment of black men, with castration even written into the penal code for a whole variety of relatively trivial and non-sexual offences; and the use of black women as sexual playthings for white men.

But what, it may be asked, of the super-ego of the (oligarchic) white man? Why should that be less troublesome to him than it is to the bigot of later years? The 'system', the actual rather than the pretended play of social relationships, permits him to deceive his wife, rob her of the closeness of her children, abuse his black women slaves and castrate, socially or genitally, his male slaves. But at a cost. The super-ego will not finally be denied. Kovel quotes Lillian Smith: 'Guilt was then and is today the biggest crop raised in Dixie.'[9] That guilt, however, remained unconscious.

> This was the triumph of the South, the principal defensive task of all its institutions to keep the minds of the masters unaware of guilt. Their guilt was unconscious, but it was realised elsewhere − in the sterile frustrations of idealised white women; in the patient suffering of black women; in the brutalisation of black men; and, principally, in the failure of the whole society, which they visited headlong upon themselves and raced toward with a desperate energy. Everyone had to pay the penalty for the crime of Oedipus; and in the endless cycle of crime and retribution, the black man had to be continually re-created out of the body of white culture.[10]

Never have repressed memories exacted so high a price.

Kovel and Freud: Theoretical Issues

It may be helpful at this point if we stand back a little from Kovel's argument and see how it relates to Freud and to the general theme of this book. It should be clear that Kovel uses two of Freud's 'stages', the anal and the Oedipal, to explain two different types of racism, practised by two different kinds of personality. Kovel does not in fact make the direct linkage of anal stage and aversive racism that I have implied, and he emphatically is not saying anything as crude as 'all aversive racists had problems in their anal stage' or 'have regressed to their anal stage'. Rather, I take what he is saying to be that you can only understand the psychic power of the aversion experienced by aversive racists if you can enter into the phantasies that all of us have experienced in our anal stage. Thus the explicand is not aversive racism as such, but rather the power that blackness comes to have over the consciousness of the white.

In the same way, his elegant and ingenious use of the Oedipal structure in 'explaining' dominative racism in general and the rape fear/neurosis in particular, is not, I take it, to be read as arguing that all *ante bellum* oligarchic whites resolved their Oedipal conflicts by splitting white women from black women and metaphorically castrating black men as both father and child (boy): but rather that that particular social structure drew its power (and ultimately via guilt its weakness or vulnerability) from the 'goodness of fit' of this solution to the Oedipal conflict and the social arrangements of Southern slave society. Admittedly Kovel is sometimes incautious: he is, after all, writing polemic rather than dispassionate analysis. Thus he says: 'Southern culture makes its unique contribution to an ageless human problem: the Southern white male simultaneously resolves both sides of the [Oedipal] conflict by keeping the black man submissive, and by castrating him when submission fails.'[11] This makes it sound too deliberate, too consciously planned. The reality surely must be that, while particular features of Southern racism (anxiety about wholesale rape, generalised punishment by castration) may indeed owe much to Oedipal anxieties, it is the seductiveness of the social arrangements in their accommodation of the memory of Oedipal anxieties that explains their power.

Of course, there are other explanations – economic, political, cultural. Kovel's argument, in which I find much truth, is that they were related dialectically to the correspondence between psychic structures and social structures. It is important to recognise that this intermediation of other social forces is by no means denied by Kovel any more than it is by any of the better writers of psychohistory. Since Talcott Parsons, it has been possible to synthesise psychology and social analysis without being forced into the quite false position that *all* explanatory power lies in one mode of discourse and none in the other. Fred Weinstein, Gerald Platt and Peter Loewenberg have all demonstrated how powerfully this synthesis, with its ability to keep open dialectic processes between the inner and the outer, can reveal the deepest origins of human behaviour.[12] That problems remain, I do not deny: I shall touch on them again briefly below.

Freud, Kovel and Memory

But where, it may be asked, does memory fit in? Freud was criticised in his own lifetime for giving too great a role to memory. Thus Laird: 'The past event to which we return in memory . . . is over and done with when we look back at it. . . . Although these events have consequences for our subsequent history, it is nonsense to say that they persist.'[13] But is it? It was Freud's contention precisely that, in one sense or another, they do indeed persist, and continue to affect the way we react and the way we relate to others.

Freud originally thought that psychological conditions such as hysteria and neurosis were caused by the unhealed memories, lodged in the unconscious, that were still 'driving' people to behave in certain ways. The task of the psychoanalyst was then to bring those memories to consciousness, encourage the patient to 'deal with' them at the conscious level and thus free themselves of the hidden compulsions that were dictating certain types of behaviour. He became aware in his later work, however, that it is not quite as simple as that. For the 'memory' as reported to the analyst may be (and in most analysts' experience usually is) an amalgam of external reality (a father, with certain characteristics of which one might be to expect high standards) and the 'patient's emotional input' (not Freud's phrase) which distorts, colours, exaggerates, gives a high emotional tone to the memory of the external reality. Freud's genius lay in examining the dynamics of this latter process: why does my 'memory' invest my father with the harshness and demandingness to which I am still responding? Perhaps I 'see' him in this light because I resent his superior power (in, for example, the Oedipal conflict) and badly want it for myself so that I can fulfil all my infantile wishes and desires. The only way I can get it is to become like him – hard-working, setting high standards, demanding the best of myself.

Now it may well be that my father plays into this at some stage by demanding something of me: perhaps in itself a trivial incident, a cheerful encouragement to 'try a bit harder' at some childish game, but one which, because of my inner processes at the time (or a little earlier or a little later), resonates profoundly and 'justifies' my projecting on to him all the terrors of exigence which will for ever deform my life.

Clearly here we are in difficult terrain. For what we have, in the account just given, is not one memory but two or possibly even three. First, there is the uncontroversial, 'objective' memory of father. Second, there is the memory of the conflict with him over possession of my mother. That is, of course, an unconscious memory now, and may even have been so at the time of the putative third memory of his 'playing into' my Oedipal resolution to become like him so that I can challenge him for my mother. In my own experience, people do remember quite easily very early incidents that can be reconstructed in the way that I have described, though they do not carry them in day-to-day consciousness (unless they are later encouraged to do so by their analyst).

Freud gave the name of 'phantasy' to the process by which I 'see' my father as excessively harsh because I am projecting on to him emotional content that does not objectively belong to him. It is important to emphasise the 'memory content' of this phantasy – and it will be no less important in the next chapter. Phantasy has elements of unconscious memory encoded in it, on to which are grafted anxieties and imaginary material with no foundation in fact. But it is the facticity that gives the phantasy its power. However far removed from actuality it may (now) be, it cannot be dismissed as absurd, irrational or invention precisely because, at some deep level, a core memory remains. Phantasy is not to be confused with fantasy or fancy or fancifulness.

Now, as we have already seen in our summary of Kovel's work, the part played by phantasy in creating relationships and, as we argued, social structures, is central. This is what Freud meant by transference – that is, the re-enactment in present relationships (supremely with the analyst or therapist) of material that is still alive in the unconscious as phantasy in the strictly technical sense I have defined. In the transference the memory or memories are repeated in a new form. The objectivity of the real world is, as it were, masticated and remoulded in the form of the repetition. Freud himself discovered this in his own self-analysis: his relationships with people of his own age tended to 'repeat' his relationship with his nephew John, who was one year older than Freud and with whom he spent much time in his early years and to whom he was very attached. In more tragic cases, one sees people who have had (or, more important, who in analysis 'remember' that they have had) loveless childhoods, repeating their relationships with their parents by courting rejection at the hands of their peer group and contemporaries; courting and eventually achieving what they most fear and detest. To such people the world seems full of loveless, unaccepting, selfish people; to them that becomes the objective fact. They have thus remoulded the world in the image they most fear. They have become the victims of their own phantasies.

By now it should be clear that when Freud (and Kovel) write of phantasy, they are not denying the reality of memory: on the contrary, they are recalling the multiplicity and polyvalency of memory, without denying the possibility that in that very multiplicity and polyvalency the objective truth of some of the memories will become distorted or rearranged. To put it more specifically, the aversive racist may well make the black the object of the transference, particularly if s/he has some unconscious memories of anal trauma or disrupted faecal play.

In that case blackness becomes more than a symbol of distastefulness: it becomes – or can become – the cause of real anguish. Aversion is then almost inevitable. In the same way the dominative racist, with his classical Oedipal resolution through splitting along ethnic lines, may well make the black the victim of the transference. The black then becomes the destructive aspects of both father and child, and those destructive aspects distort the world of the racist through fear – fear of being castrated by the father and fear of wanting to castrate the father. Out of such unconsciously remembered fears does the rape anxiety frequently arise.

A Modern Example of Kovel's Theory

I want to conclude this chapter by bringing the discussion down to earth. Kovel is writing psychohistory and although, as I have already stated, I take the view that his use of the anal and Oedipal stages in accounting for the psychic power of racism is extraordinarily fertile, the whole approach of psychohistory, with its conceptual and theorectical difficulties in holding together the matrix of causality with which it must deal, is open to trenchant criticism.[14] Let us conclude, then, by asking a simple question. Assuming that Freud's account of the four stages of erotic development are broadly right, and that his account of repetition and the transference is also roughly correct, can we find examples of these processes at work in social behaviour or structure in our own environment? I believe Ivan Ward has offered one such account, in a style and approach that is wholly consistent with that of Kovel (though in some respects it takes Kovel's argument a good deal further).[15]

Ward's study is centred on the housing policy of the London Borough of Camden in 1987. There the Labour-controlled council decided, in defiance of its own manifesto commitments, to evict squatters from a large block of flats in the borough, Goldington Court, without any guarantee of rehousing – and with neither plans nor resources to rehabilitate the flats now forcibly vacated. Large sums of money were spent first in boarding up the property and then in maintaining a round-the-clock security surveillance. Here then, on the face of it, is an irrational and inefficient act, not by an individual (whom we might easily label hysterical or psychotic) but by an institution – a council led by publicly elected part-time councillors and served by full-time professional officials. What, Ward asks, was going on?

He notices that the metaphors that marked council discussions and public utterances were two: 'the bottomless pit' and 'the black hole'. The former referred to the needs for housing which far exceeded the council's capacity to supply, and the latter to the 'rapacious demands from an infinite number of daemonic children who could never be satisfied'. Now, there are two key features of these dominant metaphors. The first is that they formed the sense of reality with which the council operated – or ultimately failed to operate, since the housing department virtually ceased to function and the Homeless Persons Unit was in effect closed down.

But second, we have to ask about the epistemic nature of these metaphors. To what do they actually point? Or, to put the same question another way, why was that particular language used to construct the reality out of which Camden Council could react? Ward strongly suggests that this language and the metaphors it expresses reflect an oral (and/or anal) level of phantasy, which is why they acquired such determinative power, both at the level of *understanding* the reality councillors faced and at the level of *deciding on action*. Thus Ward writes of the 'dominant phantasies':

It was noticeable that some of the women councillors felt a little uneasy about pursuing policies that were making people homeless for no reason. However, they too acquiesced to reality. What else could they do? The reality had an existential as well as ontological aspect – in its name you could commit acts which in other circumstances you would consider immoral. You were captured within an imaginary relation to the real situation.[16]

It is important to notice the logic of Ward's hypothesis. It flows from a relatively unstructured perception of the real world via an oral/anal set of phantasies to the restructuration of the perception of reality, accompanied by a parallel set of metaphors or language uses. In a style that is reminiscent of both Althusser or Lacan (neither of whom influenced Kovel), he ties together phantasy, language and reality, and shows how they become normative for action. Perhaps the most interesting part of his thesis – and the part that represents the most salient extension of Kovel's own methodology – is to point out the power of the phantasy and its associated effects to stand conventional morality on its head. Manifesto promises were torn up; long-held values about the needs of the homeless were forgotten; socialist principles and, one might almost say, common sense were ignored. We are, in one sense, back with the alien 'it-ness' of the Freudian id; or with Jung's reminder that 'people [even Labour councillors] think they have feelings: . . . feelings have them'. Whereas Kovel's racists, whether aversive or dominative, operate (or did at least until the 1970s) with the grain of their ambient culture, the point about Ward's Camden councillors is that they were led to operate in precise opposition to all they (thought they) held most dear.

As Ward would no doubt remind us (as would both Kovel and Freud himself), we must not be over-determinative at this point. Of course, there were other factors at work, not least the dissonance between the values of the councillors and the supposed need for managerial efficiency among the professional officials on the council's staff. No doubt some influential groups of Camden's citizens were glad to see squatters dispossessed and illegal immigrants sent packing. No doubt the police were delighted to see a trouble spot 'cleaned up'. That and much more may be admitted, but the question remains: Whence came these particular metaphors? And whence came the energy to change minds and policies on so sensitive and public an issue? We might paraphrase John Dollard's reflection in his classic study: 'What a peculiar state of affairs is to be explained and how bizarre the white [councillors'] attitude . . . seems; and we grant that some potent but not very obvious explanation is required.'[17]

Critique

And yet . . . and yet. Quite apart from the current shift away from the kind of theory they are offering in explaining social phenomena, the difficulty with Kovel and Ward is that, even allowing for non-over-determination, there is a sense in which their approach explains too much and too little. It explains too much in the sense that it makes the whole council the victim of some corporate phantasy that takes hold and becomes determinative more or less *ex nihilo* – and in a very short time. And it explains too little in the well-known sense that it is too undifferentiated. Why Camden? Why not Harringey or Lambeth or Liverpool? Why now? And, perhaps most damaging of all, if these metaphors and the phantasies from which they derive are so powerful, how is it that, within a year, the council admitted it had made mistakes and was ready to take a fresh, critical look at its own policies and procedures? Why had those phantasies become so powerful in May 1987 – and yet so seemingly powerless in May 1988? Surely the commonsensical explanation that councillors were shocked by the extent of the opposition to their policies and, like good politicians everywhere, accepted the need to trim their policies in order to avoid alienating their electorate cannot be dismissed out of hand. But that raises the objection that the cause of political behaviour is not phantasy but the need for votes: on Occam's razor, phantasy can be forgotten.

Kovel's own work is open to a similar style of objection. It is both undifferentiated, and unable to cope adequately with change. After all, the presenting symptoms of Southern racism today are not the same as they were in the 1900s, the 1930s or the 1960s. Bigots still exist, but the culture in which they operate has made their room for manoeuvre more constrained, and therefore the context within which they both exhibit bigotry and identify themselves as bigots is wholly different. If Oedipal problems explain as much as Kovel wants them to, he needs to show that they have become less severe or less widespread as the influence and incidence of bigotry has receded. That he cannot do -- and the 'cannot' is both empirical (he does not have the data) and logical (he probably never could have the data). He is too good a scholar not to realise that – and so he (in one sense rightly) appeals to intermediating factors to give his account the dynamic it otherwise lacks: to essentially economic arguments for the withering of bigotry and the insidious extension of aversion. That is honest and perhaps accurate (though too simple for a total explanation and perhaps too reliant on his notion of aversion to describe the current state of white–black relations in the USA in the wake of the firing of Los Angeles in 1992). But it falls under the same difficulties as Ward. If economics finally explains change, and psychological variables do not, precisely what need does Marx have for Freud?

This takes us back into familiar terrain, and there is no need to explore it further at this point. In so far, however, as Kovel and Ward (and, *mutatis mutandis*, the whole genre of psychohistory) are offering us new ways of understanding the power of memories and phantasies associated with primitive experiences, they are contributing to a more complete account of both structure and change. That is not to say that they furnish a complete account or that they (or anyone else) has yet produced a hermeneutic framework into which their insights can be properly integrated. But it is surely as improbable that anyone working on racism could properly ignore the Freudian perspectives of Kovel as it is that anyone working on Nazism could properly ignore the work of Adorno and his collaborators on the Authoritarian Personality. We may not yet have an adequate conceptual frame to incorporate these contributions with the disciplines of political science, economics and sociology. And they are clearly inadequate as they stand, as Kovel himself was at pains to point out in his own introduction to the Morningside edition of *White Racism*. From that it does not follow, *pace* Occam, that they can be ignored, written out of any future script on these themes.

So what positively can we derive from them at this imperfect stage of our knowledge? I suggest four things.

1.   The notion of phantasy itself, linked with the memories of primitive libidinal or erotic experiences, has huge significance not only at a clinical level but also at a social level. If Kovel and Ward are right that phantasies help shape perceptions of reality, they make our world and the way we live in it. I shall have much more to say about this in the next chapter.

2.   Whatever one may think of Kovel's exploration of Oedipal issues, the rape/castration theme is too persistently embodied in the history of race relations (and not only in the *ante bellum* Southern States) to be ignored. Freud's work on the Oedipal complex seems to offer the best way into understanding the unconscious memory material which lies behind these all too conscious anxieties.

3.   Anality/dirt/food/blackness is another similar nest of memory themes that have to be taken seriously. They have a far wider reference than aversive racism in the Kovelian sense: their relevance runs from food taboos (and therefore food distribution) to generalised assumptions of the innate superiority of the non-black to the black. To do justice to this theme would involve us in a consideration of the whole

colonial experience for both coloniser and colonised along the lines of, but at a deeper, unconscious level than, Fanon; and of the politics of post-colonial guilt from the 'winds of change' speech to the aborting of the New International Economic Order.

4. The theme of guilt is inseparable from the Oedipus conflict, and Kovel shows how it can be transferred on to a whole social order. But the guilt is unrelieved. It does not lead to penitence or change. Rather, it solidifies and makes less changeable the order that gives expression to the inner guilt. In that way guilt is not just unhelpful or spiritually deadening: it is socially deadly. The question then arises: How may that guilt be transformed? That is an issue that we shall have to deal with at greater length in the next chapter, and we shall find the notion of phantasy, with its memory overtones, again playing a central role. We shall then be in a position to carry these accounts of guilt into a more sustained discussion of the theology of guilt and redemption in Part Three, especially in Chapter 9.

6

Melanie Klein and Social Theory

In this chapter I want to look at a further development of Freud's thinking that has directly and indirectly had considerable influence on psychoanalytic theory. It has been nearly wholly ignored by Christian writers. Walter Wink's trilogy on 'the Powers', for example, does not mention it, although Wink's approach lends itself well to many of the ideas we shall encounter in this chapter.[1] Even Frazer Watts's important work on religious knowing has little on this type of theory, though Watts does recognise the significance of the work of a later theoretician in this genre, Winnicott, for an understanding of the role of religious language.[2]

Melanie Klein is in many ways less a disciple of Freud than the politics of early psychoanalysis in London obliged her to claim. Fleeing from Nazi Germany before the Second World War, she settled in London and tried to present her innovative ideas in a way that minimised her disagreement with Freud, by then the established figure in British psychoanalysis by whose standards psychoanalytic truth tended to be judged – with judgement meted out by Freud's collaborator, biographer and principal henchman, the redoubtable Ernest Jones. Although she had adopted many of Freud's ideas and methods, Klein's originality made her eventually into a theorist in her own right who would see her successors – theorists such as Guntrip, Fairbairn and Winnicott – become the key figures of a recognised 'school' of psychoanalysts, the British object-relations school.

Her originality lay in two associated directions. First, she developed a method for working with very young children, primarily by watching them at play. Second, this implied her discovery that even very young children have active unconscious lives and that most of the conflicts and traumas that will affect their development have appeared long before the Oedipal stage. In this sense she pushes the area of interest back in time, even to pre-parturition. To some people, this represents something of a methodological hurdle. They find it literally incredible that anything significant can be deduced or even intuited from the play or behaviour of infants. It is beyond the scope of this book to enter that debate, though it may be worth reminding such sceptics that there recently appeared *experimental* evidence of the ability of children of a few months old to recognise number.[3] The super-sceptic, of course, will not be impressed by the design of the experiment; but then, the super-sceptic has made up his mind to be impressed by no evidence whatever. Debate becomes futile. I must simply invite the reader, of whatever degree of scepticism, to grant the epistemological assumptions at the base of Kleinian theory and follow the argument from there.

With this insistence on the very early appearance of unconscious material goes another of Klein's discoveries which mark a major, if long-fudged, departure from Freud. He had conceived of the unconscious rather as an archaeologist conceives of a promising site, potentially layered with interesting finds. This archaeology of suffering and repression is less prominent for Klein: her major interest lies in the *continuous*, as she would insist in contradistinction to Freud, play of phantasy in the unconscious of the child. As we shall see, it is this continuity of phantasy in adult life that, on Klein's account, makes the world − and the way we relate to it.

One further prefatory comment is in order. Melanie Klein herself was not much interested in social theory. She had no 'metapsychology' such as Freud developed in *Civilisation and its Discontents*, and made only one serious attempt to relate her theories to wider issues of the development of society and culture. Like Freud in his earlier years, she was essentially a clinician, gathering data from case histories and seeking to apply her theories in a therapeutic context. It is important to emphasise that there is often a difference between what Klein herself thought and taught, and what those applying Kleinian ideas (such as Isabel Menzies or Wilfred Bion) end up with when they turn to group psychology and/or social theory. I shall not labour the point in this chapter, since to do so would require a more detailed treatment of Klein and her successors than I propose to present, but the reader should be wary of assuming that everything presented as 'Kleinian' was necessarily the precise or expressed view of Klein herself.

Kleinian Development Theory

Klein writes of 'positions', where Freud writes of 'stages'. This difference is more than semantic, and it is important to emphasise at the outset that, while we stressed in the last chapter that Freud's stages should be interpreted less as 'stage theory' than as heuristic tools, in this chapter it is crucial to understand that the individual (or, by extension, the group, as we shall see later) can and does switch readily and, under the right conditions, frequently, from one 'position' to another. There is a progression – but there is also regression. Although the later position is in some sense superior (since it makes possible an ethically superior morality), the individual or the group may alternate between the two positions identified by Klein in response to external stimuli and internal phantasy.

The first position is the paranoid–schizoid position. Its origins can be put like this. The most pervasive and powerful affect that the young child experiences is raw aggression. This aggression is experienced by the child with such power, such overwhelming force, that s/he fears that s/he will be destroyed by it. As a first step, the child projects the aggression outwards on to others (real or phantasised), but then experiences the fear of attack from those on to whom the aggression has been projected. Here the role of the person on whom the aggression is projected (usually the mother) is crucial. Does she, in Bion's phrase, 'contain' it, that is accept it, process it, psychically masticate it, and feed it, in manageable proportions, back to the infant, showing thereby that she cares, understands and can 'take' the projections? Or does she refuse the projection, defending herself against it or denying its existence? If the latter, the infant has to reintroject 'raw' aggression – something that is likely to be extremely damaging.

In either case – that is, whether the mother is 'good enough' as a container or not – the child fears the reintrojection of what it has projected. It is this that gives rise to the paranoia and its associated anxiety.

How does the child cope emotionally with this fear? Klein's genius lay in her emphasis on the child's ability to 'split' the world and attach the fear, anxiety and rage to one part of it while accepting another part as wholesome, good, loving and loved. The 'bad' part may be phantasy, perhaps attaching to one part of the child's parents or some other object with which the child is familiar. All the aggression, anxiety and hatred are then dumped through projective identification on this 'part-object', in order that the child itself may be free of them – and the rest of its world, too, may be accepted as 'good'. This ego-splitting had been recognised by Freud in an unfinished paper – *Splitting of the Ego in the Process of Defence*, written in his last years – as central to all defence mechanisms; but Klein, influenced by the work on pregenital development of Karl Abraham who had been her analyst, put it at the heart of the child's earliest experiences, its instinctive psychological response to the memory of the intolerable burden of its own hatred and anger.

Borrowing the phrase from Fairbairn, who had independently written of the newly born infant's tendency to split into idealising and persecutory modes in a paper in 1941,[4] Klein thus called her first position the paranoid-schizoid position, pointing out that the processes of splitting which allow the child to keep two parts of its world quite separate from each other is exactly what one encounters in adult schizoid patients. For thus underlining the essential continuity between both neo-nates and adults, and between healthy responses and severe mental illness, Klein was predictably upbraided by contemporaries, who wanted to preserve the comfortable myths of clear discontinuities in both psychological development and psychological 'normality'.

This sense of continuity implied, however, a further break from Freud. As is well known, Freud had come late to the recognition of the death instinct, the Thanatos that balanced Eros, the *Todestrieb*. Even then he argued that, since the infant cannot be said to have an ego (which will only develop through the oral/anal/phallic Oedipal progression), it cannot either be said to fear death, the extinction of the ego. Klein took the contrary view. She thought that the anxiety provoked by primitive sensations, especially of aggression and hatred, was so intense that the schizoid defence mechanism of splitting was vitally necessary for the psychic survival of the child – and later for the adult in the paranoid-schizoid position. Precisely because the paranoid fear of annihilation, of extinction at the hands of the (projected) 'baddies out there', was so threatening, splitting offered the only adequate defence. You do not need as sophisticated and potentially damaging a defence if the threat is not perceived as real and deadly.

Thus the infant (and later the adult or the group) projects on to part-objects (classically, 'the bad breast') its aggression, and introjects a fear that the part-object is determined to kill it. It is important to pick up the sadistic element here. The 'bad breast' takes, in the phantasy of the child, a delight in its annihilation: it is the tragic mirror image of the child's own anxiety at the memory of the strength of its aggression towards the world in general and mother in particular.

For, and this is the crucial point, what sadistically threatens the child is part of the child itself. By splitting, the child projects part of its own ego, part of its very self, into the 'bad' part-object – and then reintrojects that aggression as paranoid fear. Klein sometimes wrote as though this process were almost physical. In her *Notes on Some Schizoid Mechanisms*, published in 1946,[5] she wrote of projection (or projective identification) as a process whereby the infant 'forces parts of the ego into' the part-object 'in order to take over its contents or to control it'. How seriously we are to take this language is a matter of debate. Clearly, Klein thought she was adding something important to Freud's work on projection; perhaps, as Elizabeth Spillius has suggested, the significant difference is that Klein worked the notion of projection back to splitting the ego, and forward to the object itself: 'Impulses do not just vanish when projected; they go further into an object and they distort the perception of the object.'[6]

Just as the infant projects its aggression and makes the 'breast' 'bad', so it idealises the 'good breast'. While the 'bad breast' may be perceived in phantasy as disintegrated into the memory of a succession of would-be persecutors or bitten into pieces[7] the 'good breast' is seen as whole and wholesome. It is life-giving, and the infant's psychic struggle is to prevent it being annihilated, along with him/herself, by the 'bad breast'. S/he does this by keeping the two worlds apart, by constructing a bifurcated world in which good and bad never meet. The effort required is, of course, huge – for the reality is that there is one world and not two. It is only when the child can bear the guilt of having damaged the object into which s/he has projected his/her own aggression that s/he can take back the projections and can move on from the necessary splitting and idealisation. Then s/he can begin to experience the world as one. And that is the achievement of the depressive position.

What brings about the change – which may first take place as early as three months after birth? On that there is much debate, which can only be summarised telegrammatically here. One view puts the emphasis on good parenting, especially by the mother. By patiently accepting the child's 'bad' projections and simultaneously showing love and care (i.e., by being a good container) the mother demonstrates the irrationality of the 'bad' projections. The child has nothing to fear from her. She is good, kind, loving – and she is one whole person. The one who frustrates and deprives is also the one who cares and nourishes. The other approach is to emphasise the child's gain in cognitive skills. As s/he learns about the 'objective reality' of the world, so s/he learns that the world cannot be rigidly split into 'good' and 'bad'. Reality is not like that – and as it develops a capacity for reality testing, the child has to adapt its view of the world. Third, and possibly nearest to Klein herself, both of these factors play a role in what is essentially a normal developmental sequence, perhaps innate.[8]

From wherever it comes, the depressive position is characterised by both relief that the child has not in fact damaged the object (i.e., the mother–container) and depression and despair at the havoc s/he has wrought in phantasy on the mother and often other objects whom s/he has made recipient of his/her persecutory projections. This despair (and the guilt that lies behind the despair) is relieved by reparation. As the mother–container shows forgiveness, so the child learns how it can repair and restore the relationship with those (part-objects) s/he has sought, in phantasy, to destroy or kill or despoil. Much, then, depends on the quality of the reparation sought and the forgiveness offered. If the former is manic and the latter ungenerous or conditional (and the one may affect the other: a dialectic process can easily be put in place, albeit unwittingly), it can lead to denial and/or a quick return to the paranoid–schizoid position.

However generous and unconditional the forgiveness that is offered, however persistent the mother's efforts to re-establish relationship, the attempt at reparation by the child is dogged by pessimism (hence the depression), triggered by the memory or phantasy of previous failures at reparation Maybe the child does not have it within him/her to make adequate reparation: maybe it cannot be done. Maybe the earlier destruction and all that flows from it will have to be the last existential word. In extreme cases, the child will not be able to tolerate this and will either get stuck in the paranoid-schizoid position or at least adopt defences associated with that position, such as splitting, projective identification, idealisation or manic reparation.

With adequate containment (as a result of good, responsive mothering) and growing cognitive competence (so that it can establish whether or not that is the case) the child will hopefully learn that the anxiety is unfounded. Through both phantasy and action, s/he will make gestures of reparation and will find they are accepted. S/he learns that the healing of relationships is possible.

How far is that crucial discovery born out of guilt? How far out of fear? How far out of love? Perhaps there is no one answer to that, but Klein is clear that normally the child progresses to a point at which s/he has a genuine care for the other, the whole object, for its own sake, rather than as an actor in the child's own inner drama. To some extent, Klein believed, this transformation from self-centredness to other-centredness was the child's reaction in thankfulness and appreciation to the memory of what it had received from mother. 'Feelings of love and gratitude arise directly and spontaneously in the baby in response to the love and care of his mother.'[9] This spontaneity is exactly equivalent to the spontaneity of the anger and aggression in the paranoid-schizoid position: the two passions of hatred and love thus balance each other in each position and the child, Klein insists, is capable of experiencing both in a raw state of astonishing power. Of the latter she can thus write that the child can feel a 'profound urge to make sacrifices' for others, forego its own pleasures to give pleasure to others. As we shall see below, we have here, in the child's recollection of the mother-love it has received, the emotional origins of what in its adult form becomes one of the most basic social structures of all, a moral code that privileges altruism.

But before we can look at some of the implications of Kleinian theory, we need to introduce one more ethical term into the discussion. What, we might ask, inhibits the passage from the paranoid-schizoid position to the depressive position? Klein answers in one word: envy. In *Envy and Gratitude*, Klein gives envy a quasi-Freudian base in oral and anal sadism – that is, the despoilation of what ought to be and could be experienced as good. For her that is the root of the destructive power of envy: it denies and destroys the (potentially) good. Thus it makes the creation and maintenance of the 'good breast' in the paranoid–schizoid position almost impossible, and it makes the possibility of reparation in the depressive position quite impossible. For reparation implies a wish to consolidate the good of the other, whereas envy demands the destruction of the good of the other and the siting of all good – or any good on offer – in and for *me*. It is the familiar behaviour of the yob and the vandal. Hoggett comments how skinheads tended to break up concerts of bands *they supported*, thus representing what he calls 'a culture of envy'.[10] William Halton has more recently described the way in which envy operates at the institutional level, where different groups may all be equally committed to the goal of the institution but where envious groups will seemingly – and unconsciously – sabotage the work of other 'favoured' groups and thus undermine the work of the institution as a whole.[11]

But that is to anticipate. In Klein's development theory, envy reinforces persecutory anxiety by weakening the child's hold on his/her good objects and even by denying the possibility of good 'out there'. In the adult, the final resting place is therefore an intolerant arrogance. The victim of envy then becomes trapped in the paranoid-schizoid position – with the added horror that the defensive possibilities of splitting are much reduced. The ego is cruelly diminished, and envy correspondingly increases. The circle is vicious indeed. This is a Fall that offers scant hope of redemption. No wonder Klein thinks envy the greatest problem of all. No wonder she showed special compassion for the envious person struggling to come to terms with it.

That concludes what I want to say about Kleinian developmental theory. Critics might think it does little to advance the main argument of the book, and wonder why I have spent so long on Klein, especially given her almost total silence on the subject of memory. I beg for patience. In the next section I shall return to the relationship between phantasy, the key Kleinian building block, and memory, arguing again, as I did in the last chapter, that the two are closer and more interwoven than is immediately obvious. I shall then leave Klein's concern with the development of the individual and ask how her approach can be applied to groups. Since our basic concern is with the way memory forms us and our world, and the implications of that relationship for modern theology, we clearly need to broaden the enquiry from the development of the individual to the psychic processes of the group. I shall accordingly offer a brief discussion of some of the theoretical positions that scholars operating with a Kleinian approach have taken. This will form a preface to the consideration of two classic case studies which show how a Kleinian approach to the life of groups can illuminate the role of phantasy in social life. These case studies then should be seen as paralleling those of Stevens on the archetype of war and of Ward on Camden Council in Chapters 4 and 5, and will conclude our discussion of the strictly psychoanalytic literature. We shall then, after a brief theological reflection, turn in the last two chapters of this Part to some examples from social psychology to pursue the fundamental point of the role of memory in making our world and its implications for faith.

Klein and Memory

What role, then, does memory play in Klein's scheme? Oddly, this question has been relatively little addressed in the literature, even though it is clear that we are in very different terrain from Freud, or at least early Freud. For him, memories were part of 'the archaeology of suffering', in Lowe's phrase:[12] deep-buried repressed traumas that need to be returned to consciousness for healing. As we saw in the case of Kovel, however, post-Freudians have, like Klein, put more emphasis on phantasy as the intra-psychic material that gives shape to external reality through projection. Can we say more than that about memory? One of Klein's closest associates, analysand and co-author Joan Rivière, addressed this problem, albeit in a preliminary way. For her, the fears and anxieties of both the paranoid-schizoid and depressive positions acquire the horror of the quality they do precisely because they are an indeterminable mixture of real (i.e., objectively true) memory and false (i.e., non-objectively true) imagination. The bad object has its power to terrify and enslave not because it is imaginatively horrible – a dragon or hostile alien – but because it is a distortion of a true memory of something, or more probably someone, real and emotionally close to the client. *Mutatis mutandis*, the good object can be idealised exactly because some of its goodness actually belongs to a real person who can be experienced in the daily round.

Phantasy is, then, an indeterminable mix of reality (in the form of 'true' memory), distorted reality (in the form of false but fact-related memory) and pure imagination which has nothing to do with memory (except in so far as all imagination may be memory-dependent). But Rivière goes a step further and explains that what gives phantasy its power is its memory base in a person with whom we have close emotional ties. It is the fusion of the reality-relation of memory with the emotionality of personal closeness that generates the energy of phantasy.

The key question then becomes how we manage this energy. Commenting on the memories that underlie it, Rivière writes:

What matters is what we 'did with them inside ourselves' [a phrase used by a patient] 'in our own minds', usually much more than what happened with them outside in 'real life'. The memories to be recovered in analysis consist so much of these inner happenings, to which external events such as we consciously call memories are often not much more than labels or signposts – in a sense but 'screen memories'. As such they have their great emotional import-ance to us: just as a person's name, which is but a label, can represent his whole being to us[13]

Rivière goes on (in the article just quoted and in a succeeding essay on Ibsen's *Master Builder*) to argue that memories are, however, more than memories: they are the experience of (remembered) people in and with us. She quotes from Samuel Rogers:

. . . At moments which he calls his own,
Then, never less alone than when alone,
Those whom he loved so long and sees no more,

Loved and still loves − not dead but gone before −
He gathers round him.

The 'gathering round' is not mere recollection in a cognitive or even Wordsworthian sense:

> Those who have been emotionally important to us are still with us and inseparable from us − the unconscious truth behind the words being that they are *in us* and part of us and therefore inseparable and available to us. Memory, relating to external events and to the corporeal reality of loved figures as beings distinct from ourselves, is one facet of our relation to them; the other facet is the life they lead within us indivisible from ourselves, their existence in our inner world.[14]

The relationship between those modes of being − 'real' memory and 'life within us' − will, of course, depend precisely upon the intra-psychic dynamics of our emotional development. But it will also depend (and this is something that Rivière does not acknowledge explicitly) on the emotional load of the memory itself. Memories − real life memories − are not emotionally flat or homogeneous: each has its own affect and that helps determine the role it plays in our inner world. We should not therefore overdraw the contrast between the early Freud and the Kleinians: the archaeology of suffering may reveal more than the early Freud allowed, but the affect-laden memories of all the emotionally significant people who have crossed our path are themselves waiting to be revealed to consciousness. They play their part, for good or ill, in our phantasy, just as they play their part, for good or ill, in our conscious self-narrative.

Rivière, like Klein, was primarily concerned with the relationship between phantasy and the life of the individual patient. But that should not blind us to the fact that groups of people, from families to nations, have memories and phantasies, too, and that those play a part in determining the social characteristics of our environment. Analytically, we are in a world that parallels Jung's work on the collective unconscious; we need to ask, so to speak, about the power of collective phantasy. Although that phrase is not in common use, analysts who use a Kleinian approach are well aware of the way groups reflect the power of phantasy.[15] To that we must now turn.

Social Applications of Kleinian Theory

We need to consider the relationship between individual anxiety (whether of a paranoid-schizoid or depressive variety) and the group (i.e., a large number of other individuals with their own anxieties).[16] Does a group enable an individual to deal better with his/her anxiety, or does it reinforce it? More especially, are there reasons for thinking that membership of a group enables individuals – i.e., *all* individuals in the group – to move from the paranoid-schizoid position to the depressive position, with its possibility of what Alford has usefully called reparative morality?[17] The significance of these questions should not escape us. For, as I emphasised above, in the Kleinian model, position and its associated phantasy *make the world* in which the infant (and later the adult) operates. Translating that into post-Kleinian terminology, one might say that the phantasies shared by the group, part memory, part imagination as they are, make the group's world view – and therefore heavily influence or, at the margin, determine its structuration.

As is well known, the dominant position of Oedipal theory in Freud's theory led him and his followers to concentrate on the relationship between the leader and the group. The leader was the father figure, the group members jealous siblings. Kleinian theory does not necessarily seek to deny the possibility of Oedipal phantasies within the group, but the main developments have been in quite different directions. Wilfred Bion and D.W. Winnicott have both emphasised the way in which the group 'holds' the individual and enables him/her to defend against paranoid-schizoid anxiety.[18] In this way, Bion claimed, the group operates like a mother in the very early stages of life when the infant is fearful of disintegration. The mother almost literally holds the baby together, but also gives it space to express its needs and receive an affirming response. Winnicott emphasises the importance of this holding: 'it enables the infant's co-existing love and hate to become sorted out and interrelated and gradually brought under control from within'.[19] It is the 'prototype not only of our internal capacity to contain our experience and reach some

114

understanding of it but of an endless series of internal and external substitutions for the body of the family and the group, to the body of the motherland and to the body of Christ'.[20] So clergy hold their parishioners, counsellors hold their clients; teachers hold their pupils; and all holders, so Christians might think, look to Christ, the ultimate holder.

More particularly, Bion analysed the way a group enables its members to defend against paranoid-schizoid anxiety in great detail, arguing that in a group the individual can share both the anxiety and the phantasy and receive from the group affirmation of the classic defences of splitting and idealisation.[21] We shall see more concretely how that works when we turn below to the work of Elliot Jacques, but now it is important to put Bion's work into a more precise perspective. Fred Alford has pointed out that the individual not only shares her/his *own* anxieties in the group, but may well have a different set of anxieties that stem exactly from the fact that s/he is a member of a group in the first place. She may, for example, fear that the group is being attacked or undermined or done down by other groups, a common enough anxiety when groups are in conflict for scarce resources or when the groups that make up an institution are facing the closure of that institution – an all too common experience of public sector workers in the United States and the UK as the welfare state is rolled back.[22]

The issue, however, is whether these anxieties activate or 'plug into' deeper anxieties and become primitive, obsessive or pathological, as they reflect phantasies of final disintegration. Bion would argue that this is almost inevitable: the primitive phantasies of the paranoid-schizoid position lie so near the surface that they are easily activated by the experience of stress or conflict, especially when the survival of the group is at stake, an idea we shall meet again in the next chapter. In that case, the group enables the individual to project the anxiety outwards, to 'dump' the hatred, anger and fear on the alleged persecutors and to idealise the group itself, its allies and perhaps its clients. In much the same way, when a group is in contact with death, it will seek 'somewhere' to put both the individual and the group anger and distress. Sometimes this can be on dying patients themselves.[23]

The basic process here described has, of course, immediate resonances with the 'ingroup/outgroup' dichotomy we explored in Chapter 3, but although it includes that dichotomy the Kleinian perspective gives a far fuller and more primitive account of group defences. It helps explain the common experience of quasi-irrationality with which individuals-in-groups present their demands or react to changes thrust upon them. What is happening is clearly *more* than a reaction to the 'objective facts'. A highly charged subjective agenda operates as a sub-text, a hidden agenda, which 'makes' the subjective world in which the group objectively operates.

This account, however, is too undifferentiated: it treats of groups and individuals as separate entities each with its own dynamic. We need as a supplement an account of how the individual relates to the group to explain the common perception of the difference between behaviour of the individual as individual and individual as member of a group – a difference explored in a different cadence by Niebuhr in *Moral Man and Immoral Society*[24] and the common experience of anyone who has sat on academic or ecclesiastical committees which seem to have the astonishing power to turn decent, sensible people into monsters (or morons). Otto Kernberg has used a basically Kleinian methodology by pointing out that the group threatens the ego of the individual.[25] S/he may feel it wants to 'eat me up'.[26] To this fear (again notice how well it corresponds to Klein's accounts of paranoid-schizoid fears in early childhood) the individual responds with aggression. To defend himself against this aggression, however, he projects it outside the group on to others (the outgroup, if you will) and in doing so allies himself more closely to his own group. In this process, he may well idealise his own group and especially his leader, who can become a mother figure offering a secure relationship of dependency and security. The way this works in practice has been well documented by members of the Tavistock Clinic who consult to institutions in various degrees of crisis.[27]

Less well documented in that tradition, however, is the way these processes ensure that the individual is securely bonded to the group and will go along, usually without question, with whatever the group and its leader decide. However moral he may be at home, he is now capable of great immorality. We shall see more of the potentially terrible social implications of this in a later chapter.

Bion took that line of thought a stage further by differentiating between the group and the gang. The latter is marked by 'beta-thinking', that is, essentially unprocessed, primitive raw, unreflected, 'near sensory and somatic' types of reactions.[28] If the group, by definition capable of 'alpha-thinking' (i.e., processed, self-reflective, intellectualised), projects its anxiety on to others, that can be destructive but is not usually disastrous. If the gang does so, social mayhem is round the corner -- think of Nazi, National Front or soccer hooligans. Importantly, however, Bion never claimed to be able to say how a beta-gang was transformed into an alpha-group.

Indeed, the main thrust of the three post-Kleinians I have touched upon – Wilfred Bion, D.W. Winnicott and Otto Kernberg – is that the individual-in-the-group is incapacitated from the emotional learning that makes progress to the depressive position possible. Because the paranoid-schizoid anxieties can be so well dealt with in a group context, by the familiar processes of splitting, projective identification and idealisation, the 'natural development', as Klein saw it for the infant, to the depressive position is indefinitely delayed for the adult in the group. Thus, Bion identified the three 'basic assumptions' which the group will adopt as defences against anxiety. He and others have shown empirically how often 'work groups' move into these assumptions and thereby cease to function as groups engaged with their 'work' or primary task.[29]

Thus, while the isolated infant integrates 'good breast' and 'bad breast' into mother whom s/he has destroyed in phantasy and hopefully is able to move on to repair and restoration, if necessary by self-sacrificial acts of love, the adult-in-the-group is never likely to be faced with the need, cognitive or emotional, to make that integrative leap. Because of the group and cultural environment (and associated activities of stereotyping and scapegoating to which we shall come in Chapter 8), the outgroup remains the outgroup. Or if this particular outgroup will no longer serve as a dump for persecutory fears and hatred, another will soon be found. For the group, there is no shortage of 'bad breasts'.

The geo-political events of 1989–91 illustrate the process graphically. With the ending of the Cold War, *perestroika*, the dismantling of the Berlin Wall, the election of Boris Yeltsin as President of Russia and a thousand other significant events, it became increasingly implausible to maintain the phantasies that had an echo of verisimilitude in the days of Stalin and Khrushchev that the Soviet Union was a menace to the West. Emotionally, psychically, it could be – and was – used as a lightning-conductor which could (more or less) safely earth the projections of anxiety-ridden Westerners. Post–1990, however, you needed to be psychotic or pig-ignorant to believe that the Soviet Union was 'the evil empire' of Reagan's over-vivid imagination. Cognitively, we had to bring ourselves to accept that the 'bad breast' was perhaps not as bad as we had thought. Yet within months of the collapse of the Berlin Wall, perhaps the most symbolically significant event in this whole denouement, we had 'found' or, as I would prefer to say, 'made' another 'bad breast' in the form of Saddam Hussein and his coterie of thugs in Iraq. Without pushing the example further than it will legitimately go, three phenomena are striking: the speed and scale of the Western response; the deliberate maintenance of Hussein in power; and the absurdly exaggerated exultation in military victory with ticker-tape welcomes in New York and victory parades throughout the USA and in London. To that list might be added the complete failure in the USA and the UK to get a fair hearing for the historical claim that Iraq does in fact have on a small part of Kuwait. The 'bad breast' was needed to receive the aggression and hatred that could no longer be credibly pinned on the Soviet Union. For once emotional, political, racial, economic and military imperatives coincided. The result was inevitable.

Does this imply that everyone in the West was in the paranoid-schizoid position at this time? Clearly that would be absurd – though not so absurd that distinguished scholars have not suggested that whole nations (in one example, Britain in the late 1930s) are incapable of entering the depressive position.[30] We need to distinguish between the public and private – or the group and individual – modes of behaviour. A *group* may behave in a paranoid-schizoid way even though many, perhaps even a majority, of its members may have entered the depressive position. Group members can handle their persecutory fears and anxieties through the group. The group *qua* group 'holds' their anxieties for them. That may enable some to move on to the depressive position: it is more likely to leave the many more 'stuck' in the paranoid–schizoid position precisely because the group legitimates their anxieties and gives them concrete expression.

It is the growth-inhibiting effect of a group-life that makes Kleinian analysis less than optimistic as a political theory. If it is not possible (or even, according to Bion, healthy) for individuals to enter securely and remain in the depressive position, it is even less so for the groups to do so. We are thus faced with a tantalising tragedy, worthy of Greek mythology or Pauline agony: *if only* we could as groups, communitites, political entities, be taken by the passion for reparation, for loving restoration of relationship, for sacrificial promotion of the good of the other, free of self-interest or self-service . . . if only, how different our politics and our world would be.

It is this vision that has led some psychoanalytic and political theorists to hijack Klein for the socialist cause. By contrast with the Hobbesian or Burkeian traditions of conservatism, she seems to offer hope of a genuine social harmony out of inner freedom – rather than a Freudian repression. Michael Rustin, Graham Little and R.E. Money-Kyrle[31] have all, in their different ways, claimed Klein for socialism in one form or another. Thus Rustin draws from Klein's theory 'a commitment to the values of life, of relationship, of membership in a social community from birth, of creative development and of a normal care for others which properly form part of a socialist conception of man'.[32] And in a later essay he writes: 'The ethical cast of Kleinian thinking paralleled a moral emphasis in social-democratic political thought evident, for example, in Titmuss's forceful contrast of altruism with individualism and sectional class interests.'[33] He goes on to argue that Kleinian theory affected both literary theory via Leavis and socio-political thought via Raymond Williams, the common element between the two being a teleology that took seriously the possibilities of the 'if only' with which we ended the last paragraph.[34]

In much the same vein, Money-Kyrle sees the reparative morality as incompatible with any form of totalitarianism and, more interestingly, with capitalism. Even a moderate or reformist capitalism, tempered by the trappings of welfare state on the Swedish or British models, cannot do adequate justice to the concern for the other that is the defining characteristic of reparative morality. It is not irrelevant to Money-Kyrle's argument that, since he propounded it, both

Sweden and Britain have reformed their welfarism in the direction of a liberal individualism precisely because the 'excesses' of the 1960s and 1970s were finally judged to be inconsistent with economic efficiency under conditions of international capitalism. The more 'reparative' welfarism becomes, the more its contradictions with capitalism are revealed. Money-Kyrle thinks Kleinian theory, and its further development as object relations theory, points towards a genuinely welfare-oriented politics that leaves enough political and psychic 'space' for individuals to realise their uniqueness. He is less clear about how that may be superimposed on any known organisation of the means of production and exchange.

Perhaps the real value of Kleinian theory from our perspective is in its negative aspects. In so far as it helps explain why social and political change in the direction of altruism and compassion is so hard – essentially because groups, and particularly unorganised groups, are held in the paranoid-schizoid position – it focuses attention on the hard institutional slog of protecting and extending whatever elements of public decency we have been able to establish in our political culture.

This is to put the emphasis on the other end of the spectrum from Marcuse: he wanted an end to political and sexual repression and saw Freudian and Marxist theory fusing in the discovery of a new freedom. Perhaps Klein and her successors point in the opposite direction: in the direction of an acknowledgement of the reality of hatred, fear and anger in our own phantasies and in the projections of any group. Our task, as I claim an essentially theological task – at least until we can discover the lovingness of reparative morality – is, then, to draw the sting of those projections so that their power over us and our group becomes less destructive. Or to put it another way, Klein reminds us of the extent to which we make our political realities – and therefore of the need, one might even say the transcendent need, constantly to test those realities in any way that is open to us. Behind all political rhetoric, whether of Left or Right, communitarian, socialist or individualist, lie stereotypes that are the constructions of group paranoia or splitting. They carry our griefs, private or corporate. And they make further grief inevitable.

For example, the outgroup *makes* the stereotypes come more nearly true. Black kids underperform – so little is demanded of them and they do underperform. Feminists are abrasive – so they are discounted until they have to become abrasive to be heard. Shop stewards are bloody-minded – so they are ignored or patronised until they become bloody-minded in order to be taken seriously. In each case the stereotype is a projection, a split-off part of my fear or anxiety which can be dumped on any 'outgroup' that will carry it. In a Kleinian world, I (and by extension you and the rest of our culture) have to find a way both of integrating that fear and anxiety with the love and care of which we are capable (if you will, our psychic task): but also – and less emphasised by Klein – our political task is to check out the reality of the underperformance of black kids, the public presentation of the feminist agenda and the behaviour of shop stewards knowing as much as we can know about the perceptual blinkers our own split-off emotions bring to that task.

And that, of course, poses us a real problem and takes us back to the interconnectedness, the dialectic, between what I called in the last paragraph the psychic and political task. For we are caught by an inner contradiction: while we are the victims of our own unconscious memory-related phantasies we cannot test the reality beyond the world those phantasies create around us. Or to put it in terms of the last paragraph, the psychic task is logically prior to the political tasks; and yet part of the solution of the psychic task is the completion of the political task. It is when we unmask 'objective' reality behind the subjective reality of our stereotypes that we can begin the process of integration – but the unmasking presupposes a degree of integration already.

This should not dismay us. Iterative processes are a commonplace of psychic healing as they are in many areas of change, from engineering to geophysics or economics. And if we allow for a degree of over-determination in the last paragraph (there are other factors involved: it is not as closed a system as I have presented it), the possibilities of constructive iteration are increased. I may be trapped: but if I work at it hard, consciously and hopefully, I need not be trapped for ever.

We shall see how this operates more concretely by reference to two classic case studies, summarised below. The original focus of both these studies was to show how organisations adapt themselves to defend their members against anxieties and fears at the unconscious level. Both authors are, then, primarily interested in organisational form as defence, but it is a short step from that focus to one more immediately relevant for our purpose: to see how the unconscious memories and psychological needs of a group (for defence against primitive anxieties in these cases) become enstructured in the constitution and style of working in that group.

Case Study 1: The Nursing Profession

Isabel Menzies' study of the organisation of nursing in a London teaching hospital starts with the observation that nursing is a high-stress occupation that puts its practitioners into contact with primitive phantasies of such power that the profession has unconsciously organised itself in ways that defend it against the anxieties triggered by these phantasies.[35]

Nursing involves handling the bodies of other people; the wastes of those bodies; the pain and death of those bodies. Emotionally it has frightening, erotic, guilty, envious and resentful overtones. Menzies' argument is that this combination of external stimuli and emotional charges mirrors many of the aspects of the child's inner world. In so far as, in memory, the inner world was a frightening and anxiety-provoking place, the nurse is likely to find that her occupation generates unconscious anxiety. That is likely to be increased by the fears, stresses and anxieties that she encounters in her patients and their relatives. 'Unconsciously the nurse associated the patients' and relatives' distress with that experienced by the people in her phantasy world, which increases her own anxiety and difficulty in handling it.'[36]

For the nurse, then, her reaction to her total situation (the external world as modified by the play of her own phantasy) will determine both the quality of care she can give and her own survival in the profession. What is likely to happen is that she will project her phantasy world on to the objective situation.

Through the projection, the individual sees elements of the phantasy situation in the objective situations that come to symbolise the phantasy situations. To be effective, such symbolization requires that the symbol represents the phantasy objective, but is not equated with it.[37]

The danger is that representation does become equation – so that, for example, a dying patient comes to symbolise the death of the nurse herself. If that happens, the anxiety level is likely to become intolerable. And, Menzies argues, it is more likely to happen in nursing than in most professions because of the close resemblance between the contents of the objective situation and the contents of the phantasy world. 'Nurses will consequently experience the full force of the primitive anxieties in consciousness.'[38]

It is to defend against these anxieties that the profession is organised in a particular way, for Menzies takes it as axiomatic that, so far as doing the job at all allows, any group will so organise itself that 'the culture, structure, and mode of functioning are determined by the psychological needs of the members'. There is much more to this than simple denial – even though there is an easily recognised sense in which hospitals, like churches, may function psychically as institutionalised denials of the possibility of death. (One London hospital was, incredibly, built without a mortuary – and no one noticed until the hospital was opened.[39])

Menzies operates at a deeper level than that. She identifies the structural defences that the profession has invented (no doubt unconsciously) for itself, emphasising that although they are, for analytical convenience, described separately, they interact both in terms of the defence they offer against anxiety and in terms of the overt functioning of the system. Some examples follow.

The nurse–patient relationship is curtailed, with nurses frequently moved from ward to ward, and expected to relate to all patients rather than develop close affinity with a small number. The significance of the individual nurse is further reduced by uniforms and standardisation of style and procedures; and the nurse's professional formation encourages her to think of patients as bundles of symptoms rather than real people: 'the liver in bed No.4'. Thus identification with patients is reduced, and a brisk, reassuring manner, together with a degree of professional mystique, both puts barriers between nurses and patients, and enables the nurse to repress or at least disguise her own feelings. (Oberholzer has recently argued that the way in which the new and burgeoning generation of 'managers' in the health service separate themselves from the pain of patients, by talking about budgets and performance indicators, is overtly an excuse for never going near a patient in great pain or distress and unconsciously a classic defence.[40])

In the case of nurses, Menzies argues (and Dartington more recently concurs) that control of feelings takes many forms: from the deliberate stiff-upper-lip to harsh discipline and often a rather petty over-concern for trivia (e.g., the exact standardisation of procedures and the insistence that the standard be followed absolutely precisely; or, as Dartington puts it, that nurses be discouraged from thinking[41]).

Standardisation serves a further purpose. It eliminates individual decision-making. The more robotic the procedures, administrative as well as patient-centred, the less anxiety will be provoked by uncertainty and risk. Equally and tragically, however, the effect of these defences is to make it the more difficult for nurses to enter the depressive position and nurse out of a reparative morality. Locked in a split, paranoid world, they cannot easily bring love and tenderness to their job — which may well have been part of their original motivation.

Menzies has a particularly interesting account of what she calls the collusive redistribution of responsibility and irresponsibility. Often still very young, nurses want and need to be irresponsible some of the time. They handle this inner conflict by projecting their 'responsible' parts on to senior nurses and the 'irresponsible' parts on to junior nurses. Thus, they expect unbending discipline from their seniors, who, as it were, contain their own super-egos, but condemn young nurses as silly and irresponsible, treating them with the disdain and even severity that they feel their own irresponsibility deserves.

The inevitable result of this is that responsibility and the trickier nursing operations tend to be delegated upwards. That means that senior nurses are often overworked, while intelligent and careful juniors are allowed only to do the most routine tasks, far below their personal capacity. High wastage, of overstressed seniors and bored juniors, is the result. Interestingly, it is the brightest and most compassionate nurses who leave in disproportionate numbers.

Finally, because the system does, however imperfectly, defend nurses against anxiety, they are resistant to change. Menzies sees a direct correlation between the fearsomeness of the primitive anxieties engendered by the task and the reluctance to change styles of work, organisation and the distribution of responsibility. She was writing in 1959. In 1992 the British Audit Commission issued a report recommending that nurses see it as part of their responsibility to *know* their patients. It revealed that in only 10 per cent of wards did that already happen. The defences remain in place. The profession is caught in the same 'cultural crisis', and whereas some of the explanation for that may well lie in the wider society (as Menzies' critics maintain) it is hard to deny the pervasiveness and persistence with which the psychic pressures she describes endure.[42]

Case Study 2: Glacier Metal

Jacques' study of industrial relations in the Glacier Metal Company takes up the same point: that organisations defend themselves against anxiety by structuring themselves in response to phantasy as much as to objective fact.[43] When he came to apply this approach to one particular structural event in the life of a light engineering company, Jacques found a surprisingly good fit. Observation of the working of a joint management–worker representative committee to negotiate the switch from piece-work to hourly rates (a switch overtly agreed as desirable by all participants) revealed three ostensibly puzzling features: the contrast between heated, acrimonious debate in the committee and the generally placid, non-conflictual relations in the company at large; the distrust of the workers for their representatives, despite the fact that they had been elected by the workers themselves, in part at least in recognition of their trade union activists' credentials; and the inability of the committee to produce a satisfactory outcome to a relatively simple problem the basic solution of which all sides agreed upon. So what was going on?

Jacques thinks these features become less puzzling if we assume the workers on the shop floor had split the managers into good and bad – the good being the ones with whom they worked, the bad being the ones with whom they negotiated (even though they were the same individuals). Further, the workers had unconsciously projected their hostile impulses into their elected representatives – and the representatives redirected those impulses against 'bad' managers. Simultaneously, however, workers projected their good impulses into the 'good' managers with whom they worked day by day. This allowed them to reintroject the good relations with management and hence, by preserving an *undamaged* good object, to alleviate depressive guilt and anxiety.

This splitting was reinforced by identification with other workers. This encouraged workers' aggression against 'bad objects' – the representatives and 'bad' managers – and allowed them to be consciously represented as poor performers or sell-outs or scabs. From the point of view of the representatives themselves, anxiety about bad impulses was unconsciously reduced by accepting them (the bad impulses) as laid upon them by the workers rather than 'really' belonging to the representatives themselves. They could thus overtly justify their aggressiveness as being demanded by those they represented.

There is, however, a further dimension. For the representatives themselves knew consciously that the managers with whom they were negotiating were 'good'. How could they justify their own hostility to people who were 'good'? This guilt and anxiety were defended against by a defensive paranoid-schizoid organisation. 'This came out as a rigid clinging to attitudes of suspicion and hostility even in circumstances where they consciously felt that some of this suspicion was not justified by the situation they were actually experiencing.'[44]

And how did the managers cope with this suspicion? Unconsciously, they were anxious and guilty about the authority their position gave them. Unconsciously feared as uncontrolled and omnipotent, that authority could damage workers irreparably – and thus court dire retribution. Workers thus came to be seen in phantasy as (potential) persecutors. They must be placated and the damage (potentially) done to them by the exercise of managerial authority must be repaired. Thus, perhaps paradoxically, the hostility of the workers was met by the managers with idealisation and placation. The idealisation took the form of reiterations of the good sense, responsibility, co-operativeness and earthy honesty of the workers (when a lot of the time the truth was very different!) and placation was manifested in a refusal to 'close' the negotiating process, to keep talking, to give the representatives endless opportunities to state their position – even when that amounted to little more than unsubstantiated suspicion and hostility. Manic reparation indeed; or, as Speck has elsewhere called a not dissimilar reaction among clergy ministering to the dying, 'chronic niceness'.[45]

Notice the circularity of the unconscious process. The more the representatives attacked the managers, the more the managers placated and idealised them, were chronically nice, refusing to face the real issues. The more they did so – by keeping talking or giving way on negotiating points – the more persecuted the representatives felt and the greater their depressive anxiety, defended against by retreat into paranoid attitudes, manifested by hostility to the managers. Round and round . . . no wonder the committee made no progress on the substantive issue of pay schemes and no wonder there was so marked a contrast between the quality of relationships on the shop floor and the quality of relationship in the committee. Prior to Jacques' intervention (which helped the members of the committee to work through some – but not all – of the unconscious phantasy material), the committee was thus stuck – but stuck in ways that, at the unconscious level, served its members well. However maladapted it may have been for the overt objectives, the 'real task', of the company – to increase efficiency and therefore profit – the committee was ideally adapted to the phantasies of its members.

This is what Jacques calls the 'phantasy social form and content of an institution' and this is what enables him to conclude that 'the character of institutions is determined and coloured not only by their explicit or consciously agreed and accepted functions, but also by their manifold unrecognised functions at the phantasy level'.[46] And this leads him, like Menzies, to a sombre assessment of the chances for social change. For in so far as structures and institutions successfully defend their actors against primitive fears and anxieties, irrespective of their substantive performance, those actors are likely to be extremely resistant to change in the nature of their institutions, and/or highly adept at subverting change at the manifest level in such a way as will ensure that the institution continues to meet their psychic needs.

If we add that insight to the generalised scepticism of institutional change that comes from the interest-group analysis of structural formation, we find an almost direct parallel. Jacques argues that institutions will not and/or cannot change because they are as they are to serve the psychic needs of their actors; interest-group theorists argue that they are as they are to serve the political, economic or social needs of their actors. If these interests coincide and if they do not change over time, the chances of real social change, especially of a reparative nature, are slim indeed.

If that is not sober enough, a further reflection is stimulated by Jacques' work – and that in connection with Alford's plea for institutions of reparative justice examined above. We saw that there was an 'if only' quality about such thinking, an agonised scepticism. One source of that scepticism was the implicit need for the group as a whole to be able to move into the depressive position as a necessary precondition of a reparative politics. That seemed improbable *ab initio*. What Jacques helps us see more clearly is that the very fact of some members of the group operating reparatively is likely to lead other members to act out of anxieties of the paranoid-schizoid position – and this is especially true where there is a conflict of interest between members of the group. Then if one 'side' acts reparatively, the other is likely to respond negatively – i.e., out of the paranoid fears. This is not bloody-mindedness or ignorance: nor is the group or crowd being possessed by some kind of corporate 'id', as Freud and le Bon thought. It is the almost inevitable result of group phantasies and the way actors react to them.

From this it does not follow that social change is impossible. The staff at Glacier Metal did in fact advance to hourly rates and to a more co-operative style of management. It does follow, however, that change will be less painful and halting if the unconscious phantasies are mediated by the love and tenderness which alone make them tolerable.

Conclusion

How does the Kleinian paradigm help us in the major architecture of this book? I think there are four key insights that we need to take forward into the later discussion.

First, if we accept the role of memory in phantasy formation and the way in which others become 'part of us', in Rivière's phrase, Kleinian thinking shows the role our inner lives play in the formation of our outer lives. In that process memory is not exactly privileged but certainly significant.

Second, however, memory becomes distorted, warped, rendered dangerous by the emotionality that surrounds it. It is that that pushes us as individuals and as members of groups back into the paranoid-schizoid position and obliges us to deny the roseate possibilities of the 'if only' of the depressive position. When memory can be freed, healed, contained, our chances of living the reparative morality of the depressive position can be improved.

Third, containment offers a key that seems to operate at the psychic and transcendental levels. By making progress to the depressive position more possible (without in any way guaranteeing it), it makes a new quality of life available for individuals and for groups. The role of the container is thus not only crucial; it acquires a transcendental reference, as Winnicott himself recognised. But the containment itself has to be probed. How big a price in terms of suffocation of creativity and responsibility does it exact? The Menzies study makes that question inescapable.

Fourth, this style of thinking is not optimistic about the chances of institutionalising moral progress in the political process. If progress is to be made, it is more likely to be made by the individual or the small group. Or, to put it in a slightly more provocative way, the power of evil to subvert organisations and the people who make them up is so great that the institutionalisation of reparative morality is usually beyond us. The Kleinian tragedy is that that evil is located within us – even though we do our best to locate it elsewhere.

The last two chapters of this Part will change the focus somewhat. They will be less concerned with fundamental theoretical approaches and more concerned with applications of eclectic theory to specific problems or presenting symptoms. At this point of transition, it might be well to step a little further back from the development of the argument and reflect on the theological agenda that is slowly building up.

At one level, the issue is simple. If memory plays a nodal part in creating the narratives of ourselves and our world (and in one way or another all the thinkers that we have reviewed so far would not dissent from that), how can it be set free of whatever it is that makes it destructive? How, in a word, can memory be healed? We know the classic psychoanalytic answers to that – by bringing to consciousness repressed material (Freud); by relating to the archetypes (Jung); by adequate containment (the post-Kleinians). While not denying the significance of any of those therapies, I want to argue that they are at best partial because immanent, cast in a mould of thought that is essentially humanistic. They see salvation, freedom, liberation as the product of the human project – a perception that fails to take seriously enough the scale and source of what we need salvation from.

I shall want to argue that both the indeterminacy and the horror of human evil are such that only a transcendent solution is adequate to the task of human salvation. In other words, our memories can be healed not by (or not only by) therapeutic interventions of a classical Freudian or Jungian nature, but by the incorporation into our deepest psychic processes of the story of Jesus Christ. It is the counter-memories of his life and death and resurrection that have to be laid alongside or over the narratives derived from the conscious and unconscious memories that hold us captive. That that poses its own set of problems – essentially about the nature of the memories we have of Jesus – is immediately obvious and will need careful consideration in due course.

For the moment, the central point is that the stock of memories (conscious and unconscious; individual and collective) that conditions the behaviour of each person or group has to be extended into the dimension of the divine if salvation is to be realised. As the memories of God in Christ are internalised and deeply meditated, they become part of the self-narrative of the person and the group – archetypal, in Jungian terminology. The unhealed memories lose their power to distort and destroy as they are relativised by the memories of the gospel of God. The theological underpinnings of this approach will need to be set out in Part 3, but before we begin that task, the next chapters of this Part are concerned to look at a number of authors who have used either elements of Freudian or Kleinian theory, or drawn primarily from social psychology sources, to explore further the relationship between memory (of person or group) and behaviour. We shall be particularly interested in the next chapters to look at examples of pathological or destructive behaviour to illustrate what happens when unhealed memories are left in charge. That will form a sombre foreground against which to examine more concretely the contribution of Christian faith.

7

Narcissism and its Social Symptoms

As we saw in the last chapter, Klein was not what one might call a natural social theorist. Social theory is latent within her thinking about the very earliest experiences of the child, but one needs to extrapolate and extend her own writings to wring from them a consistent view of the relationship between psychological development and cultural change. Some have done that for ideologically partisan reasons; others, notably Alford, have been both more faithful to the texts and more creatively authentic in the way they have developed them.

In this chapter we go to the other extreme and consider a thinker whose contribution to social theory is, perhaps, greater than his psychological insight. Unlike Klein, he is not a practitioner and has no clinical evidence on which to draw. He is rather a historian and cultural critic, but one who, like Adorno and his collaborators, believes that historico-cultural developments can be explained by changes in the nature of predominant personalities. Although not a psychohistorian in the sense of Kovel or Loewenberg, his approach is nearer to theirs than to Klein or Bion.

Christopher Lasch has done more than any other writer to redirect attention to Freud's difficult essay 'On Narcissism', and has thereby persuaded us that, at the very least, it may be helpful to look at our contemporary society as having many of the characteristics of the narcissistic personality. As we shall see, I do not believe that Lasch is adequately faithful either to Freud or to later psychological explorations of narcissism, especially in so far as he ignores the self-hatred that is at the root of the narcissistic personality. None the less, despite almost total neglect for some years (perhaps as a result of the domination of American academe by the crazed disciples of political

131

correctness) and recently only the first signs of intellectual rehabilitation, his inclusion here attests to the value of his project: to relate psychological variables – and especially changes in childrearing practices – to historical and cultural variables. So let us start by looking at the myth which gives rise to this personality type and, if Lasch is right, to the particular temper of our times.

The Myth of Narcissus

Immediately we are faced with a problem. As Grace Stuart, in many ways a far more careful scholar than Lasch and pre-dating some of his insights (albeit from a British perspective) by more than quarter of a century, has pointed out,[1] there is more than one myth, with very different implications.

In Ovid's version, Liriope, a nymph, seeks to know the future of her child, sired by the river god Cephisus. The answer she receives is significant. He would live for long 'if he never knew himself'. He grows up a child, adolescent and young adult of surpassing beauty, so much so that young men and nubile women long for, and seek to attract, his love. He does not respond to their overtures: indeed, he tells Echo that he would rather die than give her the power over him that would be implied by his yielding to her advances. She pines away, mortally wounded by his heartless rejection. Young men fare little better, so that one cries for his talion punishment: 'So may he love and not gain the thing he loves.' Nemesis hears this prayer, and brings it about that Narcissus, reclining by the side of a pool, catches sight of his own reflection and falls in love with it (with all the sexual power that phrase implies). He does not initially realise that it is himself with whom he has formed this passionate attachment. Eventually the truth dawns, and with it the sense of tragic despair that leads him to exclaim: 'The very abundance of my riches beggars me.' This beggarhood is too painful for him. Like Echo whom his pride had killed, he pines away, only to re-enact his misery in the pool of the Styx in Hades, until his victims and the gods have pity on him and he is transformed into a flower.

A later version, that of Photius, emphasises the homosexual aspect of Narcissus' love, and makes the story more violent. Narcissus gives his (male) would-be lover a sword, with which he kills himself at

Narcissus' door. Discovering the truth of his plight – that he is in love with himself alone – Narcissus follows his lover's example and deliberately (in contrast to the Ovid version) commits suicide.

A third version, that of the Roman Pausanius, rejects the notion of Narcissus falling in love with his own reflection as palpably absurd. Rather, he falls in love with his twin sister whose features resemble his own in all their lustrous beauty. When she dies young, he goes to the pool for consolation, but seeing only his reflection, a constant re-presentation of the lover he could have no more, he is caught between his love of the image of his sister (in himself) and the impossibility of consummating his love. Death is the only way out.

There is much material here: let me summarise only the most salient features. First, Narcissus comes from the turbulent union of a nymph (classically not the most stable of female-types) and a river god, and is brought up by the nymph alone. Second, he is astonishingly beautiful, but unable to receive or requite the love of others, either homo- or hetero-sexually. He is closed in on himself in a way that makes it impossible for him to relate to others at any depth. This is not an act of ill will or wilful perversity – he is as he is and literally cannot accept love. But third, at least in the Ovid version (which Frazer thinks to be nearest the original), he equates love with power. 'May I die ere I give you power over me,' he cries at Echo. He is not frozen only sexually, therefore: he is frightened literally to death of any condition of dependence. His desperate need is to be subject, to be in control. In both the Ovid and the Photius versions, he is ready to kill (or its moral equivalent) to avoid surrendering his grip on his own self.

Fourth, he becomes aware of his own tragedy: 'The very abundance of my riches beggars me.' He experiences as ultimate impoverishment what other young men in his position would naturally long for. What they crave, he has in excess – and discovers it is but dust. They could enjoy what he has, but have it not: in what he has and they deserve, he can in no way find fulfilment.

And, fifth, that is the source of his anger and his violence. Narcissus is sometimes presented as a milksop, be it never so lovely a milksop. That is to castrate the story. Narcissus seethes with rage: see his treatment of Echo and his other lovers, especially Armenias, to whom he gives the sword, knowing well enough what the outcome will be.

True to classical Greek mythic form, this rage and violence is finally turned against him who practices it. Though in Ovid's version he pines passively away, Photius may be nearer the inner truth in presenting him as a suicide, the victim of his own aggressiveness, the last object of his throbbing hatred.

The Narcissistic Personality

For Freud, the myth of Narcissus presented something of a paradox. He well recognised the need for self-love: without it the ego cannot develop.[2] And yet if the love becomes obsessive or introverted, it can become destructive of both the ego and its world. It is, however, the nature of self-love to become introverted, exclusively focused on the self. To control that aspect of self-love; to keep it, as it were, finely tuned to the proper needs of the ego without sliding into self-indulgence or excessive self-regard demands a maturity and inner balance between ego and super-ego that by definition is not available in the earlier stages of development. Like the snake in Jungian archetypology, then, it is both healer and destroyer, deadly yet essential.

Later writers like Klein and Winnicott have emphasised that pathological narcissism can only arise when the ego can differentiate itself from surrounding objects. Hence the significance of the distinction between primary and secondary narcissism. The former arises when the newborn child cannot distinguish between self and mother. She believes mother is an extension of the self and that needs are met by the exercise of the omnipotence of the self. By contrast, secondary narcissism arises when the child sees that mother is a separate entity with her own agenda which is larger than merely serving the needs of the child. The child wants to have mother to him/herself: when she cannot achieve that, she is likely to react with anger or withdrawal into the self. In this latter process, the child may create phantasies of an omnipotent mother who merges with the self. By so doing, she can escape the fear, anxiety and guilt of the world as it is and create another world in which, in phantasy, the self is unchallenged master.

Now, it is central to Lasch's thesis that secondary (i.e., potentially pathological) narcissism has become a common clinical phenomenon in the last few decades.

134

The patients who began to present themselves for treatment in the 1940s and 1950s 'very seldom resembled the classical neuroses Freud described so thoroughly'. In the last twenty-five years, the borderline patient, who confronts the psychiatrist not with well-defined symptoms but with diffuse dissatisfactions, has become increasingly common. He does not suffer from debilitating fixations or phobias or from the conversion of repressed sexual energy into nervous ailments: instead he complains of 'vague, diffuse dissatisfactions with life' and feels his 'amorphous existence to be futile and purposeless'. He describes 'subtly experienced yet pervasive feelings of emptiness and depression', 'violent oscillations of self-esteem', and 'a general inability to get along'. He gains 'a sense of heightened self-esteem only by attaching himself to strong, admired figures whose acceptance he craves and by whom he needs to feel supported'. Although he carries out his daily responsibilities and even achieves distinction, happiness eludes him and life frequently strikes him as not worth living.[3]

Lasch argues that whereas, prior to the Second World War, psychoanalysts were primarily concerned to free people from over-rigid super-egos, 'today finds itself confronted more and more often with a "chaotic and impulse-ridden self"'. Patients now 'tend to cultivate a protective shallowness in emotional relations'. Sexually they are promiscuous rather than repressed, but this sexual activity tends to be joyless and unassociated with deep spiritual commitment to their partners. For they avoid intimacy, fearful that this will release in them intense feelings of rage. They thus cannot mourn, and they cannot therefore relive in memory happy or benign experiences. To do so invites the re-presentation of lost love-objects, especially parents, and therefore of the rage they feel at being deprived of those lost love-objects and at being made the more dependent. To defend themselves against that rage is their most pressing emotional need: it is accompanied (for reasons Lasch does not investigate, but presumably because of their need for emotional comforting) by feelings of oral deprivation. This deprivation they assume they have the right to gratify: 'they entertain fantasies of omnipotence and a strong belief in their right to exploit others'.[4]

Before we turn to a more detailed consideration of Lasch's understanding of the origins of this condition, it is worth pausing a moment to reflect that he presents no serious qualitative evidence for the claims that (a) this condition is 'new'; (b) that it is common; or (c) that it is so common that it can be taken, not simply as metaphor, but as constitutive of a social condition. His justification for these claims seems to rest on two somewhat shaky pillars: the professional interest in the condition as reflected in articles in the professional literature; and assertions in such literature that such presenting symptoms are 'now' 'common'. They may be: but so are other sets of symptoms, of which depression (allied to but not identical with narcissism) is the most obvious. Similarly, to assume that neurotic anxiety has disappeared from our surgeries and clinics is simply false.

Even if claims (a) and (b) alone are not as valid as Lasch likes to present them, it is not inconceivable that claim (c) may still have some interest. It may be that secondary narcissistic tendencies are indeed now sufficiently widespread to colour our culture. Capps *has* tried to collect quantitative data, not on the population (of the USA) at large, but, more interestingly, on lay and ordained Christians. What exactly his data show is less clear, not least because he couched the questionnaire in terms of the seven (or eight) deadly sins – each of which could be interpreted as pointing towards narcissistic tendencies. If they show anything, they do suggest that clegy are no less narcissistic than lay people; and Capps evidently believes that Christians are no less narcissistic than anyone else.[5] That might suggest that the culture (at least of America) is indeed deeply impregnated with these values. Before we can test that, however, we need to look more closely at the aetiology of narcissism as Lasch understands it.

Lasch on the Origins of Narcissism

He starts with an unadorned Kleinian perspective: indeed, he quotes at length from Klein's celebrated analysis of a ten-year-old boy. He goes on to argue that the child will compensate for the fears and anxieties sparked by his projection and reintrojection of his own anger by phantasies of 'wealth, beauty and omnipotence.'[6] These phantasies, allied with those of the 'good breast', become the core of his or her grandiose conception of the self, a conception that gives rise, says Lasch quoting Kernberg, to a 'blind optimism' in his or her own powers that make him or her ready to accept total independence from others. Others are threatening, unreliable, undependable. Salvation lies in independence, in preserving one's own emotional capital intact. Splitting makes it impossible for the child to acknowledge his/her own aggression or to manifest concern for others.

If the origins of narcissism are the reintrojection of the child's aggressive impulses in the shape of 'bad objects', and the compensatory phantasies of wealth, beauty and omnipotence that cannot be securely attached to 'good objects' (most obviously mother), then the memories that lie at the heart of the narcissistic personality, hovering on the borderline of neurosis and psychosis, are the memories of primitive aggression on the one hand and inadequate good objects on the other. That these memories remain unconscious in the adult is, of course, true; though the fear of rage and aggression that the narcissist knows lies below the surface may be semi-conscious or even conscious. What remains available to consciousness is the *need* for compensatory facts, fancies or fantasies that bolster the depleted ego in its own eyes and thereby defend it from its own aggression, rage and violence. Short on self-esteem, which may be overtly compensated by extravagant claims of excellence, he 'must attach himself to someone, living an almost parasitic' existence, as Lasch quotes from Kernberg.[7] But that is the trap.

For 'at the same time, his fear of emotional dependence, together with his manipulative, exploitive approach to personal relations, makes these relations bland, superficial and deeply unsatisfying'.[8] For he dare not commit himself to them. He has been hurt too deeply by the loss of his love-objects before; and so to trust another in a deep relationship, which, with all its risks and unpredictabilities, might yet give him the emotional satisfaction he craves, is beyond his emotional grasp. He compensates by promiscuous sexual relations, very possibly pansexual, and by whatever forms of temporary relief his social environment may offer, providing it does not require deep emotional commitment from him or give others an emotional hold over him.

A particular fear is thus of old age, for it represents the threat of losing control; of becoming dependent; and of losing the admiration of others, especially to younger, more dashing competitors. In late middle age, with its imminent threat of the onset of senility, the narcissist may well make a last (except it almost certainly will not be the last) attempt to satisfy his craving for the outward trappings of emotional success – a 'last' affair; a 'last' career move; a 'last' mad whirl on the boards of self-publicising theatre. Without such supports, the world is remembered as a grim and hostile place indeed.

Yet the narcissist cannot bear too much memory. One of his presenting symptoms is a blurring of time; a disinterest in the past and a fear of the future, especially his/her own. The present is all. And the fear of memory of the past and its associated concern for the future has its own inner logic. For memory can too easily bestir rage and bitterness at the rejection suffered at the hands of the inadequate good objects. Perhaps there is no more painful memory for the narcissist than rejection, for it touches in a way that can be equally shocking to the narcissist as to the onlooker a memory that lives encoded in his personality.

The inner life of the narcissist is thus remarkable for its shallowness, which gives rise to feelings of emptiness, ethical uncertainty and hopelessness. Nothing is worth doing or suffering, because nothing is worth doing or suffering anything *for*. With this shiftlessness, however, goes a desperate need for the affection and admiration of others. Clearly, at the back of all these presenting symptoms, located, it is worth emphasising, in middle-class, urban America, is the unsatisfactory handling of the separation trauma, dramatised by Freud in the 'Fort-Da' game and emphasised analytically by Kohut.[9] It need not, however, be separation from mother in a physical sense: it is rather the trauma of having to abandon the myth of self-omnipotence and therefore abandon or put in a truer perspective the primary narcissism of the very earliest weeks of childhood.

It is for this reason that Lasch gives great emphasis to the role of family, claiming that changes in family dynamics since the 1940s have left the child particularly vulnerable to the traumas of separation. He sees this in two recent developments. The first, of which he is deeply critical (and on which he has subsequently been himself much criticised) is what he calls the professionalisation of family life. Parents have been taught to believe that they are inadequate or worse, and that their offspring's best chance of emotional survival lies in the mobilisation of professional carers, from child psychiatrists to social workers, from doctors to lawyers. By definition, however, these people are professionals and their relationship with the child is that of professional: however skilled they are at winning the child's trust and even affection, they cannot and should not have the same quality of relationship as the parent to child. Accordingly, the child misses out.

Simultaneously, however, the parent or parents have been so mesmerised by the professional expertise of the pseudo-parent substitute, the professional, that they cannot give the child the kind of intense emotional commitment needed of the 'good object'. The child is thus deprived of the emotional resources to withstand the threats of the abundant and terrifying 'bad objects' he has created in his phantasy. He thus loses out again – because, notice, parents have both been persuaded that they are incompetent by the professional carers and been suborned into allowing such carers to substitute for them.

There are many sub-agendas here: I shall mention only two that have brought Lasch much ferocious criticism. The first is the implied (and occasionally explicit) allegation that it is in the professional interest of 'the bureaucracy' (sic) to undermine the confidence of parents and offer them professional services as a substitute. To most people who have worked in or alongside 'the bureaucracy' such a charge seems so absurd as to contain within it the seeds of its own refutation. While no doubt on the fringes of any profession there are those who seek to create demands for their own services, from policemen to accountants, the majority of professionals, especially those working for the public service rather than the fee-paying private client, are so hard pressed and submerged by the tide of claims on their time that to imagine they deliberately seek to increase such claims is simply wrong.

Rather than try to sustain what looks (certainly in the British context) a fallacious argument, Lasch might alternatively enquire whether, professional help and 'the therapeutic culture' aside, there may be social reasons for what he calls a 'withdrawal' by parents, and especially mothers, from the emotional commitment to their offspring. Certainly Kohut's emphasis on 'mirroring', a rather weaker form of Bion's 'containing', would identify this as the key issue. Likewise, Obholzer has suggested that the task of child rearing and educating now appears so fearsome to many averagely educated parents, bombarded by scare stories in glossy magazines, that one obvious defence is to split off that part of their responsibility and dump it on 'the professionals', 'the bureaucracy'.[10]

Lasch, however, does not want to explore this approach. Rather, he locates the reasons for the social symptoms he has described in the processes of late capitalism, arguing that the speed of technological change and the pressures of work in an international economy, where continued employment is made ever less secure, have changed the role of the father in the family, making him less available, less able to share skills and tasks with his children (especially boys) and less capable of exercising the kind of authority which would enable his sons to survive the Oedipal conflict satisfactorily. We are almost in the land of Iron John. Simultaneously, Lasch argues that feminism has devalued the role of the mother, making her dissatisfied with mothering and constantly torn between being mother and being woman. Taken together, those twin assaults on each parent have made the family a less secure, less emotionally committed environment, presenting the child with far less support at pre-Oedipal, Oedipal and post-Oedipal stages of its development. If to this is added the decline of religion, with its appeal to authority and morality, Lasch claims that the family has become an institution that is often incapable of rearing children with sufficient ego and super-ego strength to avoid pathological narcissism.

There are clearly many questions to be asked about such an analysis. Unsurprisingly, Lasch has been taken to task for seeming to lust after a romantic view of the bourgeois family in pre-industrial days, with mother at the hearth and father exercising authority over the children from his rocker. Two questions immediately arise: was there *ever* a family structure such as Lasch covets? And if there was, what is the evidence that it produced more well-adjusted and healthy children? On Lasch's own account the evidence surely points in the opposite direction: if he takes as evidence of the rise of the narcissistic personality the *decline* in neuroses and the psychic pathologies of repression, then the pre-modern 'ideal' certainly produced its own crop of disorders. If he wishes to site his ideal further back in history, perhaps to *ante bellum* United States, then he is faced by the Kovel critique of white racism.

As Ian Craib has pointed out, Lasch seems confused by the notions of patriarchy and authority.[11] You need neither an authoritarian father figure nor a hell-fire-and-brimstone religion to maintain a securely holding environment for the child before, during and after the Oedipal stage. Despite his reading of Adorno, or perhaps because of it, Lasch seems to confuse authoritarian with authoritative.

None the less, Lasch may have a point which could be put like this: modern industrial and commercial methods of production and exchange (which have much less to do with capitalism than Lasch supposes: socialist and communist regimes are not necessarily less victim of their own productive technologies) have brought about changes in family life, to which female reactions against androcracy (itself largely a product of technology) have added a further twist. In this process of change, adaptation and confusion, often marked by greater mobility and the associated reduction in the parent-substituting role of grandparents and other relatives, family patterns of authority have become less confident, less clear cut and less secure. In this context it might conceivably also be the case that parents are intimidated, further confused or made anxious by the dimly perceived knowledge that there is 'out there' a core of professional expertise on child rearing against which their own inconsistent fumblings will be found seriously wanting. That can only reduce their confidence even further, and with it the security they actually offer their children.

Shorn of Lasch's overstatement and overgeneralisation, this argument has a certain appeal. How far, however, will it function in the way Lasch wants it to function – namely, to account for the alleged reduction in the number of 'classical Freudian' presenting symptoms and the great increase in narcissistic symptoms? Lasch *assumes* the causal connection without ever seriously testing it – and for good reason. Empirical testing of such a hypothesis would be difficult and, given constraints on time and resources, practically impossible. None the less, some empirical testing is possible: is it the case that such narcissistic persons as present themselves for treatment come from families where authority figures were inadequate or where the patient had, as a child, problems with forming good-object relations? Are there class or regional or ethnic differences which might give a clue about the relationship between family life and the development of the narcissistic personality? (It is notorious, for example, that some ethnic groups have retained quasi-traditional authority patterns despite being more or less (usually less) incorporated in the modern economy.) And what about time? Is it the case that the alleged rise of the narcissistic personality coincides with the perceived changes in styles of parenting? Lasch dates the former to the '1940s and 1950s': presumably to the inter-war period in terms of the childhood of those appearing as patients in the post-war period. Yet the pressures on the father that Lasch describes, as well as the revolt against androcracy, surely come much later than that, perhaps the 1960s and 1970s. A funny muddle, one might think, for a historian.

There are, then, serious problems with Lasch's argument: some of those are inherent in the subject (problems of empirical verifiability), and some are unique to Lasch whose analysis is sometimes robbed of scholarly precision by a journalistic impressionism that titillates rather than satisfies. Should he not therefore be relegated to the dustbin of American pseudo-intellectual pap?

I think not – and for many of the same reasons that I think Adorno and Kovel should not be ignored, however easy it is to pick holes in their argument. If it is treated as hypothesis rather than fact, as an attempt to give a coherent account of social phenomena that is rooted in psychological rather than merely sociological variables, then the connections that Lasch invites us to examine are well worthwhile. In that sense (as I hinted at the beginning of this chapter) it is well to read Lasch backwards: that is, to see what he has to say about modern society and then reflect on whether this, in aggregate, amounts to, or can be illuminated by, narcissism on a corporate scale. Rather than following the classical Freudian/Kleinian route of examining the psychic entrails of scores of patients and extrapolating to social processes (which is what Lasch actually does), it might be better to start at the other end: review social phenomena and ask what kind of socio-psychological hypothesis would fit those phenomena.

For it is as cultural critic that Lasch is at his best. There is not space here to review all his observations: I shall highlight only four which seem to me especially pertinent, and even extensible to areas Lasch does not cover.

Narcissistic Society: Images

Let us start with the theme of images. Lasch argues that for the narcissistic personality, with his particular combination of phantasy and memory, reality and image become confused. Like Neumann,

Steiner and even Roethke, Lasch realises that we are on the threshold of a cultural crisis, for what is at issue is an apprehension of a credible self. Or Self.[12] Unable to relate at depth to others and therefore to the world, the narcissist cannot easily distinguish between what is real and what appears to be real. To use Jungian terminology, the narcissist cannot see beyond the persona which we all assume as protective clothing. This leads Lasch to examine the role of images in our society, quoting Susan Sontag's conclusion from her study of photography: 'Reality has come to seem more and more like what we are shown by cameras.'[13] Thus, while prosperous bourgeois families, from Holland in the seventeenth century to Britain in the nineteenth, commissioned artists to record the family's arrival on the blessed uplands of respectability, 'today the family album of photographs verifies the individual's existence: its documentary evidence of his development from infancy onwards provides him with the only evidence of his life that he recognizes as altogether valid'.[14] The truth of the self thus becomes dependent upon the image of the self captured by the camera.

If the very idea of the self is thus dependent upon and derived from the image, it is easy to see how central a role images play in social life, and how powerful become the image makers. From advertising to politics, from fashion to industrial design, from job searching to news presentation, the image is primary: the substance behind the image secondary, unimportant or definitively suppressed. In that sense reality is the image − which is not far from McLuhan's dictum that the medium is the message. Where this comes to have real historical and history-making significance is in the way our knowledge of reality, gleaned more and more from television (and therefore from photography), becomes crucially dependent upon the images we are shown. And anyone who has worked in television knows how seductive to cameraman and producer is the grabby image: their promotion depends upon it. 'One good image is worth a hundred pages of prose' is a wearisome cliché in cutting rooms and editorial conferences which is seldom exposed to a searching critique of what constitutes a 'good' image. It is seldom one that presents all the ambiguities, subtleties and caesuras of life: rather, it is stark, uncomplicated, arresting by its very simplicity. Thus the Third World is reduced to starving babies, multi-racial communities to pitched battles between police and rioters, war to jets taking off, guns firing, convoys of trucks, driven by grinning soldiers, rallying towards the front.

The difficulty with this is not only the simplification and dichoto-misation into black and white that ensues: it is the distribution of power to the image-makers and the patterns of accountability (or lack of them) that follow. The classical question of politics, allegedly solved by popular democracy, was: *quis custodiet ipsos custodes?* Who will keep control of those in power? The new question has to be: Who can guarantee that the images we see represent a genuine apprehension of reality? We do not have an answer to that question: cynics would say the only answer we can have in a late capitalist world is that the images that sell papers or air time are the images of reality. Certainly, key questions about the nature of truth and the testing for truth behind the image go by default.

We do not need to pursue this argument further. From the point of view of our enquiry, the key point is that, trapped in their own memory-world, narcissists are peculiarly vulnerable to the image maker, because they find independent truth testing difficult and distasteful. It is difficult because it implies deep relationships with others: only so can ambiguity and multi-facetedness be given space to emerge. And it is distasteful because acknowledging the inadequacy of image is to court the risk of acknowledging the inadequacy of the (image of the) self.

Narcissistic Society: Consumption

For the second example of Lasch's analysis of social symptomology, I take his emphasis on consumption. We saw how he makes a connec-tion between narcissism and oral deprivation, and so it is no surprise to find that, like Marcuse and Fromm, he sees as one of the presenting symptoms of contemporary society a fascination with consumption – in both the senses of oral satisfaction given by the (excess) consump-tion of food, drink and cigarettes and, more generally, of consumption of anything that gives status and reality to the weakened ego of the narcissist. Analytically, it may be important to keep these senses sepa-rate: oral deprivation will seek compensation through oral satisfaction. Pathological consumerism has more to do with the need to reassure the ego or, in the cadences of the last paragraphs, to buttress the self-image of the ego by surrounding it with 'pleasing' accoutrements. Economically, however, consumption is consumption, whether it be of food, tobacco or gizmos.

At this point, Lasch shows many of the perspectives of social critics of the left who see North Atlantic humanity caught in a consumerist trap. If they do not consume as required by the productive forces of the economy, they are diminished socially and psychically – *and* jeopardise their own economic security. If they do consume as required, they are on a treadmill, exploited, in Marxian terms, by the appropriation by capitalists of the surplus value they create; or, in liberal terms, forced by competition for well-paid and secure jobs to dance to the corporate tune – to become, in a word, Corporate Man or Woman.

What Lasch calls the 'propaganda of commodities' and what Marxists call commodity fetishism point in the same direction. The consumption of commodities is an analgesic, but an addictive one that extracts a high price from the addict. 'Is your life empty?' mocks Lasch. 'Consumption promises to fill the aching void: hence the attempt to surround commodities with an aura of romance; with allusions to exotic places and vivid experiences; and with images of female breasts from which all blessings flow.'[15]

Unlike the Marxists, however, Lasch is less interested in the economic significance of consumerism than in its effects on the self-knowledge of the consumer. It is not coincidental that his longest treatment of consumption occurs in a chapter entitled 'The banality of pseudo-self-awareness'. The argument is less that ever-rising consumption puts people and the ecosystem under intolerable strain than that consumption and advertising depend upon credibility rather than truth. Like images, what matters is not reality but readiness to confuse image and reality. Consumption, especially of status goods (and even necessities can be and are developed into status goods: consider the history of the humble bread loaf), is manipulated not in accordance with the intrinsic merits of the item or its potential contribution to the discovery of the good life, but in the light of its contribution to the pseudo-reality of the self. Eating the 'right' breakfast cereal or using the 'right' washing powder has nothing to do with nutrition or laundry efficiency: it has everything to do with feeling good about oneself. But a self that is properly established in

145

its own eyes needs neither bread nor washing powder to feel good. It is, Lasch implies, only the narcissistic type who needs so intrinsically feeble a prop.

There is, however, a deeper point here, missed by Lasch and explored in only a very preliminary way by Frank Pinner.[16] It is of the essence of the narcissist that s/he is relatively uninterested in the distant future; the present and the immediate future are all-important. Time horizons thus become foreshortened, even more than is culturally normal.[17] As relationships with others are problematic, so the proper care and concern for the invisible others of future generations is almost wholly lacking. To put it in the argot of resource economics, the narcissistic social time preference rate is such that the future is discounted at a very high rate indeed.

The full implications of that in an era of environmental stress are immediately obvious – and chilling. For it means that, if Lasch is right, as a society we are almost literally incapable – psychologically as well as institutionally (and, of course, the one reflects the other) – of taking the decisions now that will preserve the environment for the future. Nor should this be seen as some airy-fairy disembodied abstraction: it is incarnated in the sums that economists and resource planners do to determine whether it is 'worth' spending large sums on, for example, the reduction of CFCs, the reduction of air pollutants, the care-taking of the tropical forests and the preservation of fish stocks. Such sums are extremely sensitive to the rate at which the future is discounted and the length of the future that is considered – as we are just beginning to learn at the popular level with the full costs of decommissioning nuclear power plants emerging into the public arena. If, for example, benefits that will accrue in only seventy years' time (a reasonable period for an indigenous hardwood plantation; short for a tropical hardwood forest) are heavily discounted, it is easy to 'show' that investment is better applied to projects that yield benefits in the nearer future, even though the aggregate value of those (undiscounted) benefits is much smaller. The argument could be taken further by a consideration of the irreversibility of decisions taken now which have their full impacts in several tens of years' time. For example, you cannot make a tropical hardwood forest grow faster, no matter how much you are ready to spend on it to compensate at some time in the future for a mistake in your appreciation of the true value of future benefits. The shortened time horizon that is typical of narcissists thus traps communities in trajectories that are baneful but irreversible, even when/if the society as a whole shakes off its narcissism.

The social implications of this should need no further emphasis here, but it is worth summarising the main line of the argument to put it in context. If part of the symptomology of narcissism is hurtful memories, and if narcissism is a cultural feature, not purely a clinically individual one, then the health of the culture depends, at least in part, on the healing of memories. That healing demands a transcendental reference. It is, in short, a religious issue. Perhaps that will become even clearer after the next two examples of Lasch's analysis of the cultural impact of narcissism.

Narcissistic Society: Education

Just as Lasch argues that consumption has come to serve a narcissistic end, so he argues, in one of his most polemical chapters, that education has been adulterated for the same end.

> Institutions of cultural transmission (school, church, family) which might have been expected to counter the narcissistic trend of our culture, have instead been shaped in its image, while a growing body of progressive theory justifies this capitulation on the ground that such institutions best serve society when they provide a mirror reflection of it. The downward drift of public education accordingly continues.[18]

Here Lasch finds himself in strange company, at the opposite end of the ideological spectrum from those who condemn excess consumption and bewail its social and psychological impact. The educational conservatives, with whom Lasch appears to be aligning himself, are usually of the Right. Like Lasch they argue that 'more means worse'; they claim that there is a limited pool of bright people and that it is the function of education to select them out and prepare them for the highest academic (and, later, wider) achievement. That can only be done by basing the whole educational system on an academically rigorous foundation. If the less academically bright find that boring or too demanding, there are two solutions. One is a two-stream system, always rejected in the United States, and having been abandoned in the UK now being reinstated by the ideological Right; the other is to insist on as high an achievement as possible, even for the ungifted, so that even they may glimpse something of intellectual rigour, and acquire a more than basic accomplishment in the three Rs.

It is Lasch's argument that educationalists have abandoned this second solution, possibly because of their own narcissistic proclivities (it takes enormous ego strength to cajole and bully a class of disenchanted sixteen-year-olds into an appreciation of a Donne sonnet), or possibly because of the breakdown of parental confidence and determination that we have already discussed. Either way, Lasch is clear that *the system* (in the United States) practises what is essentially a confidence trick. It pretends to be opting for the second solution (i.e., a basic academic training for all, irrespective of intellectual capacity) while in fact it so tempers the winds of intellectual exigency to the academically shorn lambs that it releases them into the world with no sense of intellectual discipline or, implicitly, the capacity to think logically or distinguish truth from falsehood. 'When elders make no demands on the young', he writes, 'they make it almost impossible for the young to grow up.'[19]

No doubt rightly, Lasch sees the role of education as dialectically related to the culture in which it is set: it both mirrors it and it creates it. Condemning contemporary progressives for lack of any higher ideal than the former, he longs for an educational revolution precisely opposite to that advocated by Freire or Illich. He wants to return to an education that puts the development of reasoning capacity and the instilling of moral virtues at its heart and at least starts with the assumption that every child, from tenement or mansion, can respond to the challenge and opportunity.

We are back in the world of Plato and Aristotle, not, surely, in any historical epoch of modern times. Like his reflections on the family, Lasch's account of education is curiously tinged with the romantic afterglow of a past that never was. He accepts too easily the parrot cry of the educational Right: standards are falling. No doubt in some schools and in some subjects, compared with some cohort from some time in the past, such laments can be sustained. But Lasch does not ask why teachers have reacted against the dry-as-dust discipline of rote learning and grammarian gymnastics. If he did he would find that they discovered such techniques to be inefficient, inequitable and incapable of nurturing the intellectual potential of most children. That the reaction against them has sometimes been sloppily conceived and self-indulgently administered is no doubt more true than many educational liberals are yet ready to admit. But to say that is to say a great deal less than Lasch wants to say. That some teachers and educational bureaucrats have given too little emphasis to the practice of intellectual rigour and too much to self-expression does not imply that the educational system as a whole has been either the product or the cause of a narcissistic culture.

Given the analytical muddles surrounding Lasch's treatment of education, the reader might well wonder why it has been included. Part of the answer is, as I have already indicated, that despite the muddle, I believe he makes us think about the relationship between inner processes and public policy in a way that is rare (or rarely successful) among those writing out of a Freudian/Kleinian perspective. Further, his treatment demonstrates a point that I shall have to return to at more length later: namely, the inadequacy of a purely humanistic, immanent response to the problematic he describes. Education is a good example of the interrelatedness of inner and outer worlds. It shows perfectly the folly of believing that the inner can be healed in the context of an unhealed outer. The two are too closely interwoven for any such single intervention to be sustainable. That is not to deny that, at the individual level, some benefit can be had from inner work, nor that those benefits will have some outer manifestation. But that is not (only) what the Christian vision is about. That vision is about the transformation of the cosmos; and, as we shall see more extensively below, that transformation requires an external referent to deliver it from its own circularities. That that too raises problems is clear. To them we shall come in time. In the meantime, we return to Lasch for a final illustration of the impact of hurtful memories on the outer world.

Narcissistic Society: Aesthetics

For my last example of social symptomology presented by Lasch I turn to his treatment of aesthetics. The argument is subtle. On the one hand, he sees the narcissist as someone who desperately needs a hero, not in order to emulate him but rather to idealize him. Quoting from Kernberg again, Lasch describes how narcissistic patients 'often admire some hero or outstanding individual' and 'experience themselves as part of that outstanding person', who becomes, in their eyes, 'merely an extension of themselves'. Lasch goes on:

> The narcissist admires and identifies himself with 'winners' out of fear of being labelled a loser. He seeks to warm himself in their reflected glow: but his feelings contain a strong admixture of envy [significant Kleinian concept, note], and his admiration often turns to hatred if the object of his attachment does something to remind him of his own insignificance. . . . This narcissistic fascination with celebrity, so rampant in our society, coincides historically with what Jules Henry calls 'the erosion of the capacity for emulation, loss of the ability to model one's self consciously after another person'.[20]

This idealization of the quasi-hero results, Lasch argues, in the cult of the celebrity and (a phrase he does not use) what one might call the aesthetic of the spectacle. That is to say, much popular art is concerned to present the spectacle of the famous with whom the narcissist can identify. Sport becomes less a participative activity than a spectacle in this sense; popular music ceases to be the music people *make*, but becomes the music which parades the music-makers as larger-than-life figures. Film, too, ceases to be driven by plot or the subtle interplay of character and becomes a backdrop for the spectacle of the star. What the film does not reveal, the popular press and film magazines do: every intimate detail, real or imagined, is trotted out. The narcissist can almost literally make them his own: he can wear the same clothes, the same after-shave, the same haircut and the same expression. The spectacle has performed precisely what he wants.

Lasch argues that alongside this aesthetic of the spectacle goes, perhaps paradoxically, almost its reverse: the aesthetic of non-being. He sees a causal connection:

Note the close connection between a surfeit of spectacles, the cynical awareness of illusion it creates even in children, the imperviousness to shock or surprise, and the resulting indifference to the distinction between illusion and reality. . . . Over-exposure to manufactured illusions soon destroys their representational power.[21]

The result is that artistic *form* comes to merge reality and illusion, questioning which is which. Which is more illusory: the play or picture you see before you? Or the 'real' life you think you lead? The theatre of the absurd becomes the final expression of this art form. Beckett, Ionescu and Genet present us with characters dominated by isolation, despair and existential unease, on a bare stage, bereft of any attempt to create an illusory world beyond the proscenium arch. We cannot distance ourselves from their world, for it is our world, this dull wondering whether life has to be so empty. And if it is argued that that aesthetic is already out of date, Lasch could make the same point a different way – by pointing to the unconscious irony of virtual reality and its image-making powers.

Surprising in his treatment of the aesthetics of narcissism is Lasch's neglect of violence. It is as though Lasch himself is afraid, like the personality he is presenting, to acknowledge it and give it expression. Yet in any account of the aesthetics of the last thirty years surely violence, especially male violence, would have to play a major part. From artists like Francis Bacon and Kevin Kith and even, arguably, John Bellany, to popular films like *Terminator* and *Rambo*, our aesthetic culture is obsessed with violence. Although there is a strong but subdued element of violence in myths and fairy tales, the explication and popularisation of violence is relatively modern. The first comics that appeared in the 1920s rarely stressed the physical power of the main characters. But the onset of the Great Depression in 1929 saw a major change: by 1931 over half of American comics had the exercise of physical power by the hero, usually in scenes of explicit violence, as a major theme.[22] While the Second World War produced its crop of 'war movies' and associated literature, it was not until the Vietnam War that the violence theme took another leap forward. And that is hardly surprising. It was the ambiguity and moral confusion of Vietnam (in contrast to the Second World War, Hiroshima and Dresden notwithstanding) that demanded compensation by the glorification of violence as almost self-justifying. J.G. Ballard's description of the exhibition of crashed cars and the subsequent account of an actual car crash, each with its erotic overtones, is an archetype of this genre of violence, appearing in a work of fiction that has as its leitmotifs both the bombing of Hiroshima and the Vietnam War.[23]

Yet there is a further dimension here which needs careful handling. In his fascinating study of the myth of redemptive violence, Walter Wink reminds us that most portrayals of violence in popular culture follow a precise format:

> The structure of the combat myth is faithfully repeated on television week after week: an aggressive attack by a superior force representing chaos; the champion fights back, defensively, only to be humiliated in apparent defeat; the evil power satisfies its lusts while the hero is incapacitated; the hero escapes, defeats the evil power decisively, and reaffirms order over chaos.[24]

Unlike the characters of the theatre of the absurd, then, the heroes of the popular television and film myth offer a reason for living. The narcissistic *angst* of Beckett is relieved by the assurance that the self-in-the-hero can, through the exercise of violence, win the right to survive. As Wink has percipiently pointed out, the myth of our time is about *redemptive violence*: each term merits equal stress.[25]

I want, therefore, to suggest that Lasch does not take his own argument far enough in this respect. The aesthetic of narcissism is not only about spectacle and anomie. More profoundly, I believe, and certainly much more popularly (compare the viewing figures of the 24 television shows Wink lists with those of all the writers of the theatre of the absurd), the aesthetic of the narcissistic personality is about violence – and about the use of violence as a justification for life. The narcissist needs a reason for survival. He does not typically pine away like Ovid's mythic figure. He finds a justification for living in sublimated redemptive violence, a violence he knows he owns but which he dare hardly acknowledge. And if he does acknowledge it, he is more likely to act the violence than the redemption.

Lasch: What can be Saved?

We have now briefly reviewed four of the social symptoms of a narcissistic culture: the prevalence of image; the fascination with consumption; the alleged decline in educational standards; the arts, and especially popular art. We have seen that Lasch argues that what he calls 'the socialization of reproduction and the collapse of authority' has so changed the nature of family life that the inner world of the child is changed in terms of an insufficiently strong phantasy of 'good objects', leaving him bereft of an adequate sense of his own identity, a lack of ego-strength, and an unconscious rage at what he has experienced as a lack of love from his 'good objects'. We have sometimes criticised Lasch for exaggeration and imprecision; it may therefore be helpful if, before turning briefly to the final and most central topic, I summarise what seems important and valid, not just in Lasch, but in the whole current debate about narcissism, the depleted self, the minimal self and the borderline personality – all terms I am taking to be interchangeable.

We do not need to assume, *pace* Lasch, that narcissism is a recent phenomenon. What may be true is one or more of three propositions.

1. Narcissistic elements in many of us are now more strongly developed than they were, perhaps because of changes in family life or patterns of parenting

2. More people are nearing the pathological end of the narcissistic spectrum, partly for the same reasons as in 1: but partly, too, because their condition is recognized and 'the therapeutic culture', in Lasch's damning phrase, actually encourages its recognition and its deterioration.

3. Because of 1 and or 2, or possibly quite independently of them, our culture reflects more generally and more precisely the narcissistic elements in the population. This is a possibility unconsidered by most of the authors mentioned thus far but should not be too readily dismissed on that account. Suppose, for example, that most of us have (and have always had) some elements of narcissism: ego-strength is a relative concept and few people have perfectly formed egos

(whatever precisely that might mean). And suppose further that these elements in most of us were particularly easy to exploit, itself a supposition rendered the more credible by lack of ego-strength. Then the very process of the commercialisation of consumption, art, politics and technology would raise to a higher visibility what had always been latent in the culture. In that case we can dispense with possibilities 1 and 2 — and still find the same social symptoms reported by Lasch, Kohut, Sachs, Stuart et al. The engine that drives the culture of narcissism is then not changes in parenting and family structure, but of capitalist commercialisation. (And I say specifically capitalist, as competition for markets plays a key role in this process.) We would then end up with an approach much nearer to that of classical critical theory, locating the social presentation of specific psychological formations in the organisation of the economy rather than in the frankly dubious 'socialisation of reproduction'.

Such a reformulation of the hypothesis need not deny that there may well be a feedback loop from the commercialisation to patterns of parenting. The 'absent father' and the would-be liberated mother are both the products of post-war capitalist development.

How does such a reformulation effect the main thesis of this book? Hitherto we have argued, to put it more crudely than I hope appears in the text, that psychological conditions, and we have privileged memory as the leading envelope of those conditions, are incarnated in and then mediated through social structures, culture and history: perhaps the classic example is the Oedipal conflict of the *ante bellum* Southerner being incarnated in the social and sexual arrangement of Southern slave society. Now we are suggesting — as a hypothesis, not as a proven case — that social structures (commercial competition in late capitalism) select out and magnify particular psychological conditions already existent in the population. Further, a feedback may develop whereby these conditions become more pronounced and the process thus becomes self-reinforcing.

In the Lasch formulation and in the reformulation above, the *existence* of narcissism in a significant proportion of the population is not at issue. Lasch claims it has been caused by the socialisation of reproduction and the collapse of authority: I suggest that it has always been there but is made more visible and possibly more widespread and/or more pathological by specific social and economic processes.

The way in which society selects for and then institutionalises features that play to narcissism is heavily dependent upon what in Chapter 1 I called habit memory. Consider the case of consumption/oral satisfaction. A society's achievement of the 'stage of mass consumption', in Rostow's phrase, meets deep psychic needs by providing the masses with the means by which their oral deprivations can be made good. The associated consumption, however, becomes habit: cigarettes are the limit example because they are addictive in a clinical sense. The satisfactions offered by other 'good objects', other breast substitutes, become addictive in a social sense, made so in part by the needs they meet, but in part too by the very habit of satisfaction. And that need not only apply to good objects. In so far as violence portrayed in art and popular culture fulfils a psychic need for the narcissist, its portrayal becomes habitual – and self-reinforcing. Each portrayal of violence has to outshock the last or it fails not only commercially but psychically. The habit memory of narcissism is not an edifying contribution to contemporary culture. But nor are the memories and phantasies that underpin narcissism.

A Look Ahead

It is that from which the narcissist needs to be redeemed. Ovid had him redeemed by the pity of the gods who turned him into a flower that is the symbol of spring and the promise of new growth. The question that we shall have to return to in Chapters 9–12 is by what means the Christian gospel redeems him – and through him those elements of our culture that share his condition. Although it is to anticipate further developments of the argument, it may be well to put down a warning marker here. Precisely because the narcissist finds memory so painful, threatening and potentially explosive, the memory-work which is central to my understanding of redemption is exceptionally hard for him. He does indeed have to work out his salvation with fear and trembling, but the terror comes not from a vengeful or judgemental God; it comes from his own unconscious memories. That is daunting for the individual: it is more than daunting for the group or the whole society – especially when put in the context of Jacques' account, on which we touched at the end of the last chapter, of the difficulties that groups often face in dealing with those memories. Redemption, it seems, is not going to be easy.

8

Powerlessness and Genocide

As we have frequently remarked, one of the problems with a Freudian or Kleinian approach to relating social structures to memory is that their treatment tends to be highly individualistic. Heavily dependent as he is on object-relations theory, Lasch faces the same difficulty and has to rely on a process of aggregation to jump from the individual narcissistic personality to cultural formation. Although there are serious problems with the notion of the collective unconscious, so central to Jung's thinking, this device at least had the great merit of providing a logical (and not wholly empirically vacuous) connection between the individual personality and social formation. Can we find alternative bridges? Are there other ways of linking the important insights of post-Freudian theory to particular social phenomena?

It is in search of an answer to that question that I devote this chapter to two recent contributions to this general debate. Both offer explanations of puzzling social phenomena that lead back to memory, without becoming the victims of a crude psychological determinism. And both avoid the individualistic emphasis of the thinkers we have reviewed thus far by placing psychological variables more securely in a social setting. And, as we shall see, both raise theological questions about the healing of memories with unusual clarity.

Michael Lerner and Surplus Powerlessness

Michael Lerner's work might be seen as a psychodrama of memory. As we shall see, it is based on the power of memory, sometimes conscious, sometimes not, to dictate the narratives people tell of themselves and therefore the way they behave to the world around them. Unfortunately, Lerner's approach is based on an eclectic reading of Jung and Freud and has found little favour among most theoreticians. In a nutshell, he posits a three-layered model of the self, illustrated by three concentric circles. At the heart is what he calls the human essence, presumably derived from the Marxian notion of species being; and around this human essence, to be conceived as potential-always-seeking-actualization, is the childhood personality. Around that, in the outermost layer, is the adult personality.[1] Luckily, this rather contrived model is almost wholly irrelevant to what I take to be central to Lerner's contribution to the main theme of this book.

Key to Lerner's ideas is the damage that damaged parents do to the childhood personality. Larkin's celebrated poem is truer than even Larkin realised. The child's relationship with the parents is from the start a process of misrecognition. The child's Human Essence (*sic*) is not acknowledged. Instead, the parent conveys to the child that the child is a set of roles and that anything more will be too much for the parent to handle. The parent offers an implicit deal: You will get love and recognition from me of the sort I have available only if you will become that thing, that assortment of roles, in which I am seeing you. If you will be that thing, then I can give you as much love as I have to give. Lerner goes on: 'The child must lose its recognition of itself as having the Human Essence and must become the kind of partial being that will develop a Childhood Personality in response to the need for some level of recognition.'[2]

Clearly, we are in a psycho-analytic world that is, as it were, a corner of a distorted mirror of that of Klein and Bion. To Lerner, there is a little hope of adequate containment or of good-enough mothering. Instead, there is a kind of resentful struggle between child and mother from the start. If Lerner seems improbably bleak about the prospects of mother-love, he might well reply that the kind of mothers he deals with (essentially from the urban underclass) *are* often resentful and unenthusiastic about the demands children make upon them.

Three features of this psychic contract are important. First, the child's natural wish or instinct to actualise her Human Essence is put in jeopardy. The child experiences that as intensely frustrating and reacts in anger, thus immediately breaking the terms of the contract. Second, the expression of parental counter-anger or withdrawal of affection is interpreted by the child, not as just reward for its own bad behaviour, but as evidence of its own unworthiness. Although he does not use the term, Lerner seems to have in mind some concept of idealisation: the child idealises the parents and thus cannot blame them for any adverse reaction. Instead, she internalises the blame.

Third, and in some ways this is Lerner's contribution to the debate, the parents do in fact overreact, act unjustly, shrink from the fullest emotional commitment to their children, because they are themselves in pain. And their pain is a combination of the memory of the pain of their own childhood reactivated by their experience in the world in general and in the workplace in particular, and of their own repressed anger.

Thus at each 'border' – between Human Essence, Childhood Personality and Adult Personality – there is friction, pain and anger. And on each 'occasion' the instinctive reaction of the individual is to blame herself. By the time she is adult, carrying with her still both the human essence and her childhood, she has been socialised into seeing this self-blame as a perfectly normal and natural process. It is true. It is reality. *I am no good*.

Lerner presents this socialisation process at two levels. There is socialisation by external structures, the family, the Church (with its fixation with human sinfulness: I *really* am no good) and above all the school, which institutionalises failure for all but the most successful by grading, streaming, competition, examinations, ranking and reporting (just the educational techniques, notice, that Lasch advocates).

Secondly, however (and here Lerner approaches Jung), there is what he calls the social unconscious. By thus labelling it, he wants to differentiate it from the collective unconscious, but the resonance is clear. It is not, however, identical with the collective unconscious:[3]

The meaning of any physical object or event is shaped by our understanding of its relationship to all other objects and events and this meaning shapes how we perceive it. This is particularly true when we are perceiving human reality. The events of daily life do not 'speak for themselves', nor are human meanings simply 'self-evident'. In every specific human interaction the meaning of what is happening is shaped by our understanding of the world that we live in, and what is to be expected in it.[4]

We are back to hermeneutics, social interaction, communication and inter-subjectivity.

This 'universe of discourse' is clearly a social construct to which many of us contribute and by which we are all formed. It is Lerner's argument that one of the essential features of this universe of discourse is that if I am unhappy, it is most probably my own fault. This is an ideology assiduously cultivated by our 'superiors' in business and State for their own very obvious ends. It is a working assumption in our family life and is probably a necessary defence against marital or family breakdown. And it is internalised in our super-egos (a term Lerner eschews though implies) through the processes I have described. This happy or tragic co-incidence of social and psychological bias gives this part of the social unconscious its power over us. For it defines our sense of reality: it *is* our reality. And it is worked out in a near-universal sense of being trapped not by social systems but by inner inadequacy. I am powerless to change the world because I am powerless to change myself. Lerner labels this *surplus* powerlessness (to chime with Marxian surplus value and Marcusian surplus repression) in order to emphasise that it is self-generated and treatable. He is not so naïve as to think that the urban underclass with which he works will ever be powerful; but its members do not need to be more powerless than their social position makes inevitable.

Therapeutic Approaches to Surplus Powerlessness

Aware of the debate about the effectiveness of therapeutic interventions, Lerner is careful to give detailed statistical evidence of the effect that enabling people to face their 'surplus powerlessness' can have. He gives data drawn from his work with participants in occupational stress groups (OSGs) which show how the relatively uncomplicated therapeutic approach he adopts in the OSGs allows people to confront their frustration and anger and cease blaming themselves for how bad they feel. Unfortunately, he does not ask the question that will occur to any sceptical social scientist: would *any* supportive intervention, coming out of any theoretical understanding, not have the same effects? His control groups do not address that question – for they are given no support at all. None the less his results are interesting.

For example, in an experimental group of 158, self-blame dropped sharply when the participants were confronted by an enacted typical work situation by comparison with an untreated control group of 71 (multiple analysis of variance: significance of F, $P < 0.7$). Unsurprisingly, he also showed depression (as measured by a personal mood-state inventory, with all the methodological difficulties associated with that family of technique) and alcohol consumption dropped sharply for his treated group by comparison with a control group. Conversely, ability to cope with stress at home rose, as did the sense of treated participants that they could exert some power over 'society, job and union'. The statistical data merely support the strong impression of Lerner and his team:

> These changes were precipitated by our conscious attempts to undermine self-blaming, to confront the emotions and ideas that generate surplus powerlessness, and to encourage people to see the stress they were facing at work not as justified punishment for inner failures, but rather as a specific result of the ways that the world of work is organized – ways that could be changed.[5]

As self-narratives were challenged and adjusted, so behaviour patterns changed dramatically.

Critique of Lerner

It will by now be abundantly clear that with Lerner we are in a different world to any we have explored so far. Although his theory has a number of flaws to which we shall have to turn, its attraction lies in the way that it holds social and psychological factors together in a dialectic causal relation. His is neither a psychological nor a sociological determinism; rather, he analyses the explicand – the lumpenness of the proletariat – by examining the way the social, and especially the economic, environment both causes and is in turn effected by psychological processes operating through the parenting relationship. In this way Lerner both puts his version of post-Freudian theory in a wider social setting and gives an account, often neglected by Klein and the post-Kleinians, of the pressures on parents that might explain why they either give wrong or misperceived signals or issue so ungenerous a psychic contract. To use Kleinian language, they cannot contain their children's emotions for intelligible (and in a sense justifiable) reasons.

What is lacking in Lerner's account is an adequate acknowledgement of what Klein and Rivière thought were their major contributions: the vitality and vividness of the phantasy life of the child. Lerner often writes as though the processes he is describing were occurring to five- or ten-year-olds. That may be partly an expository problem (e.g., the notion of the psychic contract), but its effect is to exclude from his theory the phantasy life of the individual and the group. His notion of the social unconscious points in the same direction: that is to say, he urges us to see, surely correctly, that our constructions of reality are socially conditioned. That emphasis needs, however, to be corrected by an appreciation of the fact that our phantasies – which he would rightly insist are themselves socially conditioned by the reaction and behaviour of our (damaged and stressed) parents – also play a role in shaping our conception of reality.

Leaving aside objections that might be raised about the universalise-ability of Lerner's approach (is *everyone* the victim of surplus power-lessness? and if not, why not?), let us relate Lerner's approach to the main theme of this book by reflecting on the role of memory. Clearly, memory is central to the whole process Lerner is describing: indeed, one way of characterising his treatment would be as an analysis of the psychodynamics of the memory of failure. Working backwards from the most conscious to the least conscious memories, the parents are emotionally less available to their children because of the memory of the frustrations and miseries of work; and the inadequate compensation for that which family relations give them. These are the memories of disappointment, frustration and blocked love that touch, at a more or less unconscious level, the rage they bring from their own childhood.

And that takes us to the second level of memories – what one might call the remembered history of failure and self-blame. I remember that I was held back a grade at school; that I failed the leaving exam; that I did not get to college; that I was never elected to any office by my peer group; that my teachers disliked me – all because I am not too bright or particularly likeable.

Behind those memories lurk the memories of my reactions to

those wants or perceptions: both inner emotional reactions and outer behavioural reactions. I hated my teachers because they demanded of me more than (I thought) I could achieve and criticised me when I failed. And I put that hatred into action by absconding, by being rude and unruly – and by demonstrating thereby that I was as much of a personal disaster as I had been told and always feared. I despised my peer group (or significant figures in it) because I could find no other way of relating to them, since I could never believe that they accepted me or, much less, liked me. Why should they? I am not successful or amusing or attractive, so why should they care about me? So I was a loner who got his kicks by irritating others. The memories, however selective of objective reality they may be, constitute *my* reality of the past.

Perhaps at the less conscious level, though salients of unhappiness usually remain in the easily recalled memory, are memories of relations with parents, even from quite early childhood – memories of an over-demanding father who blamed me for fear or failure; of a withdrawn mother who insensitively destroyed a favourite toy (or transitional object); of a family row or a patronising enquiry if I 'felt better now' after a temper tantrum. Behind such recallable memories lies repressed material of the workings of the psychic contract, of how my relations with my parents may have been the best available, but were not enough. And why? Because I am unworthy of more.

At each stage, then, of the psychodrama which is Lerner's theory, memory reinforces the self-blame that convinces me that the world is as bloody as it is because I am as unacceptable as I am – and there is therefore nothing to be done about it. Note, however, that these are *my* memories; that is, they are internal to me, and remain so. Even the memories of my disappointments and frustrations in my family relationships and in my sexual liaisons are seldom shared even with those most intimately involved. One of Lerner's therapeutic techniques is to persuade clients that these memories are not unique to them; that, *mutatis mutandis*, everyone shares them: they are the stuff of the human condition. In this sense they are a corporate memory, mediated by the social unconscious. We are back, then, to collective memory, perhaps the clearest example of its significance we have met so far. Whatever one makes of Lerner's notion of the social unconscious, it is clear that his theory implies (and is much enriched by) the supposition that the experience of self-blame and powerlessness is not just an individual burden: it is a social fact, suffered by swathes of one's fellow human beings. Unlike the collective memories we explored in Chapter 1, however – e.g., of VE Day or the Queen's Jubilee – the melancholy fact of this set of memories is that, although most people have them, they are never made the subject of conversation or social interaction. In that sense they are more accurately defined as common memories rather than collective memories. The therapeutic task, then, is to draw the sting of the memories by first showing that they are indeed common to a wide swathe of the population; and second that, *pace* the social unconscious, they do not need to define reality. There are other memories, other constructions to be put on these memories. No one *needs* to be the victim of these memories; and to opt to continue to be so is to *choose* the way of surplus powerlessness. The cost of that choice falls not only on the individual: it falls on the whole community.

What is especially relevant about Lerner's work for the later chapters of this book is that, as we saw above, he is able to show that tackling the memories through a range of therapies, especially group therapy, actually works in the sense that it frees people from the compulsive behaviour patterns of opting out, excessive drinking and collusion with an oppressive regime in the workplace. Lerner's team achieves this by revealing the generality of the memory-type and persuading people of the possibility of a different set of outcomes. I shall want to argue in the succeeding chapters that the Christian gospel can act in a somewhat similar though more extensive way: that is, it can offer an alternative set of memories which can free people not only from the memories of parent–child blaming discourse, but from the wider experience of traumatic memory and phantasy that holds us captive.

Before we begin to explore that in greater detail, however, we have two additional important pieces of the jigsaw to put in place. Although Lerner's is an approach that neatly holds the individual and the socio-political together, it does not address the great political themes with which social theory has traditionally been concerned. The next section offers a way in which we can extend the analysis to such a theme.

Ervin Staub and the Roots of Genocide

My second example of a recent writer who has sought to relate social phenomena directly to psychological variables happens also, like Lerner, to give great prominence to the effects of stress. Ervin Staub's analysis of the roots of genocide[7] lacks the psychoanalytic depth implicit in Lerner, but compensates for that by a breadth of psychological references that run from group psychologists like Tajfel to 'death psychologists' like Ernest Becker. Drawing from those wide sources, he adduces a theory that claims to fit the facts of four major twentieth-century occurrences of genocide from the Holocaust to Argentina via the Armenian Turks and the Khmer Rouge. We shall not be concerned here to judge how far his theory can be validated historically: rather, we shall examine the internal consistency of the theory itself.

At the core of Staub's treatment is what he terms, perhaps a little infelicitously, 'difficult life conditions'. He obviously needs as general a term as this to cover the situations as different as the four on which he bases his work, and he necessarily assigns slightly different nuances to the term in each historical context. But the psychological import of the term is clear enough. Social stress, a paraphrase I prefer, exacts a psychological price – and that price is directly related to the memory of a 'time before', a golden yesterday when today's difficulties were unimagined and unimaginable. Such a memory leaves people feeling threatened and deprived and, more important, it may undermine their self-narratives in a way that causes them to be rewritten internally. In those rewrites, self-esteem is minimised and self-identity clouded. Since Staub's analysis is close to the social identity theory associated with Tajfel and Turner,[8] self-esteem and identity are closely linked. Indeed, self-esteem is taken to be a key psychological need.

People may handle their predicament in a number of ways. They may seek a new identity, arising perhaps from a new way of understanding their reality. Clearly Staub believes that this was one of the attractions offered by Nazism: it both explained why the Weimar Republic failed and it offered a new sense of purpose within a wider explanatory world view that absolved individuals from the sense of their own failure or moral culpability.

One might, notwithstanding the horrors of Nazism, call that the psychologically constructive way forward, in so far as it presents the psyche with new possibilities of belief, purpose and, since an ideology is by definition a group affair, membership of a wider community. Unfortunately, however, as Staub points out, the effects of social stress are such that the ideologies that emerge at such times are likely to contain elements that make genocide increasingly probable. For example, they are likely to include implicitly (but more usually explicitly) differentiation into ingroup and outgroup. The psychological process is simple: Why are we suffering – i.e., undergoing this period of social stress? Because *they* are making us suffer. 'Communists' in Argentina; bourgeoisie in Cambodia; Jews in Germany – in a sense, it does not matter how much truth there is in the claim. What matters is that the definition of the outgroup gives solidarity, security and a degree of explanation to the ingroup. From there it is but a small step, accelerated by the way categorisation *accentuates differences to the point of exaggeration*, as shown experimentally by Tajfel and Wilkes,[9] to what Staub calls the devaluation of the outgroup by the ingroup. Burlesqued by Jonathan Swift in his account of the Small Endians and the Big Endians in *Gulliver's Travels*, this psychological process culminates in scapegoating – usually of a less powerful group, of which the wider community already has some negative memory.[10]

This points to perhaps the most potent role memory plays in Staub's model: social (i.e., constructed) memories of outgroups and scapegoats. Why were the Jews so 'natural' a target for the Nazis? Because anti-Semitism had a long and inglorious history in Germany (and in other parts of Europe, including Great Britain). The Jews were corporately 'remembered' as dirty, dishonest, exploitative, cruel, exclusive, mean. It was that social 'memory', not that Jews were like that, but that enough people could be persuaded to believe they were like that, which made them an inevitable target. Perhaps every society has its scapegoat-in-waiting: the Irish in Britain; North African immigrants in France; Muslims in India; Tamils in Sri Lanka. The culturally constructed memory of their imagined shortcomings is a reservoir waiting to be tapped by an ideology of hatred.

Staub does not want to make the mistake of being over-deterministic at this point. 'Individuals differ in such psychological tendencies depending on their socialization and experience and resulting personality; societies differ depending on their history and the resulting culture.'[11] Yet the argument is that the experience of extreme social stress is so severe for the individual and for his or her group that psychological defences are set up that have within them the seeds of genocide. Such seeds will surely fruit unless there are strong counter-influences in the individual psyche (the case of the heroic objector, whom research on conformity to the group proves to be a rare breed indeed[12]), in the culture (as in Denmark and Holland) or in the leadership group (the plots against Hitler). Staub is clear that the 'system' is, as it were, open: it is not deterministic, but it is probabilistic (a term he does not in fact use), in the sense that a 'continuum of destruction' is likely to be set up which can only be resisted by exceptional people or groups. There is a sense in which we are back to the story of the Birmingham Six as we explored it in Chapter 1.

This 'continuum of destruction' is a form of learning by doing:

> Small, seemingly insignificant acts can involve a person with a destructive system. . . . Initial acts that cause limited harm result in psychological changes that make further destructive acts possible. Victims are further devalued, just-world thinking may lead people to believe that suffering is deserved. Perpetrators change and become more able and willing to act against victims. In the end, people develop powerful commitment to genocide or to an ideology that supports it.[13]

The memory of one step along the road makes easier the taking of the next step.

Defence and Aggression

But why? How do we get analytically from psychological *defence* to active aggression against victim groups or scapegoats? Staub rejects the familiar frustration–aggression hypothesis, preferring to identify a variety of motives that may generate aggression among the victims of extreme social stress. Apart from aggressive self-defence, he identifies retaliation; a sense of relative injustice; the need to achieve a sense of personal power (as a compensation for low self-esteem, a continual refrain in Staub's work, as in all social–identity theory); a Beckeresque need to feel invulnerable or even immortal; the need to associate with others and the assumption or discovery that this need is best met in aggressive situations; and obedience to authority. (This last leaves open the question of why the 'authority' should espouse aggressive or violent policies against the victim group.) One can see, however, that in so far as the authority is a mirror of the psychological needs of the ingroup, the other reasons in the list may well furnish it with adequate excuse. Once the authority *has* embarked on aggression, Staub expects the Milgram effect to be fully operational (Milgram conducted a celebrated experiment which purported to show how easily 'ordinary' people would yield to authority figures instructing them to do something they would normally find morally repugnant.[14]) Staub also cites experimental evidence, which is perhaps slightly less unambiguous than he allows, to show that devalued groups are more likely to be ill treated (i.e., be the objects of aggression) than are valued groups. To this extent devaluation itself is a *cause* of aggression.[15]

Whatever the theoretical underpinnings, Staub is clear that social stress is historically associated with aggression. He quotes the well-known data on lynchings in the Southern States, which show an increase as economic decline intensifies, and refers to similar data for Japan which show that an increase in the rate of suicide is inversely correlated with economic prosperity. There are, of course, many counter-examples, but Staub would not be embarrassed by them. He would argue, justly, that social constraints and cultures operate in different ways: his probabilistic model can take account of counter-cases. The difficulty, of course, is that the more counter-cases, the lower the probabilities must be assumed to be and the less helpful the model becomes.

The Unconscious in Staub's Theory

So far, we have presented Staub's account in broadly social-psychological categories, such as stress, scapegoating and aggression. But what of the *unconscious* roots of genocide? In general, Staub follows Tajfel and Turner in being exceedingly cautious of psychoanalytic categories, but he does make two significant and revealing references to them.

The first is in connection with one of his central analytical categories, ingroup/outgroup differentiation and the associated devaluation of the outgroup. He sees the child's attachment to mother and antipathy to strangers as a rudimentary but deeply ingrained form of ingroup/outgroup differentiation. It is habit memory that becomes an instinctual response. The more secure the child is in love of the mother, the more empathic he or she will subsequently be with the peer group.[16] The difficulty is, however, that there is no empirical evidence to suggest that the 'good parenting' (in a Kleinian or Winnicottesque sense) reduces a person's readiness to differentiate between 'them' and 'us', or to stereotype or scapegoat 'them'. The evidence does suggest that good parenting (in the limited sense above) makes the child more accepting and more positive *with the ingroup* – but that is a coded way of saying that she/he may still be as brutal to the outgroup as a less well-parented child. Indeed, attempts to associate parenting with the behaviour of tyrants have been unsuccessful. To this extent, the habit memory of in/out group differentiation must be assumed to have a genetic or instinctual origin, unmodifiable by parenting (though certainly modifiable in its effects by instruction and example).

The second example of unconscious processes that Staub cites boils down to projection. He recognises that there is a lively debate about 'the existence of classical projection and the stress-reducing function of attributive projection' (to quote the title of one of the leading contributors[17]), and recognises that it is by no means universally true that people deal with anxiety about anger or aggression by projecting them on to others. None the less, he quotes a revealing case study from Alice Miller, about a German woman who was required by her parents to forego her own bright career prospects and stay at home to look after them while her siblings made their way in the world. When she joined the Bund Deutscher Madel (the female wing of the Hitler Youth) and read the 'Crimes of the Jews' in *Mein Kampf*, she reported 'what a sense of relief it had given her to find that it was permissible to hate anyone so unequivocally'. She had not been able to express her resentment of her siblings and her parents, but 'now, quite unexpectedly, . . . it was alright to hate as much as she wanted . . . she could project the "bad" and weak child she had always learned to despise in herself onto the weak and helpless Jews and experience herself as exclusively strong, exclusively pure (Aryan), exclusively good'.[18]

In one sense this is no more than an extreme case of the ingroup/outgroup differentiation, devaluation and scapegoating that Staub has already put at the centre of his thesis. It is different only in so far as this young woman's *need* to project her 'bad self' on to the Jews arose from a family situation which obliged her to repress her negative feelings, until she was 'given permission' to express them in conventionally acceptable ways.[19] Staub does not develop this idea further, but the identification of an outgroup that can become the dump of a whole community's repressed negative feelings of fear, hatred and anxiety is obviously an important milestone on the road to the destruction of the outgroup. Clearly, the significant phase is less the repression of negative feelings than the legitimisation of the projection: we are back with ideology, its origins, its implied memories and its moral status.

Critique of Staub

It is tempting to challenge Staub's theory by counter-examples. What about, for example, England at the end of the Victorian era? Harsh parenting;[20] a militarist culture; social stress among the working class, at least until the First Boer War, and among the rural population until 1914; the emergence of a quasi-ideology that 'blamed' the bosses, the capitalists and the bankers. Yet Labour politics hardly produced a brick thrown in anger. Such a riposte is perhaps none too helpful, given the probabilistic nature of Staub's thesis and the problems of counter-factuals.

A more serious criticism can be made on the basis of empirical evidence which Staub quotes without seeing its full implications. The study is the celebrated Stanford prison simulation, in which college students were randomly designated as guards and prisoners. Symbolic uniforms were donned. No one used names of people in the other group. The prisoners were put through a humiliating reception routine and then given a long list of irksome regulations. Surprisingly quickly, the 'guards' took over the simulation, using increasingly cruel and humiliating methods on the 'prisoners'. The more cowed the prisoners, the more vicious the guards. They acted as though they had ceased to believe that the 'prisoners' were human; empathy at the human, much less the collegial, level simply disappeared. The simulation became so obscene, so threatening to the physical and psychic health of the 'prisoners', that it had to be terminated halfway through its planned duration.[21]

Remember that the 'guards' were decent American lads, who had been carefully screened for any kind of traceable psychological abnormality. They were not the victims of social stress in any significant sense. They were not overtly especially aggressive. We must assume that few if any came from unduly harsh or punitive family backgrounds; it strains credulity to imagine that all or even a significant number had so repressed hatred of their parents that they were ready to project on to the prisoners. They had no particular ideology. They had no reason to devalue or scapegoat the prisoners – except that they, the guards, could quickly identify themselves as ingroup and the prisoners as outgroup. Unlike in Milgram's experiment, they had no external authority. So what was going on? Three explanations are on offer.

Staub argues, surely unconvincingly, that the group as a whole was self-selecting:

The participants were recruited through ads in city and campus newspapers and offered fifteen dollars a day to participate in a study of prison life. Not everyone would want to participate in such a study; the personal characteristics of those who answered the advertisements may have been one reason for the intensifying hostility.[22]

That looks limp, because in an almost classically Rawlsian situation, the recruits did not know in advance whether they would be prisoners or guards. If they had been recruited *as guards*, self-selection might conceivably have played a role. Given the recruitment process and the subsequent screening, it has to be rejected.

A second possibility is that the structural form of the experiment was enough to bring about 'the sudden transmogrification of likeable and decent American boys into near-monsters of the kind allegedly to be found only in places like Auschwitz and Treblinka'.[23] That structural form consisted *only* of the formation of two groups, one symbolically differentiated, one with absolute power over the other. 'What mattered was the existence of a polarity, and not who was allocated to its respective sides.'[24] Lord Elton was wiser than he knew. Bauman claims, probably rightly, that if roles had been reversed, the result would have been the same.

Some will find so sociologistic an explanation unsatisfactory, even though Sherif's famous experiments with boys on camp might be thought to point in the same direction.[25] Others will want to ask *why* does power corrupt so quickly and so comprehensively? That takes us to the third possible explanation: that there is, in Etzioni's memorable phrase commenting on Milgram's experiment, a latent Eichmann in us all.[26] John Steiner has finessed that idea, by referring to 'the sleeper effect' which is 'the latent personality characteristic of violence-prone individuals, such as autocrats, tyrants or terrorists when the appropriate lock and key relationships become established'. Steiner believes 'all persons are sleepers inasmuch as they have a violent potential that under specific conditions can be triggered'.[27] Certainly this is consistent with experimental findings that people operate competitively even in non-competitive situations, a finding that puts the explanation back in the psyche of the individual(s) rather than leaving all the explanatory power in the identification of the individual with the group.[28]

If this is right, it puts Staub's work in a rather different light. Perhaps the collective memory of social stress and 'cultural dispositions' (e.g., a long history – i.e., social memory – of anti-Semitism) are part of the 'specific conditions' that trigger our latent violence. And perhaps the psychological preconditions that Staub enumerates, such as poor parenting or repressed hatred, are the mechanisms that determine the resistance of the trigger. The Eichmann in each of us is not equally easily activated. Some respond more readily to extreme inequalities in power relationships than others. The individual differences are then explicable, at least in part, by the psychological preconditioning that each of us brings to a particular situation. This would be consistent with the observed fact that in the Milgram experiment some 'teachers' did eventually rebel against the increasing brutality demanded of them, while others at least expressed doubts and reservations about the way the experiment was going. Power corrupts: but it does not corrupt undifferentiatedly.

If this is right, the theological task is to mobilise resources that will transform both the social memories that feed into devaluation, scapegoating and ultimately violence, and the individual sets of memories (conscious and unconscious alike) that respond to those social memories by co-opting the individual into the practice of violence.

As I shall argue in Part Three, the Christian tradition has access to a set of counter-memories that can challenge and relativise both the destructive social memories and the individual memories if they, the counter-narratives, are allowed to become part of the narrative of community and person. Concretely, I am suggesting that the communities that 'remembered' Jews, for example, as appropriate scapegoats and then acted out their own individual memories by persecution and aggression against Jews had available to them counter-memories, alternatives stories of self-identity, that would have enabled them to act otherwise. That would have entailed the deep internalisation of those counter-memories, not as learned text or familiar prose, but as deeply meditated, almost physically ingested 'stuff' that reached far into the individual and community consciousness. And even beyond consciousness. To that process we shall return in the last chapter.

Its redemptive potential is, of course, hypothesis. It cannot be proved, and the critic will get busy with counter-examples of 'good' Christians who had spent years struggling to internalise the story of Jesus's destiny – and still rejoiced at the Nazi persecutions. The Christian resistance, the confessing Church, the martyrdom of Bon-hoeffer, the long line of what Staub calls 'resisters' – all can, of course, be discounted. An empirical approach will lead us nowhere. In the next part, we shall have to return to this theme, but before we do so, we shall look at the work of two writers who have taken the possibilities of redemption seriously. One relies on sacrifice; the other on reason. We shall see how far such accounts can take us in our search for liberation from our past before having a closer look at how traditional atonement theory could be reworked to take account of the material we have reviewed in this Part.

PART THREE

9

Emancipation and Sacrifice: Girard and Habermas

We saw in the last chapter that one of the central ideas in the work of Staub is the analysis of the social and psychological processes that lead to scapegoating. We might also have noticed that 'behind' Lerner's work lurks the idea of self-scapegoating. Low in self-esteem and high in self-blame, Lerner's underclass clients do not have the ego-strength to project their hatred on to others but turn it on to themselves. Their own failure becomes the internal scapegoat which carries all their griefs. In this chapter I want first to look at the ideas of the thinker who has most famously reinterpreted theology from the perspective of the scapegoat and then turn to a philosopher who shares Girard's intent, but whose work takes a very different, but for us no less illuminating, turn.

Girard and the Myth of Sacred Violence

René Girard's basic thesis can be shortly stated, though brevity should not ignore the extent of his scholarly investigations in anthropology and literary criticsm that predate his 'discovery' of the Christian resolution of the problematic that his earlier studies had identified.[1] That problematic can be put like this. Desire is the universal and fundamental drive in human affairs (a proposition Girard thinks he owes to Freud but which actually constitutes a highly selective, not to say perverse, reading of Freud, not least because it misses the point of the Freudian duality of eros *and* thanatos). Desire, then, is for Girard constitutive; but it is also mimetic, that is to say, we learn what to desire and how to frame those desires from each other. That is part of the process of social interaction by which we know ourselves

175

and our world, and the memory of which undergirds our sense of identity and the hermeneutic we bring to the world. Girard is less concerned with that than with tracing the origins of society to 'the dynamics of mimetic desire',[2] a phrase that could almost have been invented by the high priests of social interactionism.

This learning through mimesis is an essentially cognitive process, but Girard would not deny an unconscious element in it, nor even (though he does not use the term) a kind of collective unconscious that leads us to desire the same things: possessions, mates, power, independence.[3] But, says Girard, the mimesis of desire leads inevitably to conflict. Either there are not enough 'goods' to satisfy everyone's desires, or they are mutually exclusive. Denying the possibility of a liberal 'invisible hand' to manipulate desires into compatible outcomes, Girard sees the result as a tendency to a permanent state of social conflict, with potentially lethal results for both the community and, ultimately, the individual.

The way the community deals with this permanent tendency to conflict is, *unconsciously*, to identify a scapegoat, 'deem' him or her (a 'witch', for example) 'guilty' or 'at fault' and then kill him/her. Or them. A people, a class, a colour, members of any group can become a collective scapegoat. In the process of the killing, the tensions within the community are released through some kind of catharsis, the community is enabled to survive and life continues – for a time. But as the tendency towards conflict reasserts itself, so the need for the killing of a scapegoat re-emerges.

At this point in the argument Girard is less concerned with the group-scapegoat and casts his analysis almost exclusively in terms of the individual or the small, *representative* group. As a result of the chronic need of the society for release from the tensions generated by mimetic desire, the sacrifice of the scapegoat becomes ritualised and the scapegoat becomes sacralised – precisely because it is through his/her sacrificial death that new possibilities of life are brought to the conflict-ridden community. It is holy and accursed, a 'double' that has resonances back to Freud and forward to Derrida.[4]

Central to this account is Girard's insistence that the scapegoat is innocent but is deemed, represented, re-presented, by the persecutors as guilty. As the process becomes ritualised and mythologised, the myth is always presented from the standpoint of the persecutors, the powerful. It is, in the terms we used in Chapter 1, 'social' memory, the memory of the dominant group. Whatever the 'facts' of the ethical status of the scapegoat, socially controlled memory will declare him/her to have been guilty. The witch is almost paradigmatic and the Anglo-French confusion over Joan of Arc merely highlights the point. She is 'made' 'witch' by her captors and, of course, put to death (a point Charles Peguy made long before Girard). In this sense, all human history depends on a profound but unconscious lie, a perpetual feat of self-delusion that we shall meet again when we turn to Habermas. The scapegoat cannot speak; or if s/he does, s/he is unheard or heard only in a way that condemns him/her (an experience the Guildford Four and the Birmingham Six could attest from the inside). And religion plays the role of maintaining the lie, of sacralising the 'sacrificial crisis' and preventing men and women from seeing the reality of what they are doing. For Girard as for Habermas, the role of institutionalised religion is therefore more to mask reality rather than to reveal it.

There is a kind of reductionism in Girard's development of this theme. He wants to make all human violence, all human social formation, reducible to the 'sacred violence' theme he demonstrates in anthropological studies from the Aztecs to the Holocaust, and in literary studies across an equally impressive range of literatures. He does for scapegoating what Freud had done for Oedipus – discover a hugely significant part of the human psyche and then seek to explain too much with it. But his very hermeneutic imperialism poses him with the ultimate question that takes us back to the heart of our enquiry: How may we be freed from this inner drive that is both individual and collective, and both self-delusory and utterly destructive? Or is the whole of human community made possible only by a permanent blood-letting, as human birth is made possible only by the blood-letting of the menstrual flow? And if that is the price of human freedom, how can any of us be really free in the face of the suffering of the (dead) scapegoat? – a question we shall have to face in a later chapter.

It is here that Girard privileges the Christian account of this myth. For, uniquely, the Christian story of the scapegoat is not 'social memory'; it is 'collective memory'. The story is told from the underside. Distorted it might be: but it is distorted by the victims. It is the story of the scapegoat who is not only innocent, but uniquely 'good'. The self-delusion of the persecutors is revealed for what it is, and for that very reason the Christian myth becomes formative for the whole of human history, the whole of human possibility.

It is, claims Girard, when we read the Passion and see ourselves as one of the persecutors that we are liberated from the power of the myth of sacred violence. For it then becomes possible for us to extrapolate from that experience through critical reflection of the self, seeing ourselves judged by the Gospel accounts of the Passion. As we accept our responsibility and substitute reality for illusion, we can reorder all our social relationships aware of (and therefore freed from) a myth that derives its power from always being, at the time of its acting-out, unconscious, invisible, unperceived. Girard thus argues that the Gospels' power to strip away the layers of illusion in both individuals and groups is both necessary and sufficient condition of any human society free of violence.

That there are a number of difficulties with the thesis, quite apart from its reductionism, will be immediately apparent. I shall not repeat here the criticisms made by New Testament scholars who think that Girard's account of the Atonement, so much at variance with mainline soteriology as we shall see in Chapter 10, is based on important misreadings of the Gospels, but I do want to follow Burton Mack in reading Girard against Girard.[5] Mack argues that Girard does not take his own argument seriously enough. He fails to put the Christian Gospels, which he tends to regard as more or less straight history, collective memory in our terms, in their proper sociological setting. If he had done so, he would have realised the level of tension that existed both between the Jews and the early Christians and between the Judaisers within the early Church, supremely in Jerusalem, and the advocates of the Gentile mission, supremely Paul and his allies. Further, says Mack, Girard forgets, or does not consider the implications of, the fact that the Gospels are composed, clearly with ideological intent, *after* these battles, whose intensity and gravity easily eludes us, had been fought. In other words, we need to see the Gospels not as collective memory, but as social memory, written from the standpoint of the dominant group which had emerged triumphantly from the bitter doctrinal and ideological struggle of the early Church to define its inclusiveness.

On this reading, the persecutors are the Christians and the victims are the Jews. Mack cites in evidence, for example, the conclusions of biblical criticism that have shown both the way in which the Gospels tend increasingly to incriminate the Jews and reduce the guilt of the Romans; and the way in which the trial before the Sanhedrin has come to be recognised as a possible fabrication, with too many parallels with the trial before Pilate to be credible. That leaves only the question of the 'innocence' of Jesus. As Mack puts it:

> One need not offer any apologies for the social order within which Jesus was killed in order to admit his transgression of them. One need only acknowledge that he was not killed as the innocent victim which later Christian interpretation claimed him to have been.[6]

In other words, if, following Girard's own anthropological methods, we faithfully put Jesus back into *his* historical context, of a Judaism threatened with genocide if it pushed the occupying power a fraction too far, then we can see that, in the light of his intemperate attacks on the Jewish leadership, his 'utopian dreaming' among the politically naïve social classes, and his tendency to draw large crowds and leave them excited and irresponsible, it is hard to call him 'innocent'. Naïve and foolish, maybe, rather than evil; but hardly innocent.

Why then, says Mack, did the writers of the Gospels and Paul go so far to paint Jesus as not only innocent but as divine? 'The answer lies in what we know of the social history of early Christianity.'[7] Faced with deep divisions, both within the household of faith and as between Christians and Jews, the Pauline party needed the myth of sacred violence to hold the Church (*their* version of the Church) together.[8] And the Gospels, written so much later, merely reflect the social history of the previous twenty or thirty or forty years. So, says Mack, the Gospels are as mythical as any of the other myths that Girard reviews; and the literature of the Gospels repeat the pattern he has unearthed in the other literatures he has studied. On this account, the Gospels are no more liberating than they.[9]

This leaves the search for emancipation hardly advanced. Girard himself sees the Christian gospel as the hope of delivery from the cycle of repetition of the sacred violence of the scapegoat; but that depends on unjustifiable privileging of *both* the Christian texts and the universality of the scapegoat mechanisms. Girard's work may have revealed much about the unconscious processes that generate the violence and self-destructiveness of the world: it cannot, alas, offer much hope of redemption of it.

It is instructive to read against Girard the work of Jurgen Habermas. Both share a commitment to an enlightened, justice-seeking world, where violence gives way to critical reflection on the self and the group as a means to negotiated settlement of conflict. Both are struck by the power of existing forms of social formation to make that end hard if not impossible to achieve, and both see behind social formations a fundamental difficulty in human consciousness or being. Perhaps the greatest difference between them is that, while Girard believes (in some ways, wrongly) that the Christian gospel offers a way through by way of a cognitive leap that enables humanity to rid itself of distorted ideologies and thus surrender defence mechanisms that make violence inevitable, Habermas believes that communicative action, with ideal speech at its centre, can produce rationality, truth and aesthetics. As we shall see, Habermas himself did not see communicative action as a religious concept at all, but his work has increasingly been appreciated by theologians as pointing in the direction of a deep spirituality. Perhaps to his surprise and even dismay, he is now hailed as a 'secular theologian'.[10] To him we now turn.

Habermas and Ideal Speech

Despite an understanding of Freudian theory that has brought heavy criticism from Gadamer and others, Habermas demands inclusion in this volume because, unlike any of the thinkers we have reviewed so far, including even Lasch and Girard, he integrates the psychological into a grand architecture of social functioning that has few if any serious rivals in modern social theorising. And having done so, he emerges as someone who recognises, as a fundamental necessity for the emancipatory project of critical theory and modern politics, the freeing of the memories of the victims of political processes.

No doubt his tongue was partially in his cheek when Schmidt claimed Habermas as 'the psychoanalyst of the working classes',[11] but such a soubriquet captures well one part of a dauntingly large and complex body of theory. So large and complex is it, indeed, that what can be offered here is inevitably partial, summary and foreshortened, with the resulting distortion that that implies.

The Life-world

To glimpse the senses in which Habermas may be thought of as 'the psychoanalyst of the working classes', it is well to start with his later work, where he puts at the heart of his approach what he calls the *Lebenswelt*, the life-world. This is the everyday world in which we live and move. In a 'primitive' society, it is coterminous with the whole of life, but even there it can be reviewed under three different aspects: culture, society and personality. The culture is the folk-memory, the mores, the norms, the conventions, the traditions and the aesthetic or artistic self-expression of the people, including their religious and ritual activity. The 'sacred' for Habermas is a key concept. It is essential to the culture, for it defines most or even all of what is covered by that concept. Art, for example, is not a 'secular' activity, divorced from the sacralising world view of the artist and the community.

By 'society' Habermas means the way in which people relate to each other as individuals or as groups. This can be seen as something conceptually separate from culture, though 'the sacred' may well influence the way in which relationships are patterned. Seen from the perspective of the individual actor, she or he is heir to a set of cultural data, but is also a member of a variety of groups. The more differentiated the life-world, the more groups the actor may belong to.

The actor is also, however, heir to his own personality. He can no more step out of that than he can of the cultural milieu or the pattern of relationships. In that sense he is caught or trapped in a particular set of ambitions, fears, needs, likes and dislikes. And obviously his personality impinges upon his society and his culture, both negatively and positively. He (or she) may make a contribution to the culture; s/he will certainly receive support, guidance, interpretative frameworks from it.

One can hardly fail to notice a kind of romantic glow in Habermas's description of the 'primitive' life-world. Aware that he is open to the criticism that he is rehashing Utopian socialism,[12] he none the less wants to preserve as a kind of expository device an idyllic (he would perhaps say ideal) 'time' when culture, society and personality were in some sense if not in equilibrium (a contentious and often vacuous term) at least in a harmony that allowed a full, free and healthy existence for most people most of the time. Personalities were not distorted by Marcusian surplus repression and society was not oppressed by the appropriation and accumulation of Marxian surplus value. Culture was sufficiently resilient and secure in the transcendence of the sacred to 'hold' or 'contain' the community and thus give a sense of purpose, meaning and satisfaction to its members. In that sense it was free of both Kleinian anxiety and Lerner's surplus powerlessness.

Romantic or not, Habermas sees the 'primitive' or myth-dominated life-world as one in which people have no difficulty in reaching understanding and agreement: their myths, as it were, do it for them.

> To the degree that the life-world of the social group is intrepreted through a mythical world view, the burden of interpretation is removed from the individual member, as well as the chance for him to bring about an agreement open to criticism. . . . Within such a system of orientation, actions cannot reach that critical zone in which communicatively achieved agreement depends upon autonomous yes/no responses to criticizable validity claims.[13]

Habermas wants to trace back the nature and processes of the life-world ultimately to language itself. He calls the 'primitive' life-world 'the linguistic world view reified as the world order'. His interest in such an approach is evident. He wants to argue that as, on a Chomskyan view, there are universals in language that transcend cultural (and of course linguistic) differences, so there are ethical universals (or pragmatic universals, as he calls them) operating in the life-world. The life-world is thus as *general* a phenomenon in the way it operates as is language itself.

For Habermas the whole point of the life-world is that 'it remains at the backs of participants in communication': that 'it enters *a tergo* into co-operative processes of interpretation'.[14] It is a whole unacknowledged continent of received wisdom, of world view, of assumptions, of ethical hierarchies, of technical explanations. It is thus what makes communication and 'co-operative . . . interpretation' possible, as surely as it is what makes social life, co-operative action and healthy personality feasible. Yet it remains unacknowledged, unexplored, unchallenged, unmodified and unmodifiable. It is the folk-memory that lies buried in the preconscious – and therefore intensely powerful. It is, again, quite literally the memory that makes the world.

It is significant for the larger theme of this book to note that, in so far as Habermas locates collective memories in the life-world, he sees them as having, at least in this 'stage', an entirely beneficent (one might be tempted to say redemptive) effect. The processes of reproduction that they sponsor and enable are the life of the community, and even if Habermas is guilty of romanticising elements of that life, it is a form of social life that is enduring, not only in the trivial sense of surviving through time but in the deeper sense of giving shape, form and meaning to lives that have little in the way of material satisfaction. That that does not automatically guarantee the relevant society against confusion, violence and ultimately unacceptable developmental paths is underemphasised by Habermas. A valuable corrective is the account by Fentress and Wickham of the history of the myth of the Mafia and its role in defining Sicilian identity – and, less emphasised because tangential to their purposes, the deviant ethical constructs of the *Mafiosi* themselves.[15] Memory can, then, be socially destructive as well as socially constructive.

It is worth a moment's digression here to draw a parallel that will have occurred to the reader but which has not, as far as I have been able to discover, been made in the extensive English literature on Habermas's work. Although they are using quite different philosophical tools and pursuing quite different philosophical agendas, there is none the less a striking similarity in the direction in which both Jung and Habermas point. Specifically, both are struck by the pathological results that follow when human-beings-in-community are separated from the models of meaning that have hitherto served them. Jung uses the language of the archetype; Habermas that of the life-world. Both are making the same point: when the remembered, community-stored, ritually re-enacted wisdom is no longer relevant to the needs of society, society and the individuals within it are at their most vulnerable.

Habermas is well aware, of course, that the life-world is not static. It evolves essentially as the result of the nature of language itself.

Although part of Habermas's originality lies in the account he gives of this process, we are concerned here more with the effects of this evolution. Habermas is aware of the potential conflict between a life-world dominated by the transcendent power of the sacred on the one hand and the emancipatory potential of communicative action on the other. He is clear that the latter is the more potent force and, in language reminiscent of Voeglin at his most gloomy, he writes of the 'disenchantment' of the life-world through the 'linguistification of the sacred'. As the transcendent values and assumptions of the life-world are brought under the judgement of communicative action, the irrational or non-rational features of the sacred in the life-world are gradually purged. The role of language in this process is crucial, for he relates cultural reproduction to changes in understanding or shared cognition. As cultural actors gain understanding of their world and of each other, so the culture changes. Earthquakes are no longer ascribed (only?) to the subterranean dispositions of the Great Snake but to shifts in tectonic plates. God may no longer be propitiated by child sacrifice but be content with goats or acts of mercy.

But this 'understanding' does not come out of the blue. Habermas dubs it an aspect of communicative action precisely because he wants to emphasise, as had Heraclitus long before him, that understanding (*Verständigung*) arises from communication.[16] The heuristic device he uses for this step in the argument is the ideal speech situation: that is, the search for truth by argumentation between symmetrical, non-constrained social actors who are themselves committed to remain in dialogue until truth is established. In what sometimes sounds like a recall of idealised Socratic dialogue, Habermas argues that truth, good and beauty are discoverable by rational discussion in which valid argument (rather than force, fear or projections) is the only arbiter.

Now, this argumentation is conducted in propositional language: e.g., 'the sun rises in the East', 'if A entails B and B entails C, A entails C'. This is the appropriate 'structural component' of the 'speech act' involved in the business of enlarging understanding. As social actors engage in these speech acts, as they participate in this process of unconstrained debate testing the truth and falsity of their understandings of their cultural facts, so that culture changes. Almost by definition it changes in the direction of reasonableness, that is, it becomes increasingly dominated by the faculty of human reason that is revealed in the ideal speech situation. We shall have to consider below what that implies for the development of the life-world.

In parallel, Habermas relates the aspect of society in the life-world to the illocutionary component of 'speech acts'. Put briefly, illocutionary (or performative) speech acts – 'I promise to give you a goat when my son returns'; 'I shall hit you if you say that again' – are universal types of speech that determine levels of co-ordination in the communicative community. With no illocutionary speech acts, there can, on Habermas's account, be no interpersonal commitment. Yet it is precisely that interpersonal commitment that produces social integration, the reproductive process of society in the life-world (and, of course, ultimately the commitment to the search for understanding) that lies at the heart of Habermas's theory. By thus linking a particular type of speech with the evolution of society in the direction of integration and higher levels of differentiation which that implies, Habermas is able to show how language, the universal achievement of the human species, both underlies but also drives the evolution of the life-world.[17]

Accordingly, the life-world becomes increasingly rationalised in a Weberian sense, subject to rules, rational procedures and judged by the canons of rationalisation, with the implication that means and ends come to be identified by a rational but also politically powerful agent.

The Life-world Subverted

Indeed, Habermas sees the process of rationalisation (derivable, remember, from the role of language itself) as inevitably producing, as a counterpoint to the life-world, sets of interlocking 'systems' which become detached from the life-world. These systems are dominated by what Habermas calls 'media' – money and power are respectively the media of the systems of the economy and politics. Thus the rationalisation of the life-world leads to the mediatisation of those parts of the life-world that become, through the very power of the media, semi-autonomous systems. They are *semi*-autonomous because each penetrates the other and each has a particular relationship, both dependent and aggressive, to the life-world. In a Marxian tradition, Habermas is concerned primarily with the economic and political systems, but his analysis can easily be extended to the communications media, to culture and particularly mass culture (by which I mean something wider and deeper than pop culture), and perhaps even to sexuality.[18]

The way in which those systems become detached from the life-world can be illustrated in a number of ways: Habermas's example is the supersession of the gift-exchange economy by the market economy, but we could add the supersession of various forms of participatory ('face to face') democracy by oligarchies, monarchies and dictatorships, elective or otherwise. Or, to take another obvious example from the field of communication, an 'ideal speech situation' where the best argument wins is replaced by newspaper-baron manipulation or the control of the means of mass communication by oligarchs with financial and political interests to further.

Habermas is essentially making two points here. The first is that the development of rational 'systems' as it were 'outside' the life-world is already a severe challenge to the harmonious interactions and reproductions that provide an ideal environment for human community. He looks to that development, rather than to inner processes unlinked to social change (as in a Kleinian, but perhaps not Bionesque, world), as the origins of human misery and their outworkings in society.

Note that the baneful effects occur when these collective memories are no longer adequate to the task of reproducing social and cultural formations under threat from the colonising media of money and state administration. For Habermas, this is in some ways the central problematic: How can 'reason' adapt the life-world, and its collective memories, in a way that will allow proper reproductions to take place? He assumes (against the anthropological evidence of, for example, Joutard's study of the Camisards[19]) that one cannot adapt memories: one must transcend them, perhaps reinterpret them or overlay them with new material more adapted to present contingencies. That this is a stressful and unpredictable business Habermas is certain. The finding of a new store of relevant memories and rituals, interpreted perhaps by a new rationality, is fundamental to the health, wholeness, liberation of the community – a point that cries out for the theological exegesis it will get in the next chapters.

For the very interrelatedness of his conception of the life-world, with culture, society and personality seen as aspects of the same totality, reminds us that rationalisation, mediatisation and the development of autonomous systems have implications for personality formation in itself and for the way that process (of socialisation in Habermas's scheme) relates to both society and culture. Social, cultural, economic and political change imply psychic change. More than any of the writers I have reviewed so far in this book, Habermas acknowledges that persons are the product of their whole social situation, with the result that the experience and memory of traumatic change in one 'sphere' are likely to pass their costs on to another. Thus he sites pathologies of persons and communities in the breakdown of the capacity of the life-world to reproduce itself under the stress of 'colonisation' by the semi-autonomous 'systems' of the media.

The prime philosophical interest for Habermas in the process of the colonisation of the life-world by the systems is that it marks a shift from norms determined by communicative action (e.g., in an ideal speech situation) and the level of 'understanding' achieved thereby to a set of ethics determined by the interests of the powerful, i.e., instrumental reason. This clearly relates to a wider debate than we can follow here, namely, the critique of positivism and scientism that lies at the heart of Habermas's project.

Our interest lies in the way Habermas relates the emergence of instrumental reason to the ultimate impoverishment and domination of the life-world by 'alien' norms that break down all (or most) of what gives meaning and symbolic substance to the background milieu in which ordinary people operate – and which, in the terms we have used so far in this book, makes them long for freedom or redemption. One telling illustration from Habermas will make the point. He notes the paradox of the welfare state. Conceived as a means whereby freedom from want, fear and social marginalisation would be achieved, it actually reduces freedom, partly because, in a paradoxical inversion of Weber, it has to generate ever more complex rules and procedures; and partly because, in order to cope with the complexity of real life, it has to operate not with real people and their manifold individual (and often baffling) circumstances, but with abstractions, averages, composites, hypothetical units that bear no operational relationship to how people actually are. The determination of health care by reference to 'QALYs' (quality-adjusted life years) is a topical example that Habermas would have blanched to see, the operations

of the Child Support Agency another. Such resource-allocative procedures not only do violence to the realities that people live with; they
then compound that violence by offering the only compensation the
rules allow – money. Understanding, the giving and receiving of
trust, sympathy, attention, affirmation, personal warmth and integration into a human community – these may be what people need,
but they cannot be delivered by a rational, bureaucratised structure.
Emotional need is met by economic responses. Nothing could be
more dehumanising – or ultimately more destructive. Despite good
or even noble intentions, then, bureaucracy (and its version of
rationality) has become the enemy of a reasonableness founded on
communicative action.

Habermas is not alone, of course, in his pessimistic assessment of
the social, political and psychological effects of what he calls the
colonisation of the life-world, and what others have called the breakdown of the symbolic system of Western rationalism. Indeed, one is
sometimes reminded, reading Habermas, of Yeats's remark on Blake
(which could equally, perhaps even more forcefully, apply to Yeats
himself): 'He was a man crying out for a mythology, and trying to
make one because he could not find one [ready] to his hand.'[20]
Habermas sees the world as caught between the destructive power of
the media to sabotage the life-world and the creative (redemptive,
even) possibilities of ideal speech. There is here another of those
agonising 'if only' moments equivalent to that which we encountered
in Kleinian thinking as the group keeps falling back to the paranoid-
schizoid position, unable to hold the reparative possibilities of the
depressive position.

Habermas is not optimistic about society 'reaching' the ideal speech
situation. Too much communication is distorted by ideology, by
inequality, by insincerity, by fear of allowing the argument to lead
where it will. Locked in this distorted communication, men and
women can only 'anticipate' the possibility of ideal speech.

There has been a good deal of arcane academic discussion about the
nature of this 'anticipation', some of which turns on the difficulties of
translating Habermas's abstract and dense German into comprehensible English. (Distorted communication comes home to roost!) One
of the more interesting suggestions is that we should read Habermas
eschatologically. He can be taken theologically to be pointing to the

end-time, the limiting case, to the ultimate hopefulness that is at the heart of what it means to be a language-using human being.[21] And that suggestion of Adams chimes well with Lash's claim that ideal speech is prefigured in the Eucharist – the re-presentation of ultimate love that both remembers the past and looks forward to a final consummation of the whole of creation.[22] For the Christian, the Eucharist is the ultimate myth, the myth by which the truth or transcendence of all myths is to be judged.

Habermas recognises the value of this myth making – or myth repeating. Others too are trying to make 'mythologies'. Perhaps surprisingly, he sees the new social movements, from the women's movements to the environmental groups to religious groups, as the one source of hope. For they can, he dares to believe, insert themselves along the 'seams between system and life-world'. They are asking new questions, but questions that were, as it were, already answered in the life-world prior to its colonisation. 'The new conflicts do not flare up around problems of distribution [the implication being that these are essentially 'systematic' questions] but around questions concerning the grammar of forms of life.'[23] We are reminded of Merleau-Ponty's plea for a politics of depth which seeks to build a shared social and political movement through 'a meeting at the cross-roads' which, while seeking always to define what is common and mutual, does not erode differences in thought, expression or interest.[24] Because they challenge the hegemony of the media and their systems, the new social movements, Habermas suggests, may be able to 'decolonise' the life-world, and restore to it a grammar of life which sets at a premium co-ordination and collaboration achieved by communicative action. That is not, emphatically, to dethrone rationality: it is to restore to the very notion of rationality the participation of all the actors in social communication. The scale – political, philosophical, epistemological, even – of such an undertaking is daunting. Habermas recognises that, as we shall have to in Chapter 10. He gives no guarantees of success, but he sees it as the most promising (and perhaps the only) way out for humankind and its present discontents.

It is, however, risky, a point Habermas repeats in *The Theory of Communicative Action*. 'In a rationalised life-world the need for achieving understanding is met less and less by a reservoir of traditionally artificial interpretations immune from criticism . . . the need for consensus must be met more and more frequently by risky, because rationally motivated, agreement.' This sets Habermas even further apart from both the philosophers of the Enlightenment and of the Frankfurt School. For him, emancipation from dogma, ideology and the distorted communication of the powerful brings with it the risk of stalemate, inability to agree, moral and political anarchy. As for the individual entering psychoanalysis, so for the community in search of communicatively achieved rationality in ethics and politics, free-dom has a high price.

But the question we have to put to Habermas is whether he is not over-dependent upon communicative action for discovering a way of saving the life-world. His is essentially a humanistic project that depends on the alleged universals of language to deliver rationality and the alleged counter-rationality of new social movements to discover, through 'ideal speech', a more just interpretation of rationality. But whence comes the inspiration of the new social movements? Not from language, communicative action or the ideal speech situation. It comes from memory and mythology. Both the feminist movement and the greens have their own sets of myths, their own sets of memories and their own ways of interpreting the one against the other. In that process of interpretation, language and communicative action have a part to play, as they do in any hermeneutic. And the more participative style indicated by an orientation towards 'ideal speech' may make that hermeneutic less oppressive than it might otherwise be. At the empirical level, however, the achievement of the quality of ideal speech that Habermas seems to have in mind proves more desirable than attainable – as Lerner, interestingly, dis-covered in his days with the anti-Vietnam War Left in the USA.[25] The powers of distortion are just too strong. That is by no means to deny the importance of critical self-reflection in the pursuit of free-dom from distorted communication – a point Habermas distils from an extended (and in many ways deeply flawed) analogy with Freudian psychoanalysis – but it is to argue that critical self-reflection *alone* is unlikely to achieve what Habermas is looking for.[26]

That suggests that whereas Habermas seems to put his hope for ideal speech and its redemptive possibilities in the new social move-ments (in which, remember, interestingly he includes religious groups), we need to ask how those new social movements are envisioned and nourished. That will take us, in this final Part of the book, to consider the role of myth and memory in Christian faith. For we shall want to argue that it is out of this material that the Christian Church can find freedom from the traumas and horrors that bedevil both personality and culture. Or, to put it in more Habermasian terms, we do not need to reinvent the social and psychic possibilities of the life-world: we have that potential available to us in the memories of the destiny of Jesus.

Both Habermas and Girard, it seems, have much to offer us, but neither can solve our problem. We need to combine the Habermasian notion of critical self-reflection before memory material with Girard's intuition that the internalisation of the story of Jesus's life and death (and, much neglected by Girard, resurrection) can deliver freedom from our inner compulsions to repeat the destructive games of the past. That is a task to which we turn in the last three chapters.

10

Emancipation, Redemption and Memory

In Part 2, we discovered that the source of our double unfreedom lies within us. That is to say, we behave as we do in response to other people and external events because we are as we are. And we are as we are partly because of our conscious or unconscious memories of our own identity, our remembered narratives, and partly because of the usually deeply unconscious memories we have of childhood trauma, of 'good' and 'bad' objects and of our varying capacities to relate to them. That is the first level of our unfreedom. The second level is the way in which we incarnate those memories and narratives in the institutions and structures and ideologies and languages which form the texture of our everyday lives. We saw in the case of the nursing profession (and we might very easily have adapted that model to cover the Church, often organised as a defence against anxiety) how phantasy forms the nature of professional relationships, a theme repeated in different cadence in the case of the Glacier Metal Company. And, in more sombre colours, we watched the same picture emerge in Staub's work, where memories of the supposed past combined with primitive memories of the 'good' and the 'bad' to lead to disaster.

I have tried not to present all this as a closed determinative system. Clearly, there is a wide range of other processes and mediations at work, from the historical to the sociological. Some of these other processes, especially, perhaps, interest-group theory (which stresses the influence on structure of competitive interest groups seeking to serve their own purposes in the political or economic arena), may be, at least in part, reducible to psychological investigation, as Lasswell claimed, but it is emphatically not part of my argument to suggest that all social (or individual) phenomena are reducible to psychological explanation. Nor, to repeat, do I want to deny (as Balthasar has charged Girard with doing[1], the reality of human sinfulness. I am concerned with the compulsive element in behaviour, especially of those parts of behaviour which feel 'free' but which are in fact driven. In what senses, if any, has Christ set us free of them?

I want to argue in the next chapters that if we want to give an account of what it means to say that Christ has set us free, then it is in the arena of memory that the most telling account can be given. More particularly, to those Christians, individual and corporate, who look at the world and cry; 'What does redemption mean in this mess?' or, more pragmatically, 'What can I/we do?' I want to argue that taking the theme of memory as part of a Christian doctrine of salvation gives a freeing way forward. For, unlike traditional accounts of salvation, it allows us to address those parts of our behaviour which are in one sense or another an acting out of our memories.

Before entering what will turn out to be a more complex matter than appears at first sight, let me spell out the main lines of the argument implied in the last paragraph. If, to a very large degree, we are as we are and the world is as it is because we are acting out internal memories and phantasies of varying degrees of facticity, we need to be in touch with counter-memories that can encourage and enable us to rewrite our narratives. They can do so by revealing the partiality, limitedness, illusoriness and non-ultimacy of memories that, to adapt the Jungian phrase, we think we have but which actually have us. By incorporating the counter-memories in our own narratives, either directly or in dialogue, we can allow the counter-memories to not only cut our own memories down to size but, more positively, to reconstitute them to form a self- or group-narrative that is freed of compulsive behaviour and acting out.

Jung, Hilman and Habermas, in their very different ways, imply that these counter-memories lie in the primeval, primitive or ideal past from which we have become estranged. Freud thought that the analyst, working with the analysand, could heal the memories by bringing them to consciousness and the light of reason. I want to argue that each approach is nearly right, but not quite right. That is to say – to Jung and Habermas – the counter-memories do indeed lie in the past, but not in the primitive past. With Pannenberg, I want to assert that they lie in the 'historical' past, in the life, death and resurrection of Jesus. And to Freud, I want to say: yes, the process of healing does indeed involve bringing unhealed memory to consciousness and the light of reason, but it is a light and a reason that has to be set in the context of the same history – the life, death and resurrection of this man Jesus. To omit that is to give to 'reason' a task that, *pace* the Enlightenment project, it cannot carry; or, to put it in another language, it is to invite seven more devils, more evil than the first, to move into the vacuum left by the healing of the original memory.

In Chapter 12, I shall have to face an obvious criticism that could be levelled against the argument as it will be presented in this chapter: if the story of the destiny of Jesus is what sets us free, what is the quality of that story and of the memories on which it is based? If the Lukacher argument is to be extended to the Gospels (not to mention the other distortions and caesuras in memory that we encountered in Chapter 1), what can we know about the destiny of Jesus that will help us?

In this chapter I seek to meet another objection: that the account that I give of the Atonement is too restricted to the individual. I emphasised at the end of Chapter 2 that our identities are fashioned by the processes of social interaction. We learn who we are and, to a degree, *are made* who we are by the way the community treats us – and others whom we can observe. Our selves are fashioned by our environment as well as by the inner processes of Klein and Freud: Lerner's self-blame is essentially socially induced and, at least on Baumann's (questionable) interpretation, the reaction of the Stanford 'prison guards' is likewise socially conditioned. An individualised account of salvation is therefore likely to miss much of the point. It has to take on board the role of the social environment in the process of both enslavement and liberation.

I shall argue that it is this role that the Church is expected to fulfil. Ideally (and that word hides a mare's nest in to which we shall have to venture), ideally the Church is a healed community or a community on the way to healing that allows each member to explore and consolidate the space of their own liberation. I shall argue that such an approach gives an immediacy and relevance to the theology of the Church, even though at the same time it raises some profound and troubling existential problems for us.

That, in brief, is the agenda of the remaining chapters. I want to start approaching that agenda by saying a little more about theories of the Atonement, for it is the formulation of another approach to those theories that is the ambitious aim of what follows.

As I re-emphasised above, the material we have reviewed so far should not leave us open to the charge, often made against people who take the unconscious seriously, of being 'soft on evil and sin'. Indeed, a mark of the unfreedom we experience is precisely that we are cut off from not only the deepest and truests parts of ourselves, but also the deepest and truest parts of the cosmos, God. 'Our feelings have us' and the result is that we have, in reality, no time for our neighbour or our God. And, as we have constantly pointed out, that introversion works itself out in our groups and communities as savagely as it does in the self – from Rwanda to Holocaust to labour relations.

I try the reader's patience by reaffirming all this because it is important to start from an apprehension of the reality of evil, of self-centredness, of closure to neighbour and to God when considering the theme of atonement. Though theologians differ on many aspects of the doctrine (as we shall have reason to see), at least they are virtually all agreed that the doctrine starts from a sense of the destructive power possessed by the compulsive downside of the human psyche. If Christians (and Jews) acknowledge the goodness of Creation as enshrined in the creation stories in Genesis 1 and 2, they also acknowledge, by dint of their own experience of the world, that that goodness is constantly under threat from and frequently displaced by a capacity for individual and corporate self-aggrandisement that will stop at nothing. Creation is followed by fall – and fatricide. That states the problem: how is humankind to be set free of this terrible tendency to despoil and pollute and ruin the goodness God intends for the whole of creation?

As is well known, Christianity has tended to answer that question in two different ways. Following St Paul, or at least one train of metaphors in Paul's writings, the Western Church has tended to present a forensic account that depicts a transaction between a just God and a loving, obedient Son. The transaction has the effect of satisfying the demand of God for justice but spares the 'real' culprit by offering a substitute – who is himself inalienably one with God

195

the Father. Thus, Paul uses familiar metaphors drawn from the law courts, from the slave market, from commerce and from the family to illustrate and extend the central notion of a transaction between two persons of the Trinity.

The contrast lies with the Eastern, Orthodox tradition which, no less true to other parts of Paul's writing, is less impressed by the power of the transactional metaphors and more concerned to emphasise the fact that the work of Jesus on the cross was to enable and encourage the transformation of humankind, its liberation from the sin that separates it from God and its entry into the real 'goodness' intended for it from the start. The Eastern tradition does not, as is sometimes falsely claimed, deny the significance or expositional utility of the transactional metaphors in Paul: rather, it wants to go beyond them and ask: 'Transaction for what?' It sees the demands of God the Father as being less for the upholding of an abstract principle of justice than the entry of his creation into the bliss he wants for it. The Cross is then to be seen as both the fulfilment of a life of total love and obedience, and as a precondition of the sending of the Holy Spirit who will lead creation (or the Church; emphases vary) into 'all truth', a symbol of the capacity to live at one, in the en-joyment of God and each other.

This forensic/transformational dichotomy has to be paired with another, less highlighted, contrast. It is the essence of the Western forensic tradition of atonement theory that what is at stake is ontological, the very being of humankind. Thus Gunton writes passionately about the stain of pollution darkening the soul of the whole human race.[3] He demonstrates how that is reflected liturgically in baptism where a small baby, morally incapable of guilt, is washed free of the inherited filth that would otherwise engulf it. It is incorporated into the body of Christ where it is, as it were, protected from the ontological consequences of the Fall.

On this account, then, the effects of the work of the Cross are to be seen primarily in the realm of being rather than in the realm of action, feeling or relating. One way of speaking about this is to say that, on this account, the Atonement makes little difference to what one is or how one acts in this life; the difference will be revealed only in the hereafter. A good illustration of this comes from the rigidly orthodox presentation of Professor Tom Torrance, one-time

Moderator of the Assembly of the Church of Scotland and a noted apologist of orthodoxy.[4] He writes like this:

> It was precisely into the midst of that depraved and dehumanised humanity that the Son of God penetrated by his incarnation in Jesus Christ, that is, into the very split in our human nature where we are not and cannot be what we ought to be, and where we manipulate moral righteousness in the protection of our selfish ends. Through hypostatic union and atoning union interpenetrating each other he laid hold of both sides of that split and brought them together in his own Person, removing the sin and guilt which perpetuated the split, reconciling man to God and God to man in such a way that he set the whole moral order upon a new basis. That is the moral order he embodied in himself as the one man who was and is the man he ought to be, without any trace of insincerity or hypocrisy. Through the whole course of his human life Jesus Christ was at work healing, sanctifying and humanising the human nature which he assumed from our fallen, dehumanised state, converting it from its estrangement from the Creator back to its proper relation to him. Thus through hypostatic and atoning union, fulfilled within his own incarnate Person as the one Mediator between God and man, Jesus Christ became the humanising Man who constitutes among us the creative source for the humanising of mankind.

This represents an attempt by Torrance, while remaining faithful to the tradition, to meet a criticism of the Western position: that is, that it remains so severely ontological that it is difficult to relate to the experience of everyday life. It might be that there has been a change in the ontological relationship between humanity and the Godhead, but it does not feel that I am any freer as a result. The misery of ordinary people, trapped in their Lerneresque knowledge of their own inadequacy, alienated from each other by the distortions of their communication, and suffering day by day the petty and sometimes gross cruelty of their structures – their misery is little attenuated by the knowledge that there now exists a changed relationship at some profound, mysterious level between the whole human race and the Three Persons of the Trinity. If that is salvation, it is questionable whether it brings freedom that is worth the name. We might ask, with Albert Nolan: How is the News Good?[5]

This point is worth pursuing a little further. In the same book that I have quoted from already, Torrance recounts an exchange he had, while Moderator, with a born-again Christian who asked Torrance if he too had been born again. Torrance's reply is instructive: 'This Tom Torrance you see is full of corruption, but the real Tom Torrance is hid with Christ in God and will be revealed only when Jesus Christ comes again. He took my corrupt humanity in his Incarnation, sanctified, cleansed and redeemed it, giving it new birth in his death and resurrection.'[6]

In other words, the Atonement makes little difference to the actual lived experience of 'this Tom Torrance whom you see', who remains full of corruption – and whose world remains, we have to assume, no less full of corruption. In so far as there is salvation at all, it lies in the future, 'when Jesus Christ comes again'.

This severely ontological account needs to be nuanced by a recognition that even the most orthodox exponent would recognise that the Atonement has to be appropriated by the attempts of the baptised to live, under the guidance and enablement of the Holy Spirit, a 'Christian life'. Sanctification is an idea, appearing under many guises and with many labels, that remains central to forensic, ontological orthodoxy. But it cannot by itself bring the restoration of the pre-Fall relationship between humanity and God. Justification is, indeed, by faith alone, and this type of atonement theory recoils in horror from what it is quick to brand as Pelagianism, an excessive concern with the fruits of the Atonement in the life of the believer.

None the less, since what Gelpi has called the turn to experience[7] there is a readiness, always present in the Eastern Orthodox traditions, to shift the emphasis from the ontological to the experiential. There is no need to deny or contest the ontological: but there is a need to see, like Albert Nolan quoted above, that a gospel that has no good news on the central predicament of the whole cosmos hardly deserves the name. While it may be true in some sense, that this Tom Torrance whom we see remains full of corruption and wickedness, we surely have the right to ask whether the atoning work of the Cross is really so abstracted from the real world which Jesus knew that it makes no difference to it 'until Christ shall come again'. Indeed, we might well wonder whether a view as narrowly ontological as Torrance's does justice to the Incarnation, a doctrine that, however snarled around with logical difficulties,[8] has always been seen as central to Christian belief not least because it proclaims God's desperate concern for the world as it is and for its suffering people.

An alternative account of the Atonement would be one which sits somewhat lightly to ontological questions but which expects the Atonement to have, as it were, a cash value in the life we live day by day. On such an account Tom Torrance may indeed know himself to be as full of corruption as ever, but he would hope, by the grace of the Holy Spirit, to be in the process of shedding some of the grosser manifestations of this corruption and so enlarging, like a reformed alcoholic, the space of his own freedom to love and serve God and neighbour. This is not something that he does by himself or for himself: we need to hit Pelagius firmly on the head. He does it only because he is attracted by the life and death and resurrection of Jesus where he sees humanity at its best; and because he knows himself to be wholly dependent upon the work of the Holy Spirit re-creating in him, so far as his fallen nature allows, the person of Christ. This is the familiar Orthodox idea of *theosis*, the call to enter our own possibilities of divinity, possibilities opened up to us by the Cross and resurrection of Jesus. This is no cheapening of grace, no depreciation of the quality of love that led to the Cross nor underappreciation of the power manifested in the Resurrection. But it is to shift the balance from a transaction with an angry or morally outraged creator to an anticipation of grace that makes the human spirit redeemable. 'Whilst on the Latin view, to be saved is to be justified, i.e., relieved of guilt, by Christ's sacrificial death, on the Orthodox view to be in process [n.b] of salvation is to be responding to the presence of the divine Spirit and thus gradually to be moving towards a radical new re-centring within the divine life.'[9]

Of course, we need to be careful not to overdraw these contrasts, nor to deny their cross-correlation. There are, for instance, ontological overtones in Orthodox doctrine just as there are experiential overtones in forensic, Western doctrine. None the less, I believe the two-fold dichotomy that we have now identified to be helpful, not least because it gives us a grid against which we can test a reinterpretation of atonement theory derived from the psychological material we have reviewed in Part 2. To summarise, the grid looks like this:

Type of theory	Forensic	Transformational
Effects	Ontological	Experiential

I want to start the reinterpretation by focusing on the right-hand pair of concepts, the transformational and experiential. As will become apparent, this allows the most persuasive statement of the case. I accept that it is not adequate by itself, however, and that we shall need to address aspects of the Western tradition later. But the way in to the transformational/experiential dyad is opened up neatly by a throwaway line of Hick's, in which he comments on the lack of detail in the Eastern patrisitic tradition of precisely how the work of Christ on the cross produces the inner transformation.[10] He might have added that there is an even more striking lack of detail relating how this inner transformation works out in terms wider than the individual. One of the difficulties of theosis is precisely that it is, in its logical structure, a process that has to have the individual and the personal as its predicate. We shall therefore need to extend the Orthodox tradition to give an account of the saving of the whole created order.

The appropriation of the Atonement that does justice to its emancipatory nature *and* its existential impact (and the core of my argument is that it is of the essence of a doctrine of atonement worth having that each of those elements have to be maintained) involves growth into a living relationship with the Holy Trinity that has the freedom of loving acceptance as its leitmotif. And that acceptance is dialectical in the sense that I accept myself because I am accepted; and I am accepted even though I know that I am unacceptable. Some of the emotional impact of this we have already glimpsed in the works of, *inter alios*, Kernberg, Bion and Winnicott.[11]

In the face of the material that we have reviewed from writers in the Jungian and Freudian traditions, how can I achieve (not I, but Christ in me) that living relationship? We have seen how caught I am, at the deepest part of myself, by anxieties, phantasies, fears, hatreds, guilt and envy. And we have seen how these deep (and sometimes deeply buried) emotions and the memories that hold them help me construct the world in, as it were, my own image, in a double sense. First, they make me *interpret* the world in their own light. And second, they make me structure the world to defend myself from those anxieties or to respond to the drives released by my fears or my guilt or my craving needs. What possible sense can we make of the Christian claim that we can be freed from those realities as we enter the living, loving relationship in our everyday lives with the three Persons of the Trinity? Are not these two areas of discourse, two ways of seeing the world, two, if you will, ideologies finally wholly incompatible? Are we condemned, if we believe the psychoanalytic literature, to live in that world, with the modest Kleinian hope of occasional forays into the depressive position; or, if we believe in the Christian view, to ignore the findings of depth psychology except when the unconscious unaccountably reasserts itself and leads us to experience all too painfully the reality of the Pauline 'body of death'?

I want to argue that the concept of memory that we emphasised so strongly in the preceding chapters is one (not necessarily the only one) theme that enables us to link these two worlds and give a coherent account of the process of appropriation that does justice both to the criteria I established – emancipatory power and existential impact – and to the concerns of orthodox theology to which we shall return below. By seeing the memory of the life, death and resurrection of Jesus as the source of healing counter-memories that can liberate us from the destructive power of our own unhealed memories, we can hold Jesus's Incarnation and Mediation together: we can see both as providing the raw materials for the inner and outer emancipation we crave: and we can set both in the context of the exploration of a Spirit-led, deepening relationship of acceptance in the love of God.

Although there are methodological difficulties to be faced in subsequent chapters about the nature of the memories we have of Jesus, let me spell out a little more fully what I mean by the story or, in Pannenberg's phrase, the destiny of Jesus giving us a set of liberating counter-memories. My treatment is set in the context of the way we make ourselves and the world: by story-telling, by the construction of narratives about ourselves and our environment, about our structures and institutions. Those narratives are based on remembered (or half-remembered or misremembered) interactions with others, and it is the layers of these remembered interactions that determine who we are, how we react, how our institutions actually function. I want to argue that we need to 'have in mind' not only the memories of our own interaction with the world around us, but also the memories of the story of Jesus – and by extension the whole of salvation history. This interaction between our story and the story of salvation, focused on the destiny of Jesus, plays the role that social constructionists ascribe to the discourse between the therapist and the client. This is a non-directive, all-accepting provision and sustenance of 'a discursive space' in which the client (or reader, in our case) can reconstruct a series of narratives about him or herself in the light of the conversation with the text (or therapist). We shall have more to say about this process in the last chapter; for the moment, the central point is that it is the interaction between the whole of the story of the destiny of Jesus and the believer-in-community that makes possible the refashioning I sketch out below.[12]

It is the way in which these two types of memory – the stored memory of Jesus and the conscious and unconscious memory of the individual and community – interact that is redemptive. I want to distinguish between three effects: relativising or truth-testing; containment; and explanation.

By the first I mean that, seen against the destiny of Jesus, the destructive power of our own memories is sapped, or as the Fourth Gospel would put it, judged. As we bring those memories to consciousness, whether they be of fact or of phantasy, they stand against the counter-memory of the man Jesus, so identified with the loving forgiveness of God that it made sense to call him the Son of God, freely giving himself up to the death-lust of a squalid coalition of Church and State. Staubian memories of 'better times', Lerneresque memories of failure and self-blame, Laschian memories of inadequate attachment to a primary carer, Kleinian memories of potential disintegration – all these are relativised and rendered less harmful by the remembered story of Jesus. They are robbed of illusory grandeur, of synthetic significance. That is not to deny the truth of them. But it is to refuse to take memory improperly seriously, to allow it to become the mainspring of my decisions, my actions, my relationships. In a word, it is to snatch back from those memories the power of determinacy and to reinvest it where it belongs: in the story of Jesus. When I have internalised that story through the traditional disciplines of prayer and meditation, the memory and even the pseudo-memory has to be seen *in relation to* the ultimate memory of Jesus's life and death. Whether the memory concerned be of an emotionally starved childhood or oppressive employers; or, at a group level, of wrongs done to my ingroup by an exploitative outgroup – such memories do not lose their reality, but they do lose their determinative power to rule my life. The grandeur and majesty, or, again to use Johannine language, the glory of the story of Jesus is such that it reduces the memories of injustice, hurts and inner traumas, even those of Kleinian dimensions, to the emotional power of school playground wrangling.

Transformation, then, takes place first as the believer allows the counter-memories of Jesus to become his or hers at a level of intensity that is at least as immediate as the memories of his or her own past. And that is a gift of the Spirit. The memories present themselves in a way that Walter Benjamin experienced as a shock, akin to an intense aesthetic moment, and their effects, perhaps surprisingly, are very close to what Foucault, commenting on Nietzsche, calls the 'dissociative' role of memories of the past, 'directed against identity'. 'The purpose of history', he writes, ' . . . is not to discover the roots of our identity but to commit itself to its dissipation. It does not seek to define our unique threshold of emergence, the homeland to which metaphysicians promise a return; it seeks to make visible all of those discontinuities that cross us.'[13] The discontinuity that crosses us is precisely that most radical discontinuity of all: the life and death and rising again of this man Jesus. It is the encounter with that which dissipates the well-rooted internal narratives that makes us create the world as we do and therefore react to it as we do. No wonder Foucault sees a second 'use of history' as sacrificial. For it 'sides . . . against the effective illusions by which humanity protects itself. . . . It breaks down illusory defences.'[14]

As I hinted above, much the same account can be given of the group. In so far as the group is driven by the collective memory of the past and its hurts, it can be freed from the compulsion to act them out in its social life to the extent that it has, as a group, internalised the dissociative and anti-illusory counter-memories of the destiny of Jesus. Some people would say that they saw exactly that happening in the last years of the apartheid regime in South Africa, especially among some black groups; others would make the same quality of claim for the Base Communities in Brazil and else-where; and others again for congregations and groups caught up in the protest against white racism in the USA. I would point to the way some feminist groups, especially those concerned with the ordination of women to the priesthood, have almost consciously followed this process: that is, set their own hurt and anger and sense of betrayal in the wider context of the deeply meditated Passion and Resurrection of Jesus, a history that challenges, disturbs and throws into the air all our self-narratives and world-creations. Many liturgies have appeared from such groups that express that thought in the context of worship. The contrast between the spirit of the protest of women denied ordination on the one hand and, let us say, the average strike on the other may be its own testimony to what is going on.

The second way in which the counter-memory of the destiny of Jesus transforms us experientially is through the process of contain-ment. As we saw in Chapter 5, there are two aspects of containment: the acceptance by the mother of the projections of the phantasy of the infant and the feeding back of those projections in a modified form to allow the infant to reintroject them in a non-damaging way. When the destiny of Jesus is properly internalised, Jesus becomes a container for the individual and the group in the sense that either can project their negative emotions on to him and repossess them in a way they can handle, mediated through the memory of loving acceptance and forgiveness that lies at the heart of his destiny. This is not the place for a long digression on the psychology of Mariology, but it is striking that many Roman Catholics, especially those of a relatively unsophisticated educational background, use the Virgin Mary very much as a surrogate mother to whom they can report their feelings and reactions, secure in the knowledge that they will not be harshly judged. What they may be doing in fantasy in their relations with the Virgin is available to all Christians in the counter-memories of Jesus. Because we remember him as the embodiment of loving accept-ance and constant self-giving, the power of our uncontained emotion-ality is transformed by being projected on to and received back from him – in a form and 'shape' that allows us to be free from the compulsions and drivenesses of the original emotions.

In this sense we are given a new identity, or a new set of possible identities. Our past becomes 'unreal' because we now have the possibility of a range of identities that relate to that past in quite different ways. There is, as we shall see again later, a ludic quality of this 'buffoonery of history', a playing with memory that releases us from the grip of any *one* memory-set.[15]

For example, consider the psycho-dynamics of the black in Kovel's account, and the emotionality associated with that. It has two features – first, a deep hatred of the white man who possesses his mother, wife or sister and simultaneously infantilises him, the imaginatively castrated rival: and, second, a readiness to play the part of the 'boy' thus assigned to him. Slave religion certainly kept alive the hope of emancipation in the conventional sense of the ending of slavery. But at its best it also contributed to the dignity and costliness with which Southern blacks slowly asserted their demand not just for legal emancipation but for respect as people.[16] The speeches of Martin Luther King are (for the most part) the speeches of a man whose primitive emotions of fear, hatred and anger have been contained by Jesus Christ – and who is now free to play with different self-narratives. King did not remain *just* the victim of the system. He became its critic, certainly: but also its prophet of redemption, its foreteller and foretaster of a new heaven and a new earth. The contrast with Malcolm X, for example, could hardly be more striking.

Of course, there is a sense in which the process I have just described may be thought of as one form of prayer, a form especially familiar to those who practise Ignatian contemplation with its carefully staged 'conversations with Jesus'. We should not be surprised or dismayed to find this cross-over between a theory of the Atonement that lays primary stress on transformation and experience on the one hand and prayer on the other, for it is in prayer that the processes of transformation are most readily advanced, especially in prayer associated with the nodal events of Jesus's destiny. As we shall see, the memories of the Last Supper and the Resurrection, both re-presented in the Eucharist, give praying in the context of those re-presentations special significance – a fact well recognised, albeit for somewhat different reasons, in the disciplines of the Orthodox Church.

The third sense in which the counter-memory of Jesus sets us free from the compulsions of our own memories is an extension of the first two – relativisation and containment. Taken together, the effect of these is to enable me to take responsibility for what is genuinely my affair. The history of Jesus makes me see myself in a more honest light. It thus represents a 'decisive cutting of the roots' of my original self-understanding.[17] No longer obsessed by my own hurts and disappointments, no longer overwhelmed by my emotional responses to them or their afterglow, I can withdraw my projections; recognise phantasy and fantasy for what they are; try to stop splitting the world into goodies and baddies, and become sufficiently mature (or transformed) as a person to accept my role in undermining relationships, spreading untruths, disseminating hatred and preparing the way for violence. I can then set about, deeply conscious of my need for the help and succour of the Holy Spirit in the process, putting such matters right as lie within my power or influence.

Classically, this is the process of repentance, of metanoia. Too frequently it has become strangely detached from the theory of the Atonement, yet it is the power of the destiny of Jesus to move people to repentance that is at the heart of both Western atonement theory and of Eastern theories of theosis. For how can I realise the divine within me if I do not continually repent of the evil that I have done and the evil that I continue to do?

Such repentance is, however, only possible – psychologically and spiritually – when one is sustained by the heart-knowledge of a God who forgives and accepts even the worst that humanity can do, a theme properly incorporated into Girard's account of the Cross. Within the Gospels themselves, the story of the prodigal is fundamental; and the destiny of Jesus and especially the Resurrection is the proof of its parabolic core. The experience of transformation through repentance is thus set within, again, the context of the counter-memories of that destiny.

These three elements of a theory of the Atonement that is based on the experience of transformation interact to modify the way I perceive the memories of my past – and the collective memories of my group's past. As we allow the counter-memories of Jesus to modify our emotional responses to, and thereby even the content of, our memories, so we become more open to the future and the promise of the new life that Christ holds out. The future and the past thus begin to interact dialectically. The future that is in the making drives us deeper into the destiny of Jesus,[18] and that deeper commitment to the memory of Jesus reshapes the past as we remember it: perhaps even as we are remembered by it. As the past is reshaped the future becomes more open, for we are no longer held captive by the temptation to act out our individual and corporate memories. We are free – not with licence to do as we like, but with the memory of Jesus to show us the shape of the future.

I hope this account is sufficiently distinctive to deliver me from the charge of offering a rerun of an exemplarist theory of the Atonement.[19] While I acknowledge an area of overlap and common concern, it should be clear that my approach does not simply hold Jesus up as an example to be followed. Its primary emphasis is not on Jesus as example, but on Jesus's story as a set of memories that judge my memories and liberate me from their power. In this sense, Jesus is an active principle whose story has a psychological power far greater if more subtle than that of a model who invites emulation.

I hope I have shown how, using the traditions of Part 2, it might be possible to construct a theory of the Atonement using the transformational/experiential paradigm outlined above. But what, if anything, can we say about the more traditional Western forensic/ontological paradigm? Is there any sense in which that tradition can be reshaped to be recognisably continuous but also sensitive to the processes that we have outlined? I have chosen to approach this question with the help of one of the foremost recent scholars in the field, Professor Colin Gunton, whose work on three of the central images in this tradition has won wide acclaim and whose resolute defence of Western orthodoxy cannot be impugned.

His special attraction to my endeavour is that he is well aware of the need to see the models he examines metaphorically, that is, as attempts to take the reader by surprise and reveal to him or her difficult truths that would sound either fanciful or banal if spelled out in cold prose. One useful by-product of this approach is that he needs to be less biblicist than some other Western scholars of the Atonement. That is not to suggest that he sits lightly to the biblical tradition: far from it. But, as will become apparent later, it is helpful to us to have as a guide a writer who works with the grain of the text rather than examining each mote of sawdust through a microscope. I shall

follow Gunton's order of discussion of the metaphors for its expositional ease rather than its theo-logic.

He begins with an examination of Aulen's classic Christus Victor
account of the Atonement, wherein Christ's triumph over the powers
and principalities of this present age is seen as purging the cosmos
of the ultimate triumph of evil. The possibility and prospects of
humankind have thus been changed, though each individual is still
to work out their own salvation with fear and trembling. Gunton is
rightly emphatic that we are to see this language (and its associated
New Testament analogues of demons, Satan and even the law itself) as
metaphorical. 'The texts present us not with superhuman hypostases
trotting about the world, but with *the metaphorical characterisation of
moral and cosmic realities which would otherwise defy expression.*'[20] The
question is then raised of how we, in our generation, speak of the
reality to which the biblical language is pointing. Gunton seeks to
find a way between the naïvely biblicist and the reductionist, pointing
out, for example, that we do indeed speak of people being 'demonic'
or of being possessed. Although evidently nervous of the psychological literature – and apparently though oddly regarding it as intrinsically
reductionist because 'empirical'[21] – Gunton quotes Rollo May who
defines what he calls the daemonic as 'any natural function which
has the power to take over the whole person'.[22] We are clearly very
near familiar territory. May's definition is easily extended to Jung's
aphorism about our illusion that we have feelings, while in reality
feelings have us. We are no less close to the notion of compulsive
acting out of those feelings and the memories associated with them.
Thus Gunton: 'The language of the demonic . . . is language which
enables us to to bring to expression the fact of the subjection of
human moral agents to forces they are unable to control,'[23] and he
goes on, helpfully, to point out that those human agents may not be
only individuals but may be groups (a word he in fact does not use:
he seems not to have read Bion) or societies. Zimbardo and the
Stanford prison experiment re-emerge.

Like Aulen, Gunton wants to relate the destiny of Jesus – and it
is significant for his approach that the focus of the Atonement is
broadened to the whole of Jesus's story and not just the Cross – to
the process of confronting the demonic as he has defined it. The
temptation narratives, which Gunton appears to take at their face

value as historical reportage, are thus key, for they show Jesus having to decide on how he will use power: will he use it in the service of evil or in the service of God? In much the same way, the Fourth Gospel's account of the trial is set up narratively as a confrontation with the demonic use of power. In both these narratives, 'we can *see* the conquest of the demonic happening through the decision for obedience'.[24]

While much the same point could be made with respect to the healing stories in the Gospels, some of which are explicitly expressed as encounters with the demons, this clash between the forces of moral compassion in the person of Jesus and chaotic destructiveness of the demonic in the persons of those who wish him ill comes to a head in the Passion and Crucifixion. There Jesus confronts, in absolute terms, the forces of evil and refuses to meet evil with evil. His death is at once active – for he answers the power of hatred with the power of love – and passive – for he does so by absorbing the power of hatred in the tissue of his own body.[25]

The difficulty with this account, of course, is that it leaves Gunton with all the familiar problems of an ontological account of the Atonement. 'If the Cross of Jesus is so decisive in determining the direction of the world, why is this not so more palpably?'[26] Gunton wants to argue that the role of metaphor is precisely to cut between the now and the not yet so familiar in eschatological theory. That may say something about literary style and revelation; it says precious little about the Atonement – except that, on this account, the destiny of Jesus seems to have made little difference to the way most of creation suffers, grieves and dies.

My interest in this approach is not so much to dissent from Gunton as to see how far a memory-based understanding of the Atonement can be reconciled with his more orthodox statement. With that there appears to be not too much difficulty. Jesus is precisely the one who is remembered as having outfaced the powers of darkness by the courage and faithfulness of living – and ultimately dying – by love and forgiveness. His story reveals what is divine; what divine life looks like in action; and thereby gives us not just an example (that is too jejune) but a glimpse into the nature of the Godhead. His saving power stems from his revelation, from his priestly role (see below) of holding out the gift and grace of the kind of God revealed in his life and death and resurrection. Ontologically, such a revelation ensures that the powers of darkness, the demons, have no final victory, even though they have many temporary victories all around us. This account answers Albert Nolan's question by asserting that the news is good because God has won, is winning and will finally win the upper hand in the struggle with all that leads us compulsively to violence and to estrangement from each other and from God. The more closely we identify with the counter-memories of Jesus, the more surely we will, by the power of the Spirit, come to play our part in that victory.

I want to leave the Christus Victor theme now and move to another set of theories which are more rigorously forensic and onto-logical with the same end in view – to see if a memory-based theory of the Atonement can be reconciled with the insights that have come to be associated with such a set. The central theme of this set of theories is the justice of God. It has long been recognised that all the Semitic religions (and for that matter much Greek philosophy) are concerned with the idea of a moral universe. That is to say, they are, sometimes unconsciously, motivated by a dread of anarchy and moral collapse that is not a million miles from Kleinian phantasy. One form of defence against this anxiety is to see God as the upholder of the moral universe, the ultimate authority who guarantees that anarchy will be held at bay.

In Christian theology, one way in which that has been done is to see God the Father as the equivalent of a medieval lord, one of whose obligations to his serfs is to keep law and order by punishing wrongdoers. It was this line of thinking that led Anselm to develop his now often misunderstood and much derided theory of satisfaction, in which the Son accepts punishment on behalf of humanity and thereby protects the moral order on which humanity depends for the quality of life that God intends. 'What', asks Anselm in a quotation much appreciated by Balthasar, 'could be more merciful than when the Father says to the sinner who has no means to redeem himself: Take my only begotten Son and offer him for you, and when the Son says: Take me and redeem yourself?'[27]

Like Balthasar, Gunton is aware of the limitations of Anselm's approach but is anxious to ensure that we understand what Anselm is doing: he is taking one metaphor and milking it as hard as he can in a way that will be more or less comprehensible in his own culture. Luther does much the same with the notion of justification, a process logically dependent upon the justice or righteousness of God and the fallenness of the sinner. If in the process of pursuing the metaphor of justification Luther loses sight of the cosmic agenda rightly inherent in the doctrine of the Atonement – so that Protestant understandings of righteousness have historically become overindividualised and mor-ally trivial with, among others, the results we encountered in the work of Staub – he is true to the best of the tradition in his awareness of the moral gulf between humanity and God.

This gulf is reinterpreted in a more socially responsible way by P.T. Forsyth whose work after the First World War is, after a period of relative neglect, again being read. Writing in the 1920s, he could not but be aware of the ease with which human society falls back into moral barbarism, the very antithesis of the justice of God (especially when that word is given a properly Hebrew width of interpretation rather than a narrowly jurisprudential one.) For him, then, atonement is not (or not only) a transaction between a justice-promoting God and humankind, but 'the renewal of the life of the creation'.[28] In other words, Forsyth operates out of a justice paradigm, so central to Western atonement thinking, and reinterprets it in a way that approaches what I have called the transformational/experiential. Thus Gunton summarises Forsyth:

> The Cross is at once 'the solution and the destruction of the world's moral anomalies' not because it harmonises [abstract] justice and mercy, but because as 'the creative focus of the moral world' it is 'the rightful and the real ruler of the course of history.' . . . It is God's way of so relating himself to human history that new relationships are made both possible and real.[29]

Gunton goes on to show how Barth takes this central concept further with a metaphor drawn from the courtroom wherein God leaves the judge's podium and takes his place in the dock. Humanity wants to act as judge, especially as censorious judge of neighbour and sibling, but the real judge shows the power of vulnerability by stepping into the dock and taking, in the person of the Son, the punishment that in reality belongs to judgemental (scapegoating?) humanity. 'That

Jesus dies for us does not mean . . . that we do not have to die, but that we have died in and with him, that as the people we were we have been done away with and destroyed.'[30]

Such a claim might be thought to raise empirical questions, but Barth would doubtless argue that what he is saying is entirely consistent with Pauline notions of being 'in Christ' as part of 'the new creation'. We need not interpret Barth experientially, when it is clear he wishes to be understood ontologically. The question is, however, how does our memory-based model relate to this set of theories?

The core idea of the preservation of the moral universe by an act of self-giving love that, as it were, steps beyond the bounds of the contemporary moral culture is not easily caught in a theory that puts primary emphasis on the destiny of Jesus. And yet there are in the story of that destiny sufficient resonances with that theme for it to be taken seriously. Some of these are congruent with the material we surveyed in the context of the Christus Victor theory, especially the healing and trial sequences where the confrontation of disintegration by the embodiment of wholeness is most marked. But there are other traces, too. Consider Legion, the archetype of disintegration, both personal and, if recent research on the political setting of the story turns out to be right, social. Here is a man whose chains, significantly, cannot hold, contain, him, so total is his falling apart. And the only place he is at home is in the graveyard, the symbol of death, decay and annihilation. He re-presents the ultimate challenge to the moral universe, the whole purpose of which is to maximise freedom by setting limits to licence and the anarchy it entails. His healing is a sacrament of the loving, risky salvation offered the whole of the cosmos when it seeks to turn from moral collapse to moral order.

Or take Zacchaeus, another archetype of moral disorder. Quisling, turncoat, traitor and extortioner, no less prepossessing a creature crosses Jesus's path during his ministry. His salvation lies in his discovery of himself as accepted as he is: his penitence comes only as a response to his acceptance. By offering it, then, Jesus, taking a huge risk, puts, as it were, the justice of God in Zacchaeus's hands. Zacchaeus repents and safeguards that justice. It could have gone the other way. Such is the riskiness of a way of reasserting the righteousness of God that respects the freedom of humanity to go on denying it.

Or, a last example, consider the foot-washing. The moral order of hierarchy and leadership is turned upside down and the new ethic of God's humility is proclaimed. Moral order is shown to be quite different from social ordering. The new order that is about to be initiated in the last supper together is to have at its heart an ethic that starts from vulnerability and powerlessness, a readiness to see life from the underside, the perspective of the slave.

If there are memories of Jesus that 'fit' neatly into a metaphor of justice as the leitmotif of the Atonement, it is the Crucifixion which has to be central, not least because it is the Cross which has been the focus of the family of atonement theories of this type. How well does that fit?

The counter-memory of the Cross is central to our approach less because it says something directly about the justice of God than because it makes human freedom and liberation possible by relativising, truth-testing and explaining our own memories that hold us captive. It is exactly the fact that Jesus the just was barbarically killed that gives the edge to his counter-memory – the edge which can scrape the self-indulgent fat and detritus off the hide of our own memories. Without the death of a perfectly just man, the embodiment of the loving justice and compassion of God, his counter-memory would engage with ours as ineffectively as the memory of Gandhi or Wilberforce. And the power of that death to take our memories and shake them by the scruff of their neck is both underwritten and enhanced by the remembered story of the Resurrection. We may or may not want to read that as the final vindication of the justice of God: but we shall certainly want to read it as a statement – metaphorical, symbolic even – about the absolute wrongfulness of Jesus's execution.

The third set of metaphors that Gunton highlights and which we must now subject to the same test are those around the notion of sacrifice. If one starts from the ontology of human sinfulness, then something is needed to bring new life to the dead and dying people, caught in the woeful consequences of their own sinfulness. An ancient religious way of dealing cultically with this perception was through the sacrifice of animals or even humans. Their blood symbolised the new life flowing towards the one in whose name the sacrifice was offered. Taking a cue from the Old Testament story of Abraham's sacrifice of Isaac – 'God will provide his own sacrifice' – New Testament writers and especially the author of the Epistle to the Hebrews see Jesus as both the lamb that is sacrificed (a theme more thoroughly worked out by St John the Divine) and the high priest who offers the sacrifice – of himself. With Girard, he is the willing scapegoat, offered by his own hand.

On this reading the institution of the Eucharist is a *type* of the perpetual sacrifice that Christ makes in the re-presentation of his offering of his body and blood as a source of new life for his people. The sacrifice is not some form of penal substitution, the propitiation of an angry God, but the vicarious suffering of the Son of God to change the ontological status of his people and give them the possibility of a new quality of life to be entered into in the present. For although the benefits of sacrifice may be eternal, the very fact of the re-presentation of the sacrifice 'as oft as we shall drink it' speaks of an expected benefit in the present. As Gunton points out, writers from Calvin to Irving have seen the work of the Holy Spirit in enabling the appropriation of the benefits of sacrifice as being inalienable from the work of the Cross,[31] for he is the agent of the new life that sacrifice promises.

That we have here a different set of metaphors is obvious enough. That they are sometimes combined – as, for example, in the image of the victorious lamb in Revelation or the sacrifice offered on behalf of a sinful people to a God of justice – merely complicates an already confused picture, bearing testimony as it does to the inadequacy of any one metaphor to catch the multifaceted majesty of the Atonement. The question we need to ask is how far does the counter-memory theory of the Atonement do justice to the inner truth inherent in the sacrifice metaphor?

I take two ideas to be paramount 'behind' the metaphor, both of which I have tried to bring out in my summary statement above. The first is the initiative of God. The force of the sacrifice metaphor is surely that God, in the person of the Son, provides both priest and victim to seal the new covenant between himself and humanity. Helpless to help itself, humanity can only respond to the graciousness of God who thus offers a way forward (back, if you will, to the moral universe we discussed above). The second fundamental idea is that the sacrifice is less about what it does to God (e.g., propitiation) than what it achieves for humanity, the possibility of a new quality of life.

If we concentrate on these two features of the sacrifice metaphor, we can see how they relate to our theory of a counter-memory base for the Atonement. For the source of the counter-memories is God's gracious offer of his Son in the Incarnation; and the Son's gracious living out of his destiny in loving obedience to the Father. It is no surprise that the early Fathers of the Church – Irenaeus, Clement of Alexandria, Origen, Athanasius and Gregory of Nyssa, to name but a few – embedded their understanding of the Atonement firmly in their appreciation of the Incarnation. Despite the difficulties that we shall come to in a later chapter, there is a hard facticity about the initiative of God as he enters human history in the person of Jesus and sees it to the end not just in the Cross, but in the proleptic end of the Resurrection. Or to put it another way, God gave us the counter-memories of the destiny of Jesus as a free gift, offered undeservedly and of his own volition.

And their effect is precisely to open to us a new quality of life. For it is the function of the counter-memories precisely to deliver us from the compulsions and reactions that flow from our individual and collective memories, and thereby enable us to enter a new life in which we can relate to each other and the rest of the cosmos in freedom and harmony. Perhaps more than either of the other two metaphors – victory and justice – this one leads directly into a religiously based apprehension of inner and outer liberation.

In conclusion, I have sought to show that a theory of the Atonement that places the memories of Jesus's destiny at its heart can do justice not only to transformational experiential models of the work of the Cross, but also more traditional Western, forensic models. It is, however, true that such a theory has little to say about ontology, except in a banal sense that the very fact of Jesus's incarnation changes the possibilities open to all humanity, and therefore has some ontological significance. It is equally true that this approach is necessarily confined to compulsive behaviour, acting out inner memory. It cannot, as traditional Western theory specialises in doing, take account of the ontological sinfulness of humanity. How serious a shortcoming that is will depend on the view that is taken of human nature freed from its load of hurtful memories. The more optimistic one is on that score, with, for example, Jung and Habermas and at times Klein, the stronger the claim of this approach to be considered along with other metaphors and representations.

That apart, it is generally true that the theory is stronger the more we move along the spectrum from the severe ontology of Tom Torrance towards a more experiential account that recognises what Gunton calls the cash value of the Atonement. I have tried to show that such a theory can operate with conventional theological categories, including, *pace* Hick, a full Nicene Christology and a proper recognition of the Trinitarian nature of redemption.

But what benefits does it offer? I suggest at least three. First, it enables a proper conversation between psychology and theology to take place around the central Christian claim that Christ has made us free. So long as psychology (to use that aggregative reification as a shorthand) is impressed by the unconscious springs of action, it is hard to see how conventional models of the Atonement can address that source of unfreedom – a fact that may go some way towards explaining the muted and sometimes inadequate, sometimes embarrassed response of too much theology to the kind of material reviewed in Part 2.

Second and double-barreledly, it enables a proper rapprochement between spirituality and action, especially liberative action in politics and relationships. Too often those concerned with spirituality are seen as – and sometimes see themselves, however reluctantly, as – practising a kind of up-market pietism which implies, even if it does not advocate, a withdrawal from the real world where people suffer, laugh, procreate and die. Simultaneously, those who are involved in such a world and seek to bring about a new commitment to justice, peace and non-violence find themselves without the inner resources that would enable them to endure the pressures, disappointments and projections with which they work on a daily basis. They may well ask what news is there that is good. I hope to convince the former, those who take spirituality seriously, that the memories of Jesus are the stuff of their engagement in the real world; and I wish to convince the latter that it is only to the extent that they can internalise those memories – they and their groups, both – that they will be delivered from the processes that subvert their work and be freed to work for a world transformed. Further, I want to suggest that that very process of transformation is to be found at the same source – the internalisation of the counter-memories of Jesus as an antidote to the poisonous memories that hold our world in thrall.

Third, I make no apology for shifting the balance from ontology more towards experience. In a sense that is implied in the last paragraph, but it bears separate statement. Metz has rightly complained of the abstraction and other-wordliness of atonement orthodoxy, especially those based on an understanding of Jesus's nature that places emphasis on his 'self-emptying'.[32] I fear the issue is not simply abstraction. Perhaps it is part of the pathology of our age that we have lost interest in ontology and expect, like Habermas, theory to have applications with some practical effect. Maybe. But so long as the Church continues to speak ontologically – especially when an implication of such language is a belief in a literal heavenly hereafter (where 'the real Tom Torrance will be revealed') – so long will her message be ignored as incomprehensible or absurd. To say so much is not to make doctrine the plaything of fashion, but it is to recognise that theology, as any other discipline, feeds on its cultural milieu (as any potted history of the doctrine of the Atonement makes abundantly clear[33]). If Gelpi is right in detecting a 'shift to experience' in theological method, a realignment of atonement theory in this direction may not be out of place.

If the enterprise is worth undertaking, however, we have to recognise a major problem, one much underplayed by Gunton. If the memory of Jesus's destiny is so critical, what can we say about those memories, especially in view of our earlier findings of the unreliability of memory? Perhaps, indeed, we do not have any *real* memories of Jesus at all: merely an ideologically loaded collection of stories, a social history put in place by the Early Church. It is to that issue that we turn in the next chapters.

11

The Church and Memory

Having glimpsed the role memory plays in the way we shape the world and the way we *might* shape the world if we lived in the hope and expectation of realising the divine transformation that the destiny of Jesus holds out, I shall argue in the last chapter that the proper appropriation of the memory of that destiny is the way of salvation. The appropriation of the memories of the destiny of Jesus, however, implies the availability of memories to appropriate. Those memories, then, have to be stored, sifted, re-presented, re-membered. That is almost certainly a collective activity, since it implies a tradition, a handing-on, from one generation to the next. I therefore start this chapter with a consideration of the Church as a storehouse of memories. That will lead me to look at other features of the Church which might enable it to be more than a storehouse: a community of salvation that enables and en-courages people to so appropriate the memories of Jesus's destiny that they are delivered from the effects of their own negative memories and so enter their own freedom. We shall then have to ask about the extent to which this enables groups, institutions and structures both within and outside the Church to move in the direction of freedom.

Descriptive or Normative?

We need first of all, however, to face a fact that many theologians writing about the nature of the Church too easily deny or ignore.[1] Most of us most of the time experience the Church in all her weakness, sinfulness, cowardice and triviality. We are constantly struck by the feebleness of the leadership, by the incoherence of teaching, by the perversity of priorities, and by the tendency that seems endemic to say one thing and do another. Perhaps especially, if one is inclined to give prominence to the issues of peace and justice and ecology and mutuality, one can hardly fail to be struck by the inconsistency of a Church that has some of the finest writings on these themes in the whole of literature but which simultaneously seems to collude with their opposites: violence, oppression, domination and ecological rape. Perhaps, however, hardest to bear of all is the way in which the Church – in its leadership structures and in its participative fora – constantly seems more ready to give time, space and thought to second-order issues, perhaps as a way of escape from having to confront seriously all the pain and anguish and ambiguity of first-order issues. Like many groups, the Church prefers displacement activities to its real task. As Hans Kung has put it: 'Just as the Church can be an object of admiration to one, so it can be an object of scandal or at least disappointed, irritated, sad or bitter criticism to another.'[2] Appeals for *faith* in the Church as Church almost inevitably ring hollow for the latter group. They cannot operate as though the demand for faith 'could', in the words of Pannenberg, 'replace the existing social life-world without further ado'.[3]

Seen from an object-relations perspective, that might lead us to ask whether the Church can emerge from the position where it is object-relating (i.e., comforting itself with its own theology) to object-using (i.e., allowing its theology to determine its reality testing and its reality of engagement). As Hoggett has put it in a slightly different context: 'Are its myths to be used as a material of production, as an aspect of the group's productive forces? In other words, can they be used for work or only for consolation?'[4] As far as I am aware the history of the Church has never been written from this perspective: that is, testing the history against the two polarities of work and consolation. Various radical groups from the Anabaptists to the Diggers to the Base Communities in Latin America and elsewhere today have sought to use the theology of the Church for work. It is no less easy to find extreme examples of the theology of the Church being used for consolation. In the 1950s, when the Russian Orthodox Church was a puppet of the State and the Greek Orthodox Church was conniving with the Colonels in one of the harshest repressions seen in Europe since the war, the Orthodox theologian Trempelas could claim that the Church *was* the Kingdom of God on earth.[5]

The difficulty about this is its delusional quality, a quality that causes one to ask what psychic purposes such theo-ideo-logy is being made to serve. As in nearly all delusions, there may be an escapist tendency. The pain inherent in the contrast between the world as it is and the world as it is meant to be – and seen from the perspective of the Resurrection, potentially *is* – is too great. And so we have the oddity of such phrases as the Bride of Christ and the Body of Christ, suggestive perhaps of truths about an idealised Church, sounding faintly absurd when applied to this Diocesan Synod refusing to protest at government cuts in inner-city education or that Assembly nodding through a vacuous motion on the arms trade after four minutes' exchange of platitudes.

If we take Bion's group pessimism seriously it becomes likely that the Church-as-institution will be even more locked into a paranoid-schizoid position than the individuals that compose it. *Simul peccator, simul justus.* At once both sinner and saved. Or, to quote another Latin tag that has its origins in the Reformation but which was given a significant rerun in Vatican II, *ecclesia sancta, sed semper purificanda.*[6] As we experience ourselves to be so much less than what we occasionally glimpse as our true vocation (a duality nicely caught by the Kleinian splitting and shift between positions), so we find the primary group to which we belong as Christians marked and marred by the same ambi-valence.[7] As Winnicott observed, '*shared* playing' is a more difficult and more developmentally mature process than individual playing.[8] If a readiness to 'play' with ideas is an essential requisite of creativity (and, as I shall argue in the last chapter, of salvation), then, we should not expect the Church to find that collaborative search for truth in love either easy or conflict-free.

Seen in this light, it is hardly surprising that we should be more aware existentially of the *peccator* than we are of the *justus*. I shall want to return to the former perspective later; for the moment I want to tease out some of the implications of what we have explored so far in this book for the latter – the Church as the company of the on-the-way-to-being-saved.

220

Community of Memory

Unsurprisingly, I start with the Church as a community of memory. I want to highlight four senses of that phrase. First, and most obviously, the Church is, as it were, the ark (Irenaeus uses the image of vessel[9]) in which the memory of God's dealing with his people is stored. That includes the Bible, but it also includes post-biblical history, from the great councils to the major movements of the Spirit from the Reformation to, say, the emergence of liberation theology at the Medellin conference to the charismatic renewal of Western Christendom. Some of this memory is canonical; much is written; some of it is oral or informal.[10] All but the canonical is open to revision and rewriting and even the canonical is, of course, constantly being reinterpreted.

This function of the Church as the ark of memory requires that the Church (or significant representatives of her) are, as it were, conscious of the memory. They tell the story. They hear the story told. There is an interchange between those who know the memory and those who value it but know it imperfectly. The reading of the Scriptures in Church is an obvious example of this process, but it is by no means the only one. The writing of the historians and the theologians; the recounting of the personal witnesses to current significant events in the life of the Church from both 'inside' and 'outside'; even televisual reportage of the experience of different parts of the Church – all these are instances of the story being told, of the ark being refurbished and/or replenished. 'Contained in my faith life today is the drama of Israel, the fruit of costly discussions at Nicaea and Chalcedon, what Francis of Assisi brought to fruition concerning the secrets of apostolic poverty, what thousands of unknown believers have testified as to the hope in their answers to their persecutors.'[11]

That raises the second sense of the Church as community of the memory. The memory is not just a cognitive process, highly intellectualised. It is acted memory, re-membering, re-presentation. This is most obviously the case with the sacraments, but it is also incarnated in buildings, ornaments, art, songs, movement and dance, vestment and attire. The Church is a theatre of memory, with its scripts, its scenery, its proscenium and its music. The fact that the production is often lacklustre or half-hearted or unimaginative is hardly relevant to the point. In potential, the life of the Church (and not only in its liturgy; also in its 'good works' and its prophetic witness) is an enactment of the memory of its foundational stories – and of at least parts of its subsequent history. To take one example of the latter; the Church in El Salvador still remembers through special liturgies, processions and retelling of the story the murder of Archbishop Oscar Romero in March 1980. The re-presentation of his martyrdom is also a re-membering of the history of martyrdom, not only in El Salvador but throughout the life of the worldwide Church. Similarly, when the Church in the United States (and perhaps particularly the black Churches) celebrate the anniversary of the death of Martin Luther King at Memphis, that re-presentation of his death is an enactment of the whole history of the Churches' multivalent involvement in racism in the Southern States. And behind each of those memories, of the matyrdom of Romero and the slaying of King, lurks the memory of Creation, Exodus, Captivity and Cross. For the memory of the Church is not – or should not be – finally about its own life, but only about what can be gleaned from its own life about the goodness and graciousness of the God it proclaims.[12]

More difficult to isolate and describe are the archetypal memories of the Church, that is to say, the symbols that resonate at a more profound level than the cognitive or the doctrinal; that have, so to say, their own validity that transcends the formulations of theological orthodoxy. Some of these memories may be triggered by actual physical symbols – fire, water, wine, incense, white attire, the Virgin (note) Mary – but others depend on quite sophisticated and even abstract ideas that may be represented visually but which have a substance beyond that representation. The wounded healer, the sacrificial lamb, the scapegoat, apocalyptic symbols of glory and transcendence, the wayward son, Mother Church, are six significantly different examples spanning obviously Jungian archetypes such as Mother and Healer to more Freudian ideas of super-ego and id. This is not the place to enter the debate about whether the Western Church has lost touch with its religious symbols and their archetypal power (as Jung and Berger and some of their followers certainly argue[13]), though we may note in passing that the wider culture in which these symbols are set has become increasingly distanced from them as cognitive knowledge of the tradition as well as existential knowledge of worship have both decreased in the community at large in the wake of the rise of instrumental rationality. That implies that although the Church may be a community of memory in the sense we have so far analysed, those memories are becoming increasingly detached from the wider society. And it may well be the case that this is even more true at the symbolic level than it is at the cognitive.

There is a fourth, but perhaps slightly more derivative, sense in which the Church functions as a community of memory. None of the memory-types we have identified above – the tradition-based, the representational, the archetypal – function by themselves. Each has to be interpreted, at the very least in relating the memory to the actuality of the rememberers. At one level this is the task of Church professionals, whether pastors, theologians or bishops. At a less formal level, it is a process that goes on almost unconsciously in the community of believers as its members respond (or fail to respond) to particular interpretations of the community's remembering – what in medieval times was called the *receptio*. In this way the community tests the formal interpretations of the professionals and, in the long run and differentially between Churches with different understandings and structures of authority, re-forms the content of those interpretations.[14]

This hermeneutic dynamic between professionals and people is, of course, a complex and much-debated process. In the hands of people like Edward Schillebeeckx, it goes to the heart of a fundamental debate about the relationship of papal power to the intellectuals of the Church, and the authority of each of them as they relate to the 'ordinary' (so-called) people and their allegedly simple faith.[15] The same tension compels Hans Kung to draw a rueful contrast between a papacy (and hierarchy) that is 'genuinely evangelical' with the present one that is 'juridical-formalistic and static-bureaucratic' – and he might have added, in the spirit of Menzies, deeply anxious.[16]

I am less concerned here with the way in which that process works out and what it does to our notions of truth and orthodoxy than with the way in which the community's responses to the interpretations of the professionals are themselves governed. An approach couched only in cognitive or interest terms is likely to be partial and even simplistic or reductionist. In the main, people do not respond to religious ideas *only* in the light of their economic, political or social interests, though the power of those forces should not be under-estimated, especially given the experience of the Roman Catholic Church facing the ideology of national security in Latin America in the 1960s and 1970s, or the history of the Dutch Reformed Church in South Africa. Nor do they react to them only in terms of their learned deposit of faith, nor in the light of 'raw', unmediated experience.

While by no means dismissing these elements, however, we need to recognise that the community has its own hermeneutical filters, both as individuals and as a collective, and needs to preserve them against the authoritarianisms that would decide meaning irrespective of context. One element of these filters is its own pre- or unconscious memories. Here the material of Chapter 5 is illustrative. Without necessarily adopting the full Kovelian analysis, we can see that in the *ante bellum* Southern States, with the psychological climate of racism in the ascendant, the unconscious memory-processes at work within the community were such as to make it very hard for the community to hear a gospel that was wholly antithetical to racism of any kind. To put it more crudely than the reality probably justified, on the very few occasions when the magisterium of the Church remembered and represented a Christ-memory that declared the equality of all people irrespective of race or colour, that message was, almost inevitably, filtered out in the hearing of the community by, so a Kovelian approach would argue, its own unconscious memories of unresolved Oedipal material as well as by its economic and political interests, themselves part-formed by the same memories.

Mutatis mutandis, a community that is organised structurally and psychologically to defend itself against its own primitive anxieties, in the way we explored in Chapter 6, is unlikely to be able to 'hear' the interpretations of the Christian memories offered by the magisterium that 'touch' those anxieties. If, for example, those primitive anxieties are to do with death and disintegration and the community is organised to defend against the death-wish, then the memory of a Christ who says, 'Take up your cross and follow me' (implicitly to a violent death) is likely to be filtered out by the community – *even if* the magisterium seeks to proclaim that part of the tradition-memory. And that probability is much reduced by the fact that the 'magisters' of the Church are under the same kind of psychological conditioning as well as subject to the conscious and unconscious transactions between professionals and laity.

To take a final example, a narcissistic community in the Laschian sense (Chapter 7) has a very limited time-horizon. The present is all-important; the future less so; and the distant future wholly uninteresting. Given the memories, both conscious and unconscious, that have formed that attitude to time, a community is likely to filter out of the remembered tradition reference to the eschaton – though it may replace that with a popularised and pathological interest in apocalypse, a phenomenon that does indeed seem to characterise at least some elements of the society that Lasch is writing about.

If these features of the hermeneutic process of the community – authoritarianism, filtering, defence through splitting and projection, foreshortening of time-horizons – are commonly present in the Church, we need to ask about the positive elements that may make these destructive tendencies in the community of memory survivable. It is in a closely related context that theologians like Kung and Pannenberg have refocused on the mother–child relationship as a source of basic trust out of which the child is able to develop a moral autonomy. Drawing on work of post-Freudians such as Eicke, Fromm and Benda (but, interestingly, never so much as mentioning Klein), they argue that the freedom bestowed by the experience of basic trust between child and primary carer can be extended to infuse the quality of relationships within the community. Of this happening in the Church as we know it, Kung is fractionally more optimistic than Pannenberg, who is too well aware of the huge difficulties of *any* community acting in this mode to imagine that it will be the usual experience of Christian communities. That is why the experience of the life of Christ, the metanoiaic moment of resurrection as proleptic end, is for Pannenberg the touchstone of the life of the Church. The quality of its life is therefore a *religious* question: it is not something that can be achieved by sociological or psychological manipulation. To put it more concretely, the deep pessimism of the possibilities of the human spirit in matters ethical and political (as well as matters religious) that David Selbourne reaches in his study of our days in *The Spirit of the Age* may be a fair conclusion from the evidence of the past.[17] It is not, on Pannenberg's account of the transforming power of the memory of the Resurrection, a fair conclusion from the horizon of the future. Hope for the Church as a community of memory that feeds the symbols, imagination and responses of its members and the wider society is thus based on the very memories the Church protects and proclaims. The elements of circularity here will have to be further explored in the next chapter.

The idea of the Church as the community of memory is therefore a somewhat more complex notion than is often represented.[18] Traditional representations tend to think of the Church as a library with the clergy distributing set texts which the laity have to read and on which they will be examined. A closer analogy is that of a memory-bank, with the professionals as cashiers, issuing to customers material from the bank on demand. But even that analogy, which shifts much more responsibility, albeit covertly, to the 'customer', lacks the subtlety of the dynamic that plays between the community and the memory (with its official custodians, teachers and interpreters.) It is in that interplay (and the ludic quality should not be lost), with its unconscious and archetypal processes, that we can site the Holy Spirit at work in the life of her Church. It is in the way the Christian memories are chosen from the available stock; the manner in which they are remembered and modified in the remembering; the 'life' with which they become invested in the experience of the community; the way in which they challenge, adapt, 'play with' the memories, conscious and unconscious, of the community; the feedback loop that runs from the community to the magisterium to stimulate reformulation and reinterpretation of the memories – it is in all these processes that we can give an account of the work of the Holy Spirit breaking open the community of the Church to new possibilities and new understandings of the memories held (and held dear) by the community.[19] To say that is not, however, to deny the reality of the Church's refusal to be led by the Spirit. The Spirit enables: she does not compel.

It is in these senses, I suggest, that we can term the Church a community of memory. We need, however, to look a little more closely at the first term of that phrase – community – before we can expand our ecclesiological statement by the introduction of other phrases. What does it mean to say that the Church is a *community* of memory?

Community and Communication

There is an extensive literature on the meaning and experience of koinonia, and I have little need to add to it here since it relates only tangentially to the main thrust of this book. There is, however, one aspect that arises so directly out of our discussion on Habermas that it cannot be ignored. In that discussion, we encountered Habermas's claim that it is the ideal speech situation that enables the search for truth and righteousness (a word he foreswears) to proceed most constructively. We examined some of the difficulties associated with this claim but concluded that the absence of reciprocity in communication is indeed, as Habermas claimed, an important impediment to truth-seeking.

Now, it is easy to see how that discussion relates to our concern to conceptualise the Church as a community of memory. Schillebeeckx, whose concern at the breakdown of communication within the Roman Catholic Church I have already noted, speaks of the origins of religious authority: '[a] Heideggerian dialectic of being spoken to and paying heed, of attentive listening and reactive answering so that one can oneself speak meaningfully and with authority', but goes on to brand such a view as a half-truth because it leaves masked the ideological use of language and the way the dominant power structure of the Church can manipulate both ideology and language. Concretely, he speaks of 'tragic disruptions of communication between the teaching authority and theology' and of 'a kind of witch-hunt of theologians in the Church'.[20] This suggests that, on a far broader canvas than the clergy of the Roman Catholic Church, we need to ask three sets of questions. The first is about the way power is distributed between the different member-groups of the community (the bishops, the clergy, the laity); the second is about the role of ideology; and the third is about the way any of the parties to the dialogue can be free of internal constraints and compulsions if they are to enter the dialogue creatively.

The first set of questions is familiar enough – especially in a Roman Catholic Church that is having great difficulty reconciling authority and collegiality, and an Anglican Communion that is having great difficulty defining its theology of priesthood. In so far as any consensus is beginning to emerge from these debates, it is that authority has to be conceived dialogically; that is, authority is primarily about enabling discussion to take place and progress towards an agreement.[21] Seen from the perspective of Habermas's theory of communicative action, there is an element of inconsistency here: the outcome desired is a species of ideal speech, but it is to be approached in a structural situation which is marked by non-ideal inequalities of power. To take an extreme but hardly rare example, the silencing of theologians by the Vatican is not conducive to ideal speech. Much commoner, the way power is used in much of the Church (at all levels of its life) ensures that those who control money and jobs tend to dictate the terms of debate and the form of the 'consensus' that emerges. Such a situation is neither new nor unique to the Church, but the reality of the alienation that it generates should warn us about being too fanciful when we label the Church a community. It is a group in which distorted communication takes place between persons and groups with very different degrees of power over each other. To that extent, claims about the dialogical nature of authority in the Church have to be treated carefully, more as statements of intention (perhaps sincere, perhaps rhetorical) than of achieved fact.

Now, it might be argued that such an analysis is inappropriate to an entity that makes very bold theological claims about its nature, its very being. It might be claimed that whatever the sociological analysis of the Church, the Holy Spirit is able to ensure that the Church actually operates in ways that are consistent with her true nature. And to that extent, it might be claimed, sociological theory is simply irrelevant. That, as Pannenberg for one would be quick to remind us, is to miss the point. Just as God does not override the laws of nature in answer to prayer, so he does not override human psychology in the life of organisations. The Spirit is indeed at work in her Church (just as she is in the natural order), but she works by enabling people to reconceptualise authority; to find the humility to surrender power; to discover that collaboration is more satisfying as well as more efficient than domination; to find like-minded people who are prepared to move together from a hierarchical exercise of power to one that is more participative; to move, in Mary Grey's scheme, from Logos towards Sophia.[22] We may or may not respond to that enablement, any more than we may or may not respond to the truth of Habermas's insight that unequal power relationships make 'ideal speech' impossible. As members of the Church do move from unequal power relationships towards relationships which more closely approximate the rationality and truth-revealing power of ideal speech, the expectation surely is that the memories of the community will be brought more creatively into relationship with its current experience – and therefore with truth, or even Truth.

The same point can broadly be made with respect to ideology, the power of which to distort ideal speech was of special concern to Habermas. If the Church is a community of memory, she is especially open to the power of ideology at work in her being-community as well as in the way she interprets her memories. I shall deal only with the former here. It is often said that one of the glories of the Church is that she can transcend different backgrounds, colours, races, and degrees of worldly success in her community life. And it is of course true that, faced with the ultimates of the Christian gospel in word and sacrament, social differences may lose their power to divide and antagonise. One of the ways in which Christian reconciliation actually happens existentially is in the experience of worship which, at its best, trivialises distinctions between people that in other contexts seem overpowering.

At the same time, however, it has to be recognised that time and again the Church has been pulled apart – and made a living denial of the possibility of community in the process – by ideological fixations that are palpably *not* transcended in worship. From Arianism to the Reformation to Christian radicalism of many kinds to the World Council's Programme to Combat Racism to Church unity to the ordination of women to Northern Ireland, the record is not of the Church's capacity to unite people despite differences in ideology; it is of the Church's incapacity to transcend theologically the power of secular ideology. The Church too easily becomes the institutionalised mouthpiece of the civil religion of the bourgeoisie or of the more powerful (and usually conservative) elements of it.[23] Indeed, it is hard to read the history of theology without becoming aware of the power of secular ideology to form the intellectual climate in which theology is conceived. To emphasise that is not to disparage it, nor is it to hold out the quite romantic hope that theology could or should opt out of the intellectual debates of its day.[24] It is, however, to insist that the quality of the Church's life as a community of memory is constantly threatened by the Church's tendency to allow ideology to become an idol.[25] It is when ideology (whether secular or wrapped in theological clothing) is absolutised so that it, rather than encounter with God (so far as we are capable of that) or encounter with each other, becomes the touchstone of truth that community is compromised.

That throws into relief how vulnerable, insecure and uncertain is the quality of the Church's life as community (just as her memories are vulnerable, insecure and uncertain). It is constantly threatened by the siren offer of security held out by ideology. For ideology (no matter of what persuasion) offers answers, solutions, directions, ways of looking at the world without the constant reference back to the discovery of God. It can become both a gilded couch and a slippery slope for the spiritually lazy. Its powers of seduction are therefore nearly irresistible.

But there is more to it than that. The seductive powers of ideology are the more irresistible to the extent that the Church is acting as a defence against the inner and outer anxieties of her members. If the Church is indeed the (good) Mother; if she has become a part (or whole) object to which people and groups normally trapped in the paranoid-schizoid position look for containment, two things are likely to happen. The first is that 'ideal speech' becomes impossible, for the professionals play the emotion-masticating role of the container and *reciprocal* relationship is therefore not only impossible, but actually feared. And the second is that any change, either in the outer representations of the life of the institution or in its deeper 'message', is likely to be resisted with a passion bordering on the irrational, for the threat posed by such change is nearly unbearable. Indeed, for some people, those most dependent on the Church as a source of emotional security, it is literally intolerable. It is then almost inevitable that they will resort to projections, scapegoating and all the other defensive paraphernalia we reviewed in Part 2. The community of the saved becomes the community of the damned.

If that is true of ideology, it is *a fortiori* true of the third set of questions I posed above about the nature of community: that is to say, the degree to which any of us has the inner freedom that allows us to relate to each other in dialogue free of compulsions, anxieties, phantasies and fears that distort the nature of the relationship. We are back to the Habermasian analogue of the psychoanalytic relationship that allows the analysand to discover a truer freedom, shorn of inner material that makes 'real' relationship impossible.

Again notice that many theologies of the Church assume that life-in-the-Church (or for that matter life 'in Christ') automatically has that effect. At its most extreme, this point of view is put by charismatic quasi-fundamentalists who argue that 'life in the Spirit' is such that all inner processes of distortion are swept away by the experience of conversion and incorporation in the Church. It is not part of my argument either to set limits to what the Spirit can do, nor to deny the way in which lives are sometimes changed as a result of a conversion experience. What has, however, to be challenged is the assumption that conversion and/or Church membership is a sufficient condition for giving people freedom from the damage done to them by their past and its memories. As I shall argue in the next chapter, the counter-memories of the destiny of Jesus can bring the healing of our own memories, but that requires a long, hard haul of internalising those memories and appropriating them as our own. For most of us that takes a lifetime of prayer and meditation; and even then few indeed of us can ever be sure that all the influence of our repressed bad memories has been set aside.

In the meantime, we are likely to act out some of those inner processes in the community in which, if we are lucky, we feel most accepted and least threatened. In other words, the more successful the Church is at being community for us, the more likely it is to attract the working-out of inner material that we do not feel confident enough to 'dump' elsewhere. And the more powerful for us is the symbol-world of the Church, the more readily do we attach our inner world to the outer world of the Church. To choose two illustrations from different psychoanalytic paradigms, consider the psychology of Mariology for the person (perhaps especially the male) whose experience of good objects in childhood was inadequate. Mary can very readily become for him the good object he was denied in childhood – and that implies that he will resist strongly (perhaps even pathologically) any attempt by less Marian groups in the Church to reduce the significance of the Virgin in his religious life.

Or, to extend that illustration from a Freudian perspective, let us imagine that the same man has repressed his sexual desires and subli-mated them by excessive devotion to the Virgin. For him, she is the non-threatening Woman, pure, chaste, plaster, odourless and utterly asexual. Now suppose there appears in the church a woman priest or deacon (or, less powerfully, a member of the choir) who is a living woman – alive, eminently female in figure, demeanour and smell. Perhaps she is warm and tactile, with a penchant for hugging those in need of comfort. For the gentleman with the repressed sex drive, she becomes a terrifying threat, inviting him, as it were, to face whatever trauma is making him run away from his own sexuality. Almost by definition, he is unable to do that and so he is likely to take the only route open to him: hate the real woman with an intensity that wishes her total destruction and redouble the devotion to the modest Virgin. His hatred is unlikely to stay with or inside him alone. At both the conscious and unconscious levels – the spoken and the non-spoken but intuited – it will communicate to others and thus come to jeopardise whatever degree of harmony and mutuality the community has so far achieved.

In treating the Church as a community of memory, then, we need to remember the sub-text that many of the memories of the individuals who make up the Church are likely to find expression – consciously or unconsciously – in their reactions to the life of the Church. More specifically, we cannot deal with the notion of community without acknowledging that it is a community that will experience in its everyday life the acting out of many of its members in ways in which 'ideal speech' is rendered impossible. Moreover, that acting out has to be seen in the context of the other two points made above: that power is unequally distributed, and that ideologies become fixed as part of the Church's (mis)understanding of itself. The acting out of the inner processes becomes all too easily incorporated both in the power structure of the Church and in its ideology. But this process is never complete or undifferentiated. There are different inner processes being acted out by different people with different access to power and the formation of ideology. And that can only mean conflict and confusion. It will also, unfortunately, mean pain, distress and anxiety for those for whom the Church has become a significant symbol. The community of memory is, then, a deeply flawed community.

That, of course, is the lived experience of many people in the Church. *Simul peccator, simul justus.* The Church is not a conflict-free,

harmonious and healing community that is already what it is called
to become. Rather, it is the site of the struggle to become more than
we are already. Habermas himself recognised the impossibility of ideal
speech; and if we use that idea as in some sense a benchmark for the
quality of relationships within the Christian community, it is no
wonder that we find the Church constantly falling short. Habermas
likened it to health. We find it difficult to define perfect health; but
we all know when our state of health falls short of what we would
like it to be. We feel wretched. And if the Church sometimes feels
wretched to us (who do our part in undermining the quality of
relationships within her), then all we can do is look for something
better and pledge ourselves to move in that direction.

The Community of Memory and the Future

There is, however, a more subtle point that needs to be addressed. It
arose in an exchange between Walter Benjamin and Max Horkheimer
about the 'closedness' of the past. Benjamin was discussing the nature
of historical materialism, but the development of his plea that 'the past
is not closed' has resonances with Pannenberg's plea for the openness
of the future based on the proleptic nature of Christ's death and
resurrection. Horkheimer dismissed this as romantic idealism: 'Past
injustice has occurred and is closed. Those who were slain in it were
truly slain. . . . What happened to those human beings who have
perished does not have any part in the future.'[26] This becomes relevant
when we think of the Church as a community not only of the present
generations – local, national, global in their presence – but of the
Church as a community that transcends time; or to put it in a more
traditional language, when we acknowledge the communion of saints.
If the Church is an expression of universal solidarity and unlimited
communication, at least among those who identify with her, how
can present generations, who owe the tradition they have inherited
to the prophets and martyrs of history, live with the memory of what
it has cost to give them the faith and the truth that they have
inherited? 'Is it not', asks Peukert in a parallel discussion, 'the presup-
position of happiness that the unhappiness of those who went before
is simply forgotten?' But the Church as a community of memory
cannot 'simply forget'.[27] She can *celebrate* the memory of the Cross

because it prefigures the Resurrection; she cannot in the same way celebrate the immense load of suffering of her own martyrs and those whom she has killed, or in whose killing she has connived, from the activities of the conquistadors to the IRA and AWB, in order to, as she has represented it at the time, safeguard the gospel.

How to live with that, in a spirit that is consistent with the ideals of universal solidarity and communicative action? We are surely forced back to two positions: the sense of contrition that is so deep that it comprehends the totality of human failure; and the sense of release that comes from the vindication of the destiny of Jesus in the Resurrection. For the latter promises new life for all of us, the sin-laden Church with her cruel past and unloving present included.

In the light of this we need to define the Church not just as a community of memory, but as a contrite and forgiven community of memory that is seeking to live out her forgiveness. When once that contrition and release are lost, the Church becomes a mockery of herself – triumphalistic, romantic and absurd. She may still have all the structures, appurtenances and language of Church, but she has become cut off from two essential memories: the guilty memory of her own past and the memory of the Resurrection, her foundational event.

To add the epithets 'contrite and forgiven' is important, but it is in danger of shifting the perspective of the nature of the Church too firmly into the past, a danger already present with the emphasis on memory (despite the forward reference of the Hebrew ZKR and the Greek anamnesis). To correct that tendency, then, we need to add the eschatological hope in which the community of memory lives. She may, in much of her sin-laden life, deny that eschatological hope – by despair; by displacement activities; by projecting her own guilt on to others, perhaps even finding a scapegoat to carry that guilt (the Jews, Muslims, materialism, sexuality); by an easy collusion with the *status quo*; by a reluctance to suffer; by a pathological clinging to her own bad memories or symbols of containment that make such memories tolerable. Yet the *definition* of Church is that it is a community that does not just look forward, as children to a pantomime, but which commits itself to work with every sinew for such parts of that promised future that it can now glimpse.[28]

The way in which the Church's anamnestic solidarity with the whole creation is worked out, then, is precisely in living a political theology. Metz has labelled the memory of the Church as 'dangerous' to those who wish to preserve the oppressive *status quo*.[29] In so far as the Church repeats in her own times and culture the acted proclamation of Jesus that the Kingdom of God is here and is to be found in the loving acceptance of the marginalised, she will indeed be a danger to those who deny the possibility of the Kingdom or who are repelled or threatened by its ethic.

But we should not allow ourselves to be swept away by Utopian dreaming about the Church at this point, for there is a terrible tension between her calling to live eschatologically and her being community. To put it simply if crudely, most of us do not want to live eschatologically; and if that is the demand of the community, we find ways of limiting our commitment to and identification with this community of memory. Or, to put it in Metz's terms, if the memories are *that* dangerous, we are not too sure how much of the memory we want to have to bear. Again, there is here a deeper point that needs more careful exploration.

It can be put like this: in so far as the dangerous memories of the destiny of Jesus trigger unconscious memories of our own that make us less free, our response to the community (and, by aggregation, the response of the community) will be less free, less ready to live the freedom of the new life that is proclaimed in the Resurrection. To take a relatively simple example: it may be that our notion of father is dominated by images of harshness, punishment, demandingness and emotional coldness. That may come about as a result of memories of our actual father; or through the development, perhaps as a result of an Oedipal crisis, of an over-harsh super-ego (which may or may not relate to our childhood experiences of being fathered); or as a result of an unsatisfactory relationship with 'good objects'; and/or an inadequate sense of being contained by parents in general or by a male carer. Whatever the developmental origins of this imagery, we shall resonate much more with the demands of the righteousness of God the Father than with the promises of forgiveness, restoration, acceptance and unconditional love. And because we are all too conscious of our failures to deliver on the demands of righteousness (because we have, with such a super-ego, a well-developed sense of guilt), the 'demand', as it will inevitably present itself to us, that we 'live eschatologically' will feel like a demand to experience again, perhaps in heightened form, both the failure and the guilt before a righteous-Father-God.

In that sense, Metz's dangerous memory is more dangerous than he realises, for it can freeze us in an unhealed, unfree state, beyond, as it seems, the power of the Gospel to liberate us. There can be few experienced spiritual directors who have not encountered that condition and sought to help retreatants through it by a carefully chosen diet of prayer and meditation that addresses the central issue: the image of God that we have inherited from childhood and now project on to God. No wonder Ignatius of Loyola made that the central issue in the early days of his thirty-day retreats.

We cannot pursue that line of thought further here. What is important is the recognition that the defining calling of the Church, to live the Kingdom 'in memory of me', places huge stress, at the psychological as well as the social and political levels, on her equal calling, to be community. Empirically, that has been well documented in the recent history of the Church in Latin America, South Africa and Northern Ireland.[30] In each of those places, the attempt to live the kingdom of peace, justice and unconditionality, in which each may be heard in a respectful search for truth and right, has not been abandoned. But it has led to the desertion of those who attempt it by the majority of those who want to live a less troublesome community. The unity of the Church has proved impossible to attain. In most cases even symbolic dialogue has broken down, and even approximate approach to communicative action has had to be foregone.

Provisionality and Worship

So far I have defined the Church as a contrite and forgiven eschatological community of memory. I have made no attempt to relate this discussion either to biblical images of the Church or to orthodox ecclesiologies that use categories such as one, holy, catholic and apostolic. In doing so, I am in no sense denying the validity of either, providing they are seen as ideals, as normative rather than positive. As normative statements, they can exist alongside the definition I offer, operating as it were in another dimension. I want to conclude this discussion, however, by making one final point that serves as a point of tangency between orthodox ecclesiology and the discussion above. It has two parts. The first, which need detain us least, is that the Church is a provisional creature. Although some nineteenth-century Roman Catholic ecclesiologies tended to lose sight of this and represent the Church as the final consummation of all things, the incorporation of the eschaton,[31] most authorities see the Church as destined to give way to a new creation in which the fullness of God is more properly expressed. It is worth remarking on this, as it tends to put into truer perspective the needs of those who project on to the Church their own need for security and permanence, those who see the Church as Ultimate Container. There are senses in which that is both true and false. It is true in the sense that the Church as a community of memory can offer the memory of unconditional love that will never let go. It is false in the sense that the institutional Church is no 'abiding city. For we seek one that is to come.'

And that takes me to the second point. The community of memory does not, then, exist as it were for its own benefit, but for the worship of God. And it is in that worship, with its memory-centred processes of reading the Scriptures, celebrating the sacraments and praising God for what he has shown himself to be and for what he has done in individual and collective histories, that the atoning work of Christ is appropriated. There is thus a symmetry between what the Church is – a contrite and forgiven community of memory that worships God while it awaits, and works in preparation for, the eschaton – and the re-presentation or real-isation of the destiny of Christ. The more the Church is herself, the more the Christian is exposed to the healing memories of the destiny of Christ. The more the community is enabled to 'remember this', the more the work of Christ is appropriated – and the more the Church can then become an agent of the Kingdom of God. She will still be 'very scruffy', but she can also become 'very glorious'.[32]

The Community of Memory and the Collective Memory

The Church's primary task is to worship God. In the process, she will be nourished by the memories of the history, the gospel of God. But the Church is also, as William Temple famously insisted, 'for others'. That, as we have already seen, is implicit in the doctrine of

237

the Atonement the Church proclaims and tries to live. How does the community of memory which is the Church, then, 'be' for others? And we ask that, not of some idealised Church of normative theological discourse, but of the Church as she is, with her failures, her strengths and her sometimes strong, sometimes feeble sense of her own vocation. And we ask it not for individuals – they can 'join' the Church and expose their own memories to the counter-memories of the destiny of Jesus in ways that we shall explore more fully in the next chapter – but for communities, institutions and structures. If the Church as community of memory has within it the power of salvation through its recall of the destiny of Jesus, can it offer any salvation to the wider social groups of which its members may or may not be members? Does a memory-based account of the Atonement have anything to say to them? I shall explore two types of answer.

The first is the case where communities are split or at war as a result of long-held resentments enshrined in some form of collective memory. Northern Ireland is the obvious example, but the destructive power of history extends from New Zealand to Peru, from South Africa to Bhutan, from former Yugoslavia to the Baltic States. It permeates industrial relations, political allegiances and agendas, class relationships and the agrarian structure not only in the UK (which seems to be a particular victim of its own history) but in the United States and every major country of Europe. What does the community of memory have to offer these chronic structures of remembered resentment? I suggest two things.

The triad of ways in which personal memories are healed by being put alongside the counter-memories of the destiny of Jesus which we explored in Chapter 9 can also be applied, *mutatis mutandis*, to community memories. They can be relativised by being put alongside the Church's memories of Jesus's destiny so that they begin to lose some of their compulsive power. Such a process does not deny the sense of injustice or of hurt or the reality of past and present suffering. But it undermines the ultimacy of those emotions, denying them the absolute value that they easily acquire – and which is essential if they are to be maintained over any length of time. Once they can be reduced to relativities, they become both emotionally handleable and negotiable. That is not to say that success in negotiation is guaranteed: there may, in fact, be no negotiable 'solution'. But it is to say that there is a tectonic shift in the possibilities of communication once the absolutes have been dethroned.

The same can shortly be said of containment. The more securely the Church can contain, in Bion's sense, the resentment, anger, accumulated bitterness and griefs of the communities concerned, the more free they will be to move from the paranoid position to the depressive where reparative morality can replace *lex talionis*. If the communities are allowed to continue to believe that they are not heard, that they are not valued, that their case and claims are not taken seriously by anyone, that they are locked into their own understanding of their history and its emotional burden without any 'outside' inter-mediation, then the chance of them surrendering their resentments and their paranoid fears of 'the other' are slim indeed. The danger clearly is that the Church becomes the non-critical, non-reflexive storehouse of the community's complaints, and indeed may come to play a major role in perpetuating and embittering the associated memories. This is what seems to have happened in Northern Ireland and in the former Yugoslavia and in parts of South Africa, on both sides. That is fatally to misunderstand what Bion meant by containment. Bion's understanding of containment is not partisan support or emotional side-taking. It is, rather, accepting the rawness of the emotion and allowing the container to reintroject those feelings in a way that enables the subject to deal with them in a non-pathological way. That implies accepting the pain and distress, but not being dominated by them or absolutising them or seeing them as the last word. Above all, the process of containment implies a recognition of the fact that it is the subject's pain, not the container's. It is for the subject to learn how to deal with it in a constructive and freeing way, rather than getting stuck in pathological reactions of violence, hatred and fear.

That needs a level of emotional, cognitive and relational learning that the Church, as community of memory, should be able to provide – if, but only if, she has achieved sufficient freedom herself from her own bad memories. The evidence from Northern Ireland is that that is difficult and rare.

The final leg of the triad I called judging and explaining. The two go together as there is an explanatory rather than a condemnatory load to the judging. The memory of the Church makes violence an unacceptable response to resentments and injustice, and those who resort to violence have to be re-minded that the hatred and/or cynicism that lead to violence are judged in the light of the eschaton as revealed in the Resurrection. This is not moralistic preachments to the men of violence by those who have never experienced and have no individual or collective memory of the injustices of which they complain: it is, rather, a lived expression of the ethic of the Kingdom that is central to the foundational memories of the Church. But the judging has to be extended back, from the current violence, to the cause of the violence, the fears and hatreds that are now sedimented in the memory of the community prone to violence – and that in a way that does justice to Merleau-Ponty's call for a recognition of the 'plurality of negativities'.[33] The ethic of the King-dom *was* violated by the Cromwellian invasion of Ireland and the alienation of land that followed it, by the ethnic violence practised by the Croats under the protection of the Nazis, by the Boers and the Nationalists under Verwoerd (or by the 'English' at the time of the Boer War). However wrong the violence now, there is a historical (or 'historical') reason for it, and the collective memory of that reason has to be honoured, as well as judged. For out of that may come some relativised understanding of the sources of the present violence which in no sense justifies it, but helps to explain the strength of the myths that make it so appealing.

In this sense, the present memories incarnated in the Church act both backwards and forwards: they expose the evil of the present; they trace its origins to evil in the past; and they insist that the future does not have to be made by the past. Indeed, they make the impossible claim that the future can remake the past – and that the future that can do so has already been glimpsed in the Resurrection of Jesus Christ.[34]

The sceptic might claim that this argument has a certain appeal only because it is applied to the extreme case of inter-communal or inter-ethnic violence. What about the community malaises of which Lasch complains – shallowness in education, a foreshortening of time-horizons that makes the management of natural resources impossible (and/or irrational), or mysogyny, or excessive consumerism that triv-ialises both production and appetite – and diverts resources from needs of the poor to wants of the not-poor?[35] How can the community of memory address the presentations of the narcissistic culture?

In those terms it cannot – directly. What it can do is to address the origins of the narcissism by re-presenting a memory of a God who loves unconditionally and who offers himself as an unfailingly good object to make up the deficiencies in the inner world of each member of the whole community. While there may well be a role for the relativisation of the demands of the narcissistic culture, and for its judging and explaining by the memory of Jesus's destiny, the most significant part of the process is the containment of the narcissistic elements of the culture in a secure relationship with God through the Church. Again, the object is not to justify the emotional superficiality of the narcissist or her culture: it is to enable her to feel sufficiently secure and accepted so that she can begin to explore her own emotional world more deeply.

But there is a deeper sense to be uncovered here. The narcissist (and I use that as a shorthand for the narcissistic elements in each of us) allows and encourages the trivialisation of politics. Unable to commit himself to serious political endeavour at a level deeper than the adulation of political heroes or excoriation of political foes, he takes part in a long-running assault on the seriousness of purpose of the State itself. Obsessed by his own needs, he demands that the State meet those needs – for housing, employment, health care and education, certainly, but, at a deeper level, for fulfilment, acceptance and ultimately meaning. The State pretends to do the former – but can never do so properly because such needs are infinite but resources are finite – and cannot even make an honest claim to be able to attempt the latter (except in the kind of totalitarian environment analysed by Staub when the offer of meaning through a State-centred nationalism is almost always sinister).

The danger of this narcissistic demand for the State to meet needs is that the legitimacy of the State itself comes to be associated with its capacity to meet those needs. For that becomes the nature of democracy: the notion of God (or any other transcendent referent) as the legitimiser of the political order (still more or less in place in Stuart times in England) is 'replaced by the people and its infallibility'.[36] The legitimacy of the State then becomes internalised as in the celebrated 'circle of justice' in which the State is legitimated by its upholding of justice, but justice is defined as the will of the State. There is literally no way out of the cul-de-sac. Anarchy or yobdom are at the gates. Recent political developments in France, Germany, Italy and Britain point unambiguously in this direction.

How can the Church as a community of memory make any difference? The answer surely lies for the community where it lies for the individual – in the 'rediscovery' of the transcendent claims of God's reign and the internalisation of God's model of power as demonstrated in the life, death and resurrection of Jesus. The legitimacy of the state is not to be defined in the meeting of *my* needs but in the creation of a community that loves and forgives and looks forward to the End as both invitation and model. To say that is not to demand the reimposition of a fundamentalist theocracy such as Iran under Khomeini or Sudan under an ever more desperate Numeiri,[37] but it is to insist that a society that looks for its own legitimacy only to its own politics is doomed to failure – and the alienation that results either in apathy or in violence. And, of course, that is to lay upon the community of memory an awesome burden: the revivification of religious language, symbols and discourse in a way that invites and attracts the discovery of ultimate reality in the transcendent rather than the immanent. It is to some of the implications of that task that the last chapter of this book is addressed.

I want now to move to the second way in which the Church as community of memory, contrite and forgiven, can offer salvation to the wider community. The biblical triad of repentance, forgiveness and reconciliation is at the heart of the memories of the Church, running through both Old and New Testaments as well as in the experience of the Church herself. And as Alan Falconer has pointed out, the drama of the triad in action is usually accompanied by anamnesis in which the people are specifically called to remember the tradition of graciousness and forgiveness that makes possible both the repentance of the sinner and reconciliation with God.[38] Furthermore, as Dag Hammarskjöld commented, forgiveness implies sacrifice – the sacrifice of the giver of forgiveness in living with the consequences of the evil action for which forgiveness is needed. The forgiver cannot rewrite history: as the victim of the Holocaust knows, he has to live with its consequences. The community of memory, then, has the memory of that dynamic in action – of forgiveness

242

asked and granted, but granted at a cost and yet still with total acceptance and self-giving, as a prelude to and condition of reconciliation. Perhaps there is no greater religious truth of which the practical consequences are less generally realised than this memory which lies at the heart of the Christian faith.

And that implies that the community of memory has also to be the community of forgiveness, not only in its own practice but in keeping alive in the wider community the knowledge of the creative power of forgiveness. By accepting the consequences of the action of another without rancour or resentment, the one who forgives (whether that is an individual or a group or a community or a nation) allows the other (the sinner) to discover a freedom from the past and its memories,[39] and an openness to the future and its possibilities. As Hannah Arendt has put it: 'Forgiving . . . is the only reaction which does not merely re-act but acts anew and unexpectedly, unconditioned by the act which provoked it and therefore freeing from its consequences both the one who forgives and the one who is forgiven.'[40] In this sense, past, present and future interact in ways with which we are becoming familiar. But, as in all such interactions, the initiating process – forgiveness, in this case – has to be continuous. It is not a one-off event that can then be forgotten. So the community of memory becomes a community that remembers the act of forgiveness and its liberating power, not, as too often happens in Churches caught up in inter-communal conflict, a community of memory that hangs on only to the initial wrongs.

And the good news is that it can be seen at work – among the black community in the United States and, to take one example at random, among the ex-'guerillas' in Zimbabwe.[41] As Donald Shriver comments, in his postscript to Brian Frost's study of the politics of forgiveness: 'Western theologians [and he could have widened that to include anyone from our culture] reading this book are likely to be discomforted by the notion that forgiveness – or any other term signifying a claim central to religious scripture and religious history – is a 'fact' comparable to the facts of science.'[42] While both Frost and Shriver are at pains to emphasise that the Church has no monopoly on the memory or practice of forgiveness, they recognise the inseparability of Jesus's life, death and resurrection on the one hand and the 'fact' of forgiveness on the other.[43] Like all religious truth that holds together the individual and the social, false dichotomies arise so that forgiveness is too easily confined to the personal, but Frost's book is a measured statement of the political power of forgiveness, and of the wisdom of politicians in recognising that. That is a memory the Church enshrines.

Conclusion

I have sought to show that the Church contains within its tradition, its memory-bank, memory-resources that, given the condition of real communication within the Church and between it and the rest of the world (a very demanding condition, as we saw), can act as a counter to the destructive collective memories of communities. As long as those memories stay on the shelf of the bank, dusted by studious clerics, they can achieve little. In the last chapter, then, we need to think more about how they may properly be appropriated so that their healing power may be released among us – churched and unchurched alike.

12

Memory and Appropriation

Memory and Ideology in the Text

In the last chapter we saw that the Church is an ark which contains the memories of Jesus on which we draw to confront the memories from which we need to be set free. It is in laying alongside our own memories the counter-story of the destiny of Jesus that the power of our memories (both conscious and unconscious) to shape our actions is cut down to size. Such was our argument when we discussed theories of the Atonement and sought to shift the balance in favour of the existential. But in making that argument we were uncomfortably aware that we had skated round the question of the status of those memories. Are they historically true? Are they wholly unreliable? Are they somewhere in between and, if so, how do we know? It may be helpful to recall some of the material about memory which we reviewed in Chapter 1.

There we looked at collective and social memory – the latter the more ordered and 'official' version of the former – and saw that they were characterised by three features. First, they depend on a community and especially on the community's 'remembrancer' to keep them in being and to pass them on. The way that passing on is done can vary greatly, but we were especially struck by the role of ritual and re-presentation as ways in which the community may keep in touch with its memories. Second, we saw that the official memory may well differ from and be deliberately manipulated by the official rememberers, both in terms of what is remembered and more particularly in terms of what is forgotten or repressed.

Third, and most immediately relevant for our purposes, though dependent upon the foregoing features, we also saw that memory is unconsciously (as well as consciously) manipulated by both community remembrancers and by 'official' historians. And, in a weaker sense than Lukacher's example of the Freudian analysis, we can seldom if ever get back to the 'real truth' that lies behind the memory as it is currently collectively or socially recalled. Even if we have fairly full documentary evidence, we would, in the light, for example, of studies of the accuracy of testimony of judicial witnesses, be wise to suspend judgement about the historical accuracy (whatever precisely we take that phrase to mean) of the memories presented to us, not least because we do not know and the rememberers cannot know the unconscious filtering and rearranging that has gone on.

This kind of general theorising about the nature of collective and social memory has to be applied to the Gospel narratives. It is likely to lead us to recognise that the very process of Gospel remembering is, like every other act of collective and social memorising, open to radical doubt based on the very nature of the remembering process itself. I want in the following paragraphs to explore the nature of that doubt and, as it were, take it in the flank.

It is now a commonplace of biblical scholarship that the Gospels are not naïve diaries of events, but very carefully constructed accounts, each with its own audience and its own set of ideas or emphases that it is seeking to convey. The Gospels are written with clear ideological intent and in that sense are, in Habermas's terminology, 'distorted communication'. Wendt has shown, for example, how the power of the Romans is variously interpreted,[1] and there is a wide literature on the way the evangelists treat the Jews, their leadership and the common people.[2] At a more detailed level, it is clear that stories of miracles and healings have a precise theological purpose. Even non-narrative bits of teaching, so-called pericopes, have been shown to serve a particular doctrinal or ecclesiological purpose, crafted, often out of assorted materials, with a particular audience in mind.[3]

To take a more extended example to which we shall return below, it is clear that Luke-Acts has the purpose of presenting the Jesus movement as unthreatening to the Roman Empire, at a time when persecution of the sect by the Roman authorities was increasingly harsh. This led Luke to 'clean Jesus up', an objective he achieved in part by the genealogies and birth myths at the beginning of the gospel which give a veneer of respectability to Jesus and his parents by linking them with the Davidic kingship; by disguising the humble and disreputable origins of Mary; and by pietising Jesus's bastardy by the device of the Immaculate Conception and perhaps the creation of Joseph as a cover for the possibility that Mary was a single parent. Perhaps oddly with this ideological intent, he does not disguise the radicality of the agenda of the Jesus people, even putting into the mouth of Mary a freedom song that would have had, for many Jews and some non-Jewish observers of Jewish and Roman-imperial history, echoes with earlier, unsuccessful revolts by groups of Jews. But as Josephine Massyngberde Ford has pointed out,[4] there is a remarkable discontinuity between the military revolutionary sub-text of the infancy narratives (which some critics at least see as Luke being faithful to 'history') and the rest of the Gospel, where the ideological intention of the Gospel, essentially reassuring the ruling classes that the Jesus movement does not present much of a threat to them and their interests, reasserts itself:

> From now on [i.e., after the end of Chapter 2] in his Gospel, Luke will take almost every opportunity offered him to show that Jesus, contrary to all expectations as seen in the infancy narratives, is a preacher with an urgent message to his generation and to the generations to come, the powerful message of non-violent resistance and, more strikingly, loving one's enemy in word and deed.[5]

Two points need adding to that. The first is that the very fact of ideological intention implies that much has been excluded – and is therefore forgotten. It is not simply that it is easy to overlook how short are the Gospels, masterpieces of compression. There is much we do not and cannot know about the narrative of Jesus's life. We do not know it precisely because knowing it would add nothing to the theological points that the evangelists wish to convey. We might have more diary: we would have no more theology. But at a more serious level, it is the absences from the text, from the narrative, that are themselves ideologically loaded. Terry Eagleton writes of the text being 'hollowed' by its relation to ideology. The text, he says, 'is driven up against those gaps and limits which are the product of ideology's relation to history'.[6] Materialist critics have argued that one of the significant gaps in the Lukan account is precisely that the

Jesus movement was, at least in potential, a working-class freedom movement that was in ideo-theological revolt against both the Romans and their comprador allies among the Jewish leadership. On this account the revolutionary potential implied in the first two chapters is gently honed away, leaving the story emasculated of its politico-social message.[7] This ideological load, this distortion in the Church's communication of its own story, has served the Church, or significant parts of it, well.

The second point is about disaggregation. It might be said, for example, that while the structure of each of the Gospels is carefully managed to make theological or ideological points, the individual stories – parables, bits of teaching, miracles, specific events – each stand on their own feet as 'hard' memory, with, the implication would be, a one-to-one relationship to historical accuracy. Take, for example, the overthrow of the money-changers in the Temple, set by different evangelists in different parts of their narrative to make very different points about the nature of the relationship between the mission of Jesus and the Jews in general and Temple worship in particular. The fact that the event is used structurally in different ways does not, it might be claimed, impugn the reliability of the memory of the event.

Even the fact that different evangelists emphasise different details and so tell a slightly but subtly different story does not invalidate that claim. There is, of course, an element of truth in it. It is, however, easily exaggerated, for at certain critical points, of which the Resurrection stories are the most notorious, detail becomes of the essence. Who precisely found the empty tomb? How empty was it? Did they 'see' Jesus there or not? It is not enough to indicate a vague consensus that the tomb was discovered to be empty: if the memory is to lay claim to any degree of credibility it needs to be more precise and consistent than that. Recent developments in what has come to be known as rhetorical criticism have further suggested that even the disaggregated story or literary unit has its own special features that stem from the process of literary or poetic composition. 'The kind of words used and the way they are put together make every unit a new creation.'[8] And from this it follows that 'every text [i.e., literary unit] requires its own hermeneutics'.[9] And in that case, disaggregation helps us little to get back to some kind of primary, 'real' or reliable memory.

There is further the objection that disaggregation is itself a distortion. Architects design buildings, not bricks. And while it might be useful, even necessary, to look critically at a brick, the intention of the architect, the message s/he wishes to convey by this particular building in this particular location, cannot be derived from a study of individual bricks. As Farley puts it: 'These literatures are not simply aggregates of discrete units [texts]. They concern each other as resources for portrayal.'[10] In other words, the impact of the Gospel narrative depends upon the way the literary bricks relate to each other – and the gaps between them – and to seek to derive something of the primary memory of Jesus from individual stories is to misread not only the Gospel but the nature of narrative itself.

We must therefore approach the Gospels not in the expectation that we have memories of the same logical order as television reportage (ideologically loaded and subject to premature closure as that is). Rather, we have memories that are at times much closer to the memories that in analysis are released from the unconscious – significant, full of (ambiguous or polyvalent) meaning, possibly distorted by affect, certainly distorted by teleological intent, not necessarily in the right order or over-accurate in detail (which is not the same as over-detailed, which they may or may not be), full of gaps and unanswered questions. How can we, who carry our own memories and are 'made' by them, read the text that contains such memories? I shall answer: 'In much the same way as they are written.'

Memory and Ideology in the Reader

Since Gadamer's reappraisal of 'the Enlightenment's prejudice against prejudice'[11] it has become a commonplace of literary criticism that, just as the writer cannot escape her own ideological, theological and contextual conditioning in the writing process, so the reader is subject to the same influences in the process of reading. We all read through our own mental lenses – and for the most part we are nearly or wholly unconscious of them. That degree of unconsciousness may or may not imply repression: it may simply be that I have never realised that I tend to associate with the dominant group or that I tend to see things from a male perspective, and that when it is pointed out to me I can, perhaps with difficulty, consciously correct my own biases. It may, on the other hand, be that I am repressing memories of a poor relationship in the early months of life with my mother, with the result that I will resist any suggestion that I need to correct such biases in my reading. I would therefore be relatively happy with the patriarchal, androcentric *writing* of most of the Bible that feminist literary critics are revealing; and I would be resistant to their suggestions that I need to 'correct' the text in order to eliminate or relativise that bias in it.

This is one example of a much wider phenomenon – the interconnection and interpenetration of unconscious processes, the formation of ideology and the reading of the text. We have explored the link between the first two elements of that triad in the foregoing chapters: recall the archetypes of war and militaristic ideologies in the work of Stevens; the Oedipal conflict and the racism of the southern states in the USA in the work of Kovel; the depressive position and the adoption of an altruistic ideology in the work of Klein, as three very different examples. And then consider how people caught in the paradigmatic expression of these psychological and ideological states will read the text. Raboteau's classic study of the slave religion of the *ante bellum* slave states is illuminating not only for how the slaves' religious consciousness developed but no less so for what the slave-owners *thought* the gospel (and its hired preachers) was saying to them: essentially that obedience, cleanliness, sobriety and the cheerful acceptance of the *status quo* were the will of God for his black children. Caught in their own ideology of racial supremacy by, *inter alia*, their Oedipal experiences, they could not imagine that the gospel might be read (as it clearly was by many slaves) as the promise of freedom.[12]

This contrast is exactly the point. It nicely illustrates the insistence of Heidegger, Gadamer and Ricoeur (and, in a slightly different mode, of feminist theologians such as Schussler-Fiorenza and Mary Daly) that our way of reading the text is not just a question of epistemology: it is a question of ontology. We are both the captive and the creative subject of 'our ownmost possibilities'.[13]

Take another somewhat more contentious example. Assume that Lasch is roughly right: that ours is a culture of narcissism in the sense that our predominant cultural norms are self-regarding, shallow and highly individualised, with little interest in or capacity for deep personal relationships or social transformation. Then consider the conventional reading of the opening chapters of Luke's Gospel. It fails to challenge Luke's ideology: indeed, it wants Jesus 'cleaned up'. It wants an insipid, milk-and-water Mary, purged of any notions of her as a ghetto-raised, single-mother revolutionary. And so it sets her freedom song to Anglican chant or multi-part settings and thinks: 'How beautiful.' Taking Lasch (and for that matter Galbraith) seriously, it is no wonder that we, by which I mean middle-class North Atlantic, Anglo-Saxon males, read the Bible in as ideologically loaded and politically castrated way as we do, for we are as much victim of our unconscious processes as anyone else. (We are also, of course, the victims of history and in this particular case of at least fifteen hundred years of ecclesiastical interest in calming whatever anxieties the political powers might have entertained about the security risk posed by the Church.)[14]

To imagine, then, that the text *gives* or that, even if it did, we could *appropriate*, undistorted memories of the life, death and resurrection of Jesus the saviour is simply mistaken. We can do no such thing. What we have is rather a highly selective, carefully slanted account made up of an assortment of sources and literary devices, some of which, perhaps very many of which, are based, to an uncertain degree, on more or less precise memories of first-hand witnesses. And we bring to this assembly our own conscious and unconscious biases and preconceptions, always unaware of the absences or gaps in the text; and no less unaware, much of the time, of the gaps and slants in our own perceptual or ideological approach to the text.

Does this mean that we have to read it with total scepticism, as a series of caesuras and indeterminacies? This is the way of negativity that says with Jacques Ellul: 'The Christian God is a *hidden God*. Nor can any image of Jesus be preserved or imagined. We have here a religion of the Word alone, and Jesus is the totality of the Word, living and not ritualized.'[15] The Barthian overtones are clear, but is that all there is to be said?

I think not. I want to suggest that we take the text as we find it, with all its uncertainties, its polyvalencies and its caesuras, recognising that unconscious processes have been at work in its formation – as well as ideological, doctrinal and literary processes. Take the text as *that thing*, that subjective object, and work with it in the same spirit of adventurous play which lies behind its creation. And work with it in the expectation that the 'memories' of Jesus's destiny that it portrays may function as history, or as myth, or as symbol, or as interrogation. Or as any combination of those, variant and unpredictable over time, place and reader. But in each case we bring to the text the hope, the anticipation of the healing of our own memories.

For as I shall argue in the next section, what matters is not, in fact, the facticity of the memories we encounter in the text, but what we do with them. Like Joan Rivière's patient, we find that what matters is 'what we do with them inside ourselves' – for it is out of that that salvation can come. In a word, we are back to hermeneutics. Interpretation is, it seems, all.

It is therefore appropriate to complete this book by looking at a hermeneutic style that takes emancipation seriously.

Reading the Text against the Grain

A recent writer who has faced some of the questions posed by such a hermeneutic is Itumeleng Mosala in his book *Biblical Hermeneutics and Black Theology in South Africa*.[16] In this book, written before the collapse of the apartheid regime, he faces the contrast between the conservative, pro-*status quo* ideological load of some biblical writers (he is only marginally less concerned with analysing how those writers have in fact been read through the ages) and the ideological commitment of black South Africans to the end of the racist (and, he would add, multinational capitalist) regime. How, in short, can black South Africans relate to a set of texts that are written from an ideological standpoint precisely opposed to their own? He rejects two possible solutions: that they should forget the text and get on with the revolution: or that they should forget the revolution and learn, like the white slave-owners hoped would happen in the Deep South, to live at peace with the existing political 'realities' – and therefore the text. Both of those solutions, greedily grasped by different factions in South Africa, define the problem away. Mosala, however, is too good a scholar to fall for them. So what is to be done?

Mosala suggests that black South Africans have to approach the text in three ways.[17] The first he calls political and puts it this way: 'It asks: What is the role of this . . . text in the signification of the Jesus practice?', and by signification he means something close to the attachment of an ideological load to the praxis of the followers of Jesus. Reflecting on the welter of social, political and religious forces that were already locked in conflict at the time of Jesus,[18] he asks how the evangelists came to make their choices of the forces they recognised and the forces they either did not recognise or chose not to include in their narrative. What ideological load was at work shaping the way they 'remembered' Jesus and invited their audience to remember him? And how did that remembering process form the (transmitted) identity of Jesus? Looking at the way Luke and the other evangelists describe John the Baptist, for example, Mosala is struck by the extent to which he is presented to us as an exponent, like the Essenes and later the Desert Fathers, of the principle of resistance-by-withdrawal. In that description it is the withdrawal rather than the resistance that gains the most attention – both in the writing and, we might add, in the reading by most white Christians of today.

Secondly, black theology has, Mosala says, to learn to engage the text appropriatively. 'By this I mean that black working-class Christians, using the weapon of black theology, must interpret the text *against the grain*' (my italics). By deliberately inverting the common hermeneutical guide to interpret 'with the grain' of the text, Mosala means that black Christians have to learn to play with the text and its ideological structure against their own experience. That experience has its own discourse, its own narrative and ideological commitment; and that discourse of the experience of people engaged in the struggle (or for that matter just suffering the impact of the regime and its outworks) needs to be 'bounced off' the Gospel discourses. In the process the gaps and caesuras in the texts will be discovered; so will the gaps and caesuras in the people's appropriation of and reflection on their own experience. It is in that sense a two-way street, a mutual discovery of truth, of fudge, of confusion and of dishonesty. It is close to Fred Dallmayr's 'probing of opacity . . . to decipher the signals of a precognitive or prereflective practice' and/or to Vico's advocacy of poetic wisdom.[19]

Mosala's third hermeneutic approach is what he calls projective.

It interprets the text in ways that intend effects conductive to the victory of the liberation struggle – notwithstanding the class character and ideological commitment of the text. . . . The usefulness or otherwise of the agenda of the text cannot be decided *a priori*. It has to be tested on the basis of the demands and experience of the struggle of black working-class people.[20]

I would highlight 'demands' in that explanation, for what Mosala is courageously saying is that if the gospel is to be received and experienced as genuinely (rather than pietistically or schizoidly) good news, it has to accord with the demands (not just with the experience) of the oppressed and the abused and the exploited. They have the right to demand that of the gospel: only so can they speak of a gospel that takes their salvation seriously. If it does not do that, it is like salt that has lost its savour and is good only for the tip. For it is demanding that they live their religion in a split-off world – split off, that is, from the world in which they live, suffer and die.

But let us be clear how far-reaching is the implication of this projective hermeneutic. It is making the human demand for emancipation the yardstick by which the gospel is to be judged. To the Barthian, raised on the primacy of the Word, that sounds almost blasphemous. Yet it follows logically from the insistence that the Word as we have it, the narrative as we have it, is an ideological construct which must be challenged, played with, bounced against if it is to yield good news for this generation (and this class) of readers.

I would want to argue, however, that a projective hermeneutic is likely to be the more liberating if the projections that the reader brings to her reading have already been subjected to as much self-reflection and criticism as possible. We are back to Habermas, and perhaps even more to Martin Buber. What is required is that our relation with the text and its discourse should be as free from distorted communication as we can make it. If we are to have genuine dialogue with the Word in a free relationship of the I/thou class of total inclusivity, then we need to be as free of our own inner distortions that will undermine the nature of the relationship as we can manage – without falling into the Pelagian trap of thinking that we can save ourselves by our own efforts.

That will involve a degree of aggressiveness, for it means that we are obliged 'to break through the limitations of [our] assumptions or to challenge the 'squatting rights' of the colonizer within one's own internal world'.[21] For, as we have seen from a number of perspectives, one's internal world has been occupied by a variety of more or, usually, less welcome guests, from the unexamined, precritical under-standings of childhood to quite unconscious assumptions and attitudes associated with developmental difficulties that have never been tran-scended. They have all to be challenged in the search for 'ideal speech' with the text – and with the self. And that requires the courage to discover the connection between aggression and explor-ation that Winnicott traces back to the foetus in the womb, kicking the restraining walls of the placenta.[22]

It is also deeply anxiety provoking. Some will be able to contain this anxiety better than others. Some will want to hang the more desperately to the comforts and comforters of the past. The polarity between fundamentalism and openness is thus established. But whether fundamentalist or liberal or post-modern, our language betrays what is going on: we speak of understanding as 'grasping', as 'getting to grips with', as 'getting on top of'.[23] But sometimes understanding can only come through an initial letting go.

In the next section we shall ask how we may adapt Mosala's hermeneutic for our time and place.

Reading the Text: Projection

I shall call the adaptation I propose 'projective play', and want to discuss each of those terms at some length.

By 'projection', I mean a number of things. First, like Mosala, I mean that we must be ready to confront the text with our deepest desires; or, since we often are not sure about our deepest desires as individuals or as communities, with our need to gain clarity about what those desires are. In doing so, we shall of course project on to the text and our reading of it unconscious material or conscious material that we are unaware of projecting. In a number of senses, we shall be projecting our very selves; and again, that has to be interpreted at both the level of the individual and of the community. The group of Christians that projects on to the text a deep resistance to change may be projecting on to the text its own anxiety. The group that projects on to the text its hostility to the ordination of women (or their election as bishops) may be projecting on to the text something about their own sexual anxieties that may well include unresolved Oedipal conflicts or their female equivalents. The group that projects on to the text their longing for peace and prosperity in, say, Rwanda may be projecting certain forms of idealisation and/or guilt at half-perceived collusion in structures and policies that have brought violence and starvation to that country.

I want to emphasise that such projection is perfectly proper and healthy. It is proper theologically because it avoids hypocrisy. And it is proper psychologically, in that it does not encourage us to suppress or repress parts of our selves and our experiences that need airing if they are to be healed. Such an approach does, however, contrast with current conventions that are predicated either on a mental/emotional *tabula rasa* or, even worse, an assumed piety that detaches the reader from his or her own reality; or, again, commits the reader to reading the text through the eyes of the dominant class or caste, with whom s/he may have next to nothing in common.

Much has been written about the methods of biblical reflection adopted in the Base Communities of Latin America and elsewhere,[24] and it might be thought that I am advocating an Anglo-Saxon version of that. That is both true and false. It is true in so far as the Base Communities approach the text out of their *'realidad'*, a word rubbed threadbare of meaning by its repetition in this context. It is false in so far as the Base Communities become the victims of their own ideologies and their own group-think, so that they paradoxically become (or can become) divorced from their real desires. (Or they become sectarian, attracting and including only those who share, at a deep level, their ideological stance.)

And that raises an important issue – namely, that my real desires may conflict with the prevailing ideology of the Church or of significant sections within it. Indeed, such seems to be a common scenario: consider the history of the Church in South Africa, Nicaragua or inner urban Britain. To pursue the implications of this conflict would take us too far from our present theme and over some of the ground discussed in the last chapter. Maybe all that can be said here is that whether as individuals, or as small, incohate groups or as large sections of the Church, we somehow need to find the courage to 'speak' if not 'ideally', then as firmly oriented in that direction as we can find the courage to be. We shall never encounter the text (or be encount-ered by the text) as long as we allow ourselves to be 'distorted', to tell our self-narrative the way it is *not*.

I do not wish to pursue that further here. Rather, I want to explore the second sense in which I am to be understood to be using projection. As we approach the text, we need to be in touch with our fears, our anxieties, our griefs and our guilt, all the material in a word that derives from the conscious and, as far as we are able, the less-than- and un-conscious memories that we can bring forward for reflection. As we bring our *desires* forward, expecting them to be honoured in the encounter with the text, so we bring our *negative feelings, our Shadows* and our underlying memories, expecting them to be mirrored in the text, that is, shone back to us with new light. We stand before the text, whether as individuals or as a group, with all our negativities (and the wounds associated with them) revealed to the text.[25] Nothing is or can be hidden. As the writer incorporated his Shadow in the construction of the text, so we incorporate ours in the reading of it. To read the text insulated from that material is to read it as an escapist novelette – and to expect as much from it. In orthodox terminology, this readiness to project on to the text the memories of our own negativities is to take seriously the doctrine that Christ redeems us as we (truly) are, that Christ identified with the whole of the human condition in the Incarnation and not just its masks or personae.

Part of that process of bringing our negativities, through critical self-reflection, to consciousness will put us in touch with our own symbolic world. It is in symbols, both as artefacts and as language and images, that we are reminded of (or have re-presented to us) the events, people and encounters that have helped to form us, to write our stories as we have interacted with them. Some of this may be dream imagery, some of which Jungians will see as archetypal; more is likely to be derived either from direct experience or from literary or artistic activity or exposure. Most refer directly or indirectly to memories living at some level of consciousness.

The linkage of memory and symbol thus becomes a crucial cogni-tive process the undertaking of which is part of our preparation for an encounter with the text. In Jungian terminology again, this involves us in linking our consciousness with archetypal material which 'holds' the most powerful symbols for us. It is only when we are in touch with the power of our own symbols – and as it were, behind them, their archetypes – that we shall be able to respond fully to the symbols and archetypes in the text, and thereby break out of the 'magic circle' in which language and mimesis holds us captive.[26] To live non-symbolically, in an entirely logical or analytical world, is to cut ourselves off from the poetry, the possibility of transcendence, of the text and, at a deeper level, to blinker or castrate the religious sensibility of both reader and text.

Let me try to illustrate that. In a post-Kleinian world, 'transitional objects' assume a key role in defending against anxiety. They can take many shapes, including linguistic forms[27] and organizational structures, as we saw in the work of Menzies and Jacques. Most of us most of the time remain unaware of the transitional objects in our lives, accepting them, as it were, at face value. And that in turn means that when we come to the text, we may well remain unaware of the power of the text's symbolism for us. Take for example Psalm 22:9–10.

For you brought me forth from the womb, made me safe upon the breasts of my mother,
Upon you was I cast from the womb; from the womb of my mother, God are you.

Phyllis Trible has shown[28] what a powerful verse this is, combining and ultimately eliding images of human and divine midwife, mother, womb and breast, yet preserving the transcendence of all those images. To suggest that we read this verse aware of our (need for) transitional objects is not an invitation to make God into a divine comfort-blanket. It is rather to suggest that the text can come alive in quite new ways when, by paying attention to our symbols, we project on to it our normally unconscious needs – in this case, for a substitute for the good breast. We are back to Bion's containment – and, perhaps surprisingly, Julian of Norwich's 'keeping'.[29]

Again, to repeat, this is as true of the community as it is of the individual. The symbols of Armistice Day, red poppies and wreaths, are linked very consciously with the memories of war and mass destruction; and perhaps less consciously with absent father, anxious mother, physical danger half-comprehended and deprivation directly experienced. To maintain the Kleinian paradigm, here we are in touch with symbols of primitive anxiety of the paranoid-schizoid position that threatens us, we know not why or whence, with total obliteration. It is with these deep fears and their symbols in our collective remembering that we need to be in touch as we approach the text. Or, to take another example, this time with overtones of Lerner, the symbols of Labor Day or the Durham Miners' Gala are linked consciously with unemployment and the conflicts between the interests of capital and labour; and less consciously with the experience of father's self-blame as he lived in the twin embrace of a bullying foreman and consumerist media – and drank himself to oblivion of both.

In a third sense of projection, the consciousness of memory and symbol, and of symbolic or symbolised memory, may be projected on to the wider community. It was not only my father who found himself in Lerner's trap. It was not only her father who was absent at the war when she needed him most (with the result that she has been unconsciously looking for him ever since). These were common experiences for our class and age cohort and are shared, consciously or not, by many others. The projection involved here is of an anamenistic empathy, a recognition that we share memories with a wider group which may never identify itself. And as we share the memories, so we share with that group a need for salvation. The archaeology of suffering has to be met with the eschatology of redemption. The reading of the text is not *my* reading alone. It is the reading of the text for all of us, whether the others are part of the physical reading process itself or not.

There is a fourth sense to be attached to the idea of projection – its more literal sense of throwing forward. The desires, symbols, memories and solidarities that are recollected and brought to consciousness are thrown at the text, and specifically at the Gospel texts of Jesus's life and death. Now much emphasised by some variants of reader-response criticism, this process lies in stark contrast to the tradition that sees the reader as the still, silent receptor of the text. Rather this is active engagement with the text, not (or, perhaps better, not only) on its terms but on ours. In 'anticipation' that our level of consciousness of ourselves and the world will be shifted, the text is to be challenged, to be confronted, to be brought face to face with our agenda, our needs, our hurts, the symbols of suffering of individuals and communities.

The text is, however, not only the recipient of our play, the rag doll of our imaginative *bal masqué*. It has a life of its own. That life is defined by the words, the memory-associated spaces between the words and the refusal of the words and the language that contain them to go wherever we want them to go; and it is often expressed in symbol. As Milner put it when writing of free imaginative drawing, 'the line as it were answers back and functions as a very primitive type of external object'.[30] In much the same way, the text acquires its own life. It does not reveal itself uniformly. It indulges in metaphor, allegory, allusion, pun, word-play, symbolism, association and caesura. And it does not accept our projections at face value. As we saw earlier, it challenges *them* as surely as it is challenged by them, and in the challenge there might well lie relativisation and judgement as well as healing. The memories may be shown to be one-sided, to be incidental, to be partial. The symbols may be exposed as hollow, as straw men, as romantic or self-indulgent. The memory or the symbol may 'feel' to be true: but it might still be revealed as false. For the text has its own symbols as well as its own memories, and the play may well end up by investing the text's symbols with far greater credibility than our own. Thus the ideologies by which our needs are structured, and projected on to the text, are brought to judgement, or, as I would rather put it, to healing.

Paul Hoggett has an appropriate analogy for this process, that of a pianist addressing her piano. 'She may have an idea of what it is that she wishes to produce but she cannot produce this idea instantaneously; the piano stands between her and its realization.' She will have to work with the instrument, accepting its limitations and possibilities as part of the creative task. Thus she comes to 'adopt an attitude of respect, a position of humility before the recalcitrant partner in her musical endeavour'.[31] It is when our demands meet the contingencies of the text that creativity and finally healing can take place.

A further, factual illustration. In analysis a close friend 'discovered' (to be interpreted now – though it was not at the time – with all the Lukacherian reservations) that at the moment of birth, his mother kicked the new-born him away, screaming: Take it away, take it away. She had been having an affair with the local doctor and was frightened that her baby's physical appearance would reveal that he was the doctor's son, rather than her husband's. (It did not.) This sense of rejection and lovelessness has had, predictably, a number of effects in his life, usually of a negative or potentially (and actually) destructive variety. In the light of the findings of the analysis, he has tended to 'blame' his mother for much of this and the suffering that it has brought to him and to others. It has only been when he has been able to read the verse of Psalm 22 quoted above and cognate verses – Genesis 49:25; Numbers 11:12 – against the whole 'experience' that he has had to withdraw that blame as an easy way out of accepting responsibility for his own actions and failures. For God is revealed in the text as his *real* mother and Her love has never been in doubt.

Reading the Text: Play

With that, I want to leave discussion of the projective part of 'projective play' and explore more carefully the idea of play. To most of us, brought up in a culture and a theology which depends heavily upon Aristotelian ideas of logic and upon a *theological* notion of a Word that discloses itself in the text in a non-ludic way, the concept of play in the text may seem strange. But the psychotherapeutic value of play has long been recognised, as has its link with the courageous aggression that we identified at the end of Chapter 10. Critical thought, critical self-reflection, crucially depend on a species of play, play in which a willingness to knock down the sandcastle or the Lego village and start again is a necessary part. Without it 'is a relationship with external reality which is one of compliance, the world and its details being recognized but only as something to be fitted in with or demanding adaptation'.[32] If we are to face the full force of the text both critically and openly, we have to move beyond that 'relationship . . . of compliance', that 'meddling without passion'.[33] I therefore want to illustrate play from two other sources.

The first is Stephen Moore, whose book *Mark and Luke in Post-Structuralist Perspectives: Jesus Begins to Write*[34] is one of the most illuminating and original essays on the 'play' in the text. It has, perhaps inevitably, little rooting in existential context and so illustrates more of the play than the projection and has to be read with that in mind. But perhaps we can supply some imaginary context as a kind of experiment. Suppose the following paragraphs, or a reading of the text informed by them, to be read by an archetypal narcissist, anxious about his relationships and their lack of depth; about always finding himself (or herself) on the outside of groups, looking in but unable to trust himself to them; fearful of death and any kind of physical weakness or incapacity; becoming aware, perhaps, of why many therapists call his personality type 'borderline'. Let us suppose that s/he has just finished an unsatisfactory affair, and has an image of her/himself, a symbol, as being a permanent outsider.

Let that be the context of this bit of biblical play. Written in dialogue with Derrida, Lacan, Joyce and Foucault as well as the evangelists, it is uncommonly hard to summarise, even in flavour: what follows is no substitute for, but hopefully an inducement to begin, reading Moore's text.

Moore is discussing Mark's parables and therefore the Markan secret: 'To you the secret of the Kingdom of God has been given: but to those who are outside everything comes by way of parables so that (as Scripture says) they may look and look and see nothing: they may hear and hear and understand nothing: otherwise they might turn to God and be forgiven' (Mark 4:11,12). He notices that Derrida finds the terms used by writers to describe writing – *pharmakon* in Plato, *supplement* in Rousseau, *hymen* in Mallarmé – have a contradictory, double sense, so that, for example, *pharmakon* is *both* poison and cure. Is the same contradictoriness or Janus quality of ambiguity to be found in Mark's parables? Moore quotes from the literary scholar J. Hillis Miller on the prefix *para*. Miller writes:

A thing in para . . . is not only simultaneously on both sides of the boundary line between inside and out. It is also the boundary itself, the screen which is a permeable membrane connecting inside and the outside. It confuses them with one another, allowing the outside in, making the inside out, dividing them and joining them. It also forms an ambiguous transition between one and the other.

This gives Moore the clue. Parables keep outsiders out and allow insiders in, but oddly they also rupture their own membrane, allowing

outsiders in and confusing the insiders who do not understand them
and thus define themselves as outsiders. Indeed, parabolic words and
deeds become so confusing that as 'deranged doormen, [they]
threaten to make outsiders of us all'.

That is the point. The parables do not respect outsiders and insiders.
They turn language inside out like a pocket, 'one that turns [the]
inside[r] out'. Or perhaps Mark is more like a laced shoe, double
knotted. 'Through Mark's eyelets, ever watchful, disciples and readers
are threaded relentlessly: outside then inside, then outside again; left,
then right, then left (clueless) again.'

After an aside on the parallels between Lacan and Jesus in which
he quotes Clement on Lacan – We thought about what he had said
but even more about the enigma of what he might have meant –
Moore returns to Jesus's use of parables. They issue from deep in
Jesus's interiority, from the very depths of his being, but they turn
into unincorporable exteriority. 'Let anyone with ears to hear, hear,'
cries Jesus. But no one has ears big enough. So parables unsettle
speech; they throw language into disarray and leave interpreters
unsettled, the bed-frames of hermeneutical schema roll uncontrol-
lably. Parable is close to *parablos*, counterfeit or false. It is close enough
to be worrying, but not close enough to void it of truth.

So the insiders get their share of the truth; they can look in. Jesus
is identified as the Son of God by God himself (Mark 1:1, 9:7), but
also by the demons (Mark 3:11, 5:7) and supremely by the centurion
at the foot of the cross. But although the demons have inside information on Jesus, they cannot be seen (or perhaps they can?) as
insiders. The women draw closer to the inside, until parable (of act)
leaps out to greet them from the inside of the tomb and drives them
back outside again.

Because even the most inside of the disciples cannot accept the
fact that suffering lies at the heart of redemption, all the insiders are
in the end outsiders. The only exception is the centurion, a gentile,
a Roman, an oppressor among the oppressors who is allowed to look
on the inside. 'Sent to dispatch Jesus, he executes a reading as well . . .
abruptly pulled inside to substitute for the disciples [insiders become
outsiders] who should themselves have been at the foot of the cross,
if not hanging on other crosses round about.' And what has brought
the centurion from the furthest reaches of the outside to the climactic

inside – which may well have ended at least one edition of the Gospel? 'Paradoxically, the centurion's recognition of Jesus as Son of God follows on Jesus' anguished declaration that God has cut him adrift (Mark 15:34). It is the declaration of the book after the author has expelled it from his body. Having read the book, the centurion believes. A writing of absence and inarticulation accomplishes what plain speech could not (Mark 8:32), speech that should have been laden with plain, self-evident meaning. . . . Understanding occurs only at the moment Jesus becomes absent, and when his speech decomposes as it is delivered up to death.'[35]

There is a temptation to dismiss this kind of deconstructive play as specious cleverness. Its critics sometimes claim that it does nothing to reveal 'truth', but strips language of meaning and retains only 'the worthless residue'.[36] Lyotard's 'pragmatics of language particles', which clearly have resonances with Moore's approach and its many derivatives and emulations, are charged with failing adequately to criticise the canon or the society which contains it, but rather, by its narcissistic superficiality, its over-conscious striving for effect, its determined flight from unambiguous meaning, become exemplars of the worst features of the culture of narcissism, the culture of contentment and the culture of the image – exactly the cultures they thought they were reacting against.[37]

Perhaps deconstructive play is not for everyone. Perhaps the imaginary narcissist for whom we played it cannot in the event respond to the inside/outside explorations even though they precisely reflect his own position. Each person has to find their own species of play, to break down the givenness, the hard objectivity of the text, which we have already seen is no objectivity at all. Just as Nietzsche, Heidegger and Derrida (and, in different modes, James Joyce and Kierkegaard) are anxious to break open the Cartesian dualities that hold our culture and our metaphysics in thrall, so a reading of the memory of the life of Jesus with emancipatory intent has to tease, taunt, jolly the text into a departure from the engrained half-truths of ecclesiastical and Sunday-school learning. Such half-truths, with their precipitate closure and over-determinations, their *dependable* meanings, have to be recognised as the barnacles on the furry bottom of the bark of faith, slowing progress – but perhaps keeping some of the planks in place. Faced with all the ambiguities of memory, including the 'irreducible core' of facticity at the most improbable places, we need to hear Derrida's challenge to 'overthrow the hierarchy' of conventional hermeneutics in order to make space for 'the irruptive emergence of a new "concept", a concept which no longer allows itself to be understood in terms of the previous regime'.[38] To hear that challenge and indulge in play is to begin to explore the subversive potential of ludic fantasy and thus find hope where there was formerly only despair.[39] It is thus an act of abandonment of false sources of hope and a return to reality – perhaps an odd claim to make in the context of the last two chapters, but one that is to be made none the less.

Precisely how we get beyond conventional hermeneutics is, at this level, a question of *techne*: the Ignatian use of the imagination is an older tradition that, in the best hands, has more than a tangential relationship to the deconstructive play that I have already illustrated. For the imagination works less logically than mythopoetically, encouraging us, in Jorge Luis Borges's phrase, to 'invert our eyes and practise a sublime astronomy in the infinitude of our hearts'.[40] Spontaneously acted or mimed re-creations of Gospel memories can have the same effect for a group. Some types of dream work, and the use of paint, clay, collage, and puppets in 'dialogue' with the text can break open the text for individuals and sometimes for groups.

This play that challenges, perhaps defies, the conventional pseudo-understanding of the text inevitably involves the projection of our own memories and unconscious material on to the text in much the same way as we saw above in consideration of the projection of our needs on to the text. Play is ludic(rous) and part of that ludic quality is the introjection into the text of signs and symbols that do not belong there – pockets, pocketbooks, shoes and shoelaces in the example from Moore. They may or may not survive as the play gathers pace or, to change the metaphor, moves along the score. What matters is that they come out to play, that they are given the chance to play around, to dance in the sunlight. For the object is to get away from an imitative, mimetic quality of understanding with its one-to-one relationships of meaning and its tired dualities – true/false, historical/legendary, one/many, Jew/non-Jew – into a poetic or, as Hopper calls it, theopoetic quality. And that is something that each person and community confronting the text has to be prepared

to take the risk of doing. It is like writing their story as a cartoon
rather than as Macaulayan history. Or singing their story to Captain
Pepper rather than to Wagner.

Hopper calls this a step back, a deliberate unlearning.[41] He quotes
Charles Peguy, who in a poem has God say:

It is innocence that is full and experience that is empty.

. . . . .

It is innocence that knows and experience that does not know.
It is the child who is full and the man who is empty.
Empty as an empty gourd and as an empty barrel:

. . . . .

Now then, children, go to school.
And you, men, go to the school of life.
Go and learn
How to unlearn.

Paul Hoggett quotes a nice example of unlearning from the
musician Steve Lacy. Asked if, during his performance, his mind went
blank, Lacy replied: 'Not exactly a blank – more like a blink. You
try and stay out of the way. You try and not lose touch with the
music, and let the thing happen. It's not you that does it – it's IT
that wants to be done. . . . It can only go one way, and it's not you
who decides. It's IT.'[42]

This may seem in strange contrast with the emphasis that we have
so far been putting on the significance of bringing experience – the
sedimented memories that make us what we are – into contact with
the text. But we should not confuse Peguy's innocence with naïve
empiricism. His innocence is precisely the critic of that kind of
naïvety. It is the innocence of the 'child' (clearly a symbolic figure)
who has not yet been tainted by the unacknowledged ideology incorporated in the contemporary 'naïve empiricism' and is therefore
better in touch with John Lyons's 'genetic anamnesis' of human
possibilities. It is to aver that the cartoonist can sometimes see more
of the truth than Macaulay (or even, perhaps, Kovel).

In this sense it is a call *back*, back to a deeper level of consciousness
where the current dichotomies and representations hold no sway, back

perhaps to the primary symbols,[43] for it is there that the memories that hold us in thrall are to be relativised, judged and put in context.

Reading the Text: Moving Forward

Hopper contrasts that with the necessary steps that follow the backward step; the step down and the step through. The step down is even more demanding than the step back, for it involves the shattering of 'the protective wall of the conscious ego [including that of Freud] to become open to the deep Self [Jung]'. Leaving aside the question of whether this juxtaposition is entirely accurate, we glimpse what Hopper has in mind: the letting go of the security of ego-strength, even of identity itself, as we come face to face with as much of the inner material that we are projecting as we can bear. It is a constant struggle of pain and anguish to reach beyond the obvious, the known, the accepted and acceptable to uncover new depths of ego-resistance – until we cry with Ezra Pound: Shall we look for a deeper or is this the bottom? It is, of course, never the bottom: there is always more unconscious to unpack; more false consciousness to surrender; more distortions to unravel; more of the suffering of the world to share empathetically. Perhaps only the mystic and the rare poet comes anywhere near the bottom; and then finds both nothing (No-thing) and everything simultaneously. This is the moment of Zen Buddhism when the whole of Creation is revealed (like Julian of Norwich's acorn) in the simplest representation.

In a sense, the text – Jesus – becomes the analyst which/who stands with us and enables us to 'see' the false constructions we have put on others and on ourselves in our memories, as we have sought to protect the fragile self in masquerade of the real Self.[44] He takes us through critical self-reflection until we confront the distortions in our communications with others and the sedimentation of such distortions over the years.

Because the text fights back, courage and honesty, even aggression as we have already seen in a slightly different but closely related context, are required in the step down. That is why it is important to see Jesus the Saver as centrally involved in the step down; we need courage and honesty beyond us if we are to take it. Or to put it in a language that chimes with older traditions of spirituality, it is in the step down that trust in the loving graciousness of God becomes determinative. If, to use Bion's terminology, I am not able to feel 'held' or 'contained' during that process, I am likely to be so dominated by (usually) unconscious fears and anxieties about what I shall find as I step down, that I shall pull back. I shall want to return to the comfortable womb of conventional religiosity which protects me from the experience of suffering and so makes change – inner *and* outer – impossible. That is to trade death for life, to refuse the possibility of new life. It is the final denial of faith in a good God who wants his people free. The (conscious) fear of confusion, of getting 'it' wrong, of finally not having the courage to live it out . . . such fear and anxiety are natural, indeed both healthy and inevitable. But they, too, lead us back finally to faith in a gracious God who will, in one way or another, alone or more usually in and through company, pull us through. We are back to Christ the container, the 'keeper' of Mother Julian, whose containment can give us the capacity for Keatsian patience: 'When a man is capable of being in uncertainties, mysteries, doubts, without any irritable reaching after fact or reason.'[45]

How, though, do we relate this theopoetic approach to the analytical approach of Chapters 4 to 9? If the step down (and through, for the two inevitably elide) is a step towards a new consciousness, how does it relieve me of the unconscious drives that were leading me to structure my world – and therefore leading *us* to structure *the* world – in this way? That will become clearer when we have explored a little more the third step – the step through.

Despite the effort involved in getting to its threshold, the step through is gift. It is 'the step through into the newness of the whole where the presencing of Being is experienced. This is that "creative advance" of which Whitehead has spoken.'[46] And not only Whitehead. As we saw in anticipation above, it is the moment of the mystic and of the poet. But it is, too, the moment of the therapeutic client who suddenly 'sees' in a quite new way, of the scientist or cosmologist who is enabled to step beyond the boundaries of the subject and intuitively grasp a new way of looking at the world that will take years to set down in comprehensible mathematics or cold prose. It is Meister Eckhart's discovery of God beyond 'God' where 'theology becomes theopoiesis', using metaphor as 'diaphor' (movement through) in which 'new meaning emerges from juxtaposing particulars of experience, and it is the new meaning of sacred Presence that speaks'.[47] It is epiphany: but it is also diaphony, the transparent moment that reveals all in outline. We (for it is not a moment reserved to the religious or literary expert) no longer see in enigma: we see face to face.

In so far as this diaphor brings together, in a powerful fusion, the memories of our (individual and corporate) past and the memories of Christ's death and resurrection, it performs precisely the task that Marcuse (falsely) thought memory alone could achieve: 'a mediation that can momentarily at least break through the omnipresent power of the given facts'.[48] It is Metz's vision of a 'definite memory that breaks through the magic circle of the prevailing consciousness'.[49] It calls into being 'the possibility of seeing the present from the point of view of the past, from the moment when this present . . . was entirely contingent . . . not the reiterative unreality of reverie, which emptily rewrites history'. We are thus obliged to see ourselves again as the 'partial origins of our own history' and to become again the origin of possibilities, 'as having had a history which was history and not fatality'.[50]

Face to face in memory with the acting out of total self-giving, we find our fears, anxieties, traumas and self-blames relativised to insignificance. What once seemed to demand reaction, which seemed to possess us (while we imagined we possessed it/them) and create us in its own image, can no longer pretend to such power. Contained by a love so absolute, so unconditional, we discover that judgement issues not in condemnation but in forgiveness. The ice-stiletto which once threatened our rib-cage with penetration and death melts to a few drops of harmless water and flows back into the sea. We are on the way to freedom from compulsion.

Elsewhere I have called this diaphor 'radical contemplation', since it is radical in at least three senses: it gets to the root of the ego, deep into the psyche beyond the defences that condition meaning, domesticating it so that it serves our (infinitely subtly disguised) purposes; it deals radically with the text, refusing a premature closure but always plunging deeper in the expectation that new levels of meaning and challenge are waiting to be discovered; and it radically changes our view of ourselves (our Selves) and our world, snapping our collusive attachment to the structures of power and language that hold us captive. It is radical precisely because it will not collude with the *status quo*; for now it is free to glimpse the Kingdom. And it is contemplation because it emerges from the patient waiting (as well as the projective play) in hopeful anticipation, which is the stance of the contemplative. It takes us back to Rilke's 'arrow [that] endures the string, to become, in the gathering outleap, something more than itself. For staying is nowhere.'

After the Text . . .

Now we are in a better position to answer the question posed above about the relationship between the 'fruits' of projective play and the fundamental questions of this book. For what I have suggested is that projective play with the text opens consciousness not only to unconscious material, but to a process of relativisation and transcendence that destroys the destructive power of the unconscious material. Father may still be an enigma and an incompletely resolved sign or symbol in our lives: we do not need to be led by the Oedipal nose. Pre-Oedipal fears and anxieties do not disappear as morning dew, but they no longer need be determinative of the way I structure my relationships or my understanding of the world. Anima may still seduce or demand attention: she need not control me. The narcissist may still be 'outside'; but s/he discovers that s/he is not alone and therefore does not need the hatred and anger that total exclusion makes inevitable. Lerner's clients may still feel that they 'could have done better'; but they do not have to internalise all that self-blame because the pressure to 'do better' has been relativised – not in relation to neighbour or foreman, but in relation to the discovery of ultimate redeeming love. The stereotyping, outgroup thinking and resentful memories of Staub's analysis become almost literally impossible from the standpoint of the step down and through. And Girard's scapegoat is redundant, not because there will in future be no griefs to bear, but because they can be borne without anger or blame.

And if that is true at the individual level, it is no less true at the group level – despite the pessimism of Bion and Alford. For the containing power of the counter-memories of Christ are often sufficient to allow cell-churches to advance from the paranoid-schizoid position to the depressive position and find there, perhaps for only short periods, the capacity for altruism and sacrificial love. In South Africa, Brazil, Nicaragua, the Philippines; with the womens' movements, the ecology lobbies, the peace movements; in L'Arche, in Corrymeela, in the Catholic Worker communities, in many, many less publicised little associations of people who hold in common a radical openness to the contemplation of Jesus's memory, we have seen it happening. These are new social movements with hope – in a far more radical and purposeful way than Habermas ever envisaged.

Like us as individuals, they are left with their memories. But they are no longer destroyed by them.

Notes

Chapter 1

1. M. Halbwachs: *The Collective Memory*. Trans F.J. Ditter. San Francisco: Harper and Row, 1980.

2. But some long-established groups may have very little collective memory. For example, the Karen of Burma, who may have been in their present location for 1300 years, have been called 'a people without a history' because they have virtually no oral tradition of their origins or exploits. See Jonathan Falla: *True Love and Bartholomew: Rebels on the Burmese Border*. Cambridge: CUP, 1991, p.15.

3. L. Passerini: *Fascism in Popular Memory*. Cambridge: CUP, 1987.

4. Milan Kundera: *The Book of Laughter and Forgetting*. Trans. M. Heim. Harmondsworth: Penguin, 1983, p.159.

5. James Fentress and Chris Wickham: *Social Memory: New Prespectives on the Past*. Oxford: Blackwell, 1992, p.13.

6. *ibid.*, p.116.

7. Terence McCaughey: *Memory and Redemption: Church, Politics and Prophetic Theology in Ireland*. Dublin: Gill and Macmillan, 1993. And compare John Beckett: *The Anglo-Irish Tradition*. Belfast: Blackstaff, 1983, p.53.

8. For a recent discussion, see Gillian Cohen: *Memory in the Real World*. Hove: Lawrence Erlbaum, 1989, esp. pp.156–60.

9. Paul Connerton: *How Societies Remember*. Cambridge: CUP, 1991.

10. W.B. Yeats: *Mythologies*. New York: Macmillan, 1959, p.345. See, too, Mircea Eliade: *Images and Symbols: Studies in Religious Symbolism*. New York: Sheed and Ward, 1952.

11. In Thomas Butler(ed.): *Memory, History, Culture and the Mind*. Oxford: Blackwell, 1989.

12. See N. Chomsky: *Language and Problems of Knowledge and Freedom*. Cambridge, Mass.: MIT, 1988; and for an earlier statement, modified by 1988. *Language and Mind*. New York and London: Harcourt Brace, 1968.

13. John Lyons, recognising Chomsky's acknowledged affinity with Platonism, has felicitously called this 'genetic anamnesis'. See his excellent

272

introduction to Chomsky: *Chomsky.* 3rd edition. London: Fontana, 1991, p.165.

14. So much so that it now seems that Chomsky himself deliberately underplayed his break with Bloomfieldian behaviourism in his early *Syntactic Structures* (1957). See Lyons: *op. cit.*, Appendix 2, pp.226–9.

15. E. Thomas Lawson and Robert N. McCauley: *Rethinking Religion: Connecting Cognition and Culture.* Cambridge: CUP, 1990, p.183.

Chapter 2

1. Philip Roth: *The Facts, A Novelist's Autobiography.* New York: Harper, 1988, p.8.

2. Theo Platinga: *How Memory Shapes Narratives.* Lamperer: Mellen, 1992, p.45.

3. E. Loftus: *Eyewitness Testimony.* Cambridge Mass.: Harvard UP, 1979, pp.86–7. But see also G.M. Stephenson, H. Brandstatter and U. Wagner: 'An experimental study of social performance and delay on the testimonial validity of story recall', *European Journal of Social Psychology,* 13, 1983, pp.175–91, and G.M. Stephenson, D. Abrams. U. Wagner and G. Wade: 'Partners in recall: collaborative order in the recall of a police interrogation', *British Journal of Social Psychology,* 25, 1986, pp.341–3.

4. The phrase is that of I.M.L. Hunter in *Memory.* Rev. ed. Harmondsworth: Penguin, 1964, p.183.

5. See Cohen: *op. cit.*, pp.201 ff.

6. Platinga: *op. cit.*, p.3.

7. Ned Lukacher: *Primal Scenes: Literature, Philosophy, Psychoanalysis.* Ithaca: Cornell UP, 1986.

8. F. Nietzsche: *On the Advantage and Disadvantage of History for Life.* Trans. P. Preuss. Indianapolis: Hacken, 1980.

9. There is, of course, another side to that argument: that forgetting – especially of humankind's capacity for evil, for example in the context of the Holocaust – is deliberate suppression that can lead to repetition of disaster. See Stefan Kander: *The Eighth Sin.* New York: Berkeley, 1978.

10. See Wolfhart Pannenberg: *Anthropology in Theological Perspective* (hereafter ATP). London: SCM, 1985, p.494. F. Tupper: *The Theology of Wolfhart Pannenberg.* London:SCM, 1972, pp.103, 104.

11. Wolfhart Pannenberg: *Basic Questions in Theology.* Vol 1. London: SCM, 1970, p.79.

12. See, for example, A.R. Luria: *The Neuropsychology of Memory.* Washington, DC: Winston, 1976, p.238. And Oliver Sacks: *The Man who Mistook his Wife for a Hat.* London: Pan/Picador edition, 1986, pp.104 ff.

13. Rom Harré: *Social Being: A Theory for Social Psychology.* Oxford: Blackwell, 1979; and *Personal Being.* Oxford: Blackwell, 1983. And Alistair McFadyen: *The Call to Personhood: A Christian Theory of the Individual in Social Relationship.* Cambridge: CUP, 1990.

14. M. Main, N. Kaplan and J. Cassidy: 'Security in infancy, childhood, and adulthood: a move to the level of representation', in I. Bretherton and E. Waters (eds): *Growing Points of Attachment Theory and Research*. Monographs of the Society for Research in Child Development. Vol. 50. 1985, pp.66–104.

15. John Lyons: 'Deixis and subjectivity. Loquor ergo sum', in Robert J. Jarvella and Wolfgang Klein: *Speech, Place and Action: Studies in Deixis and Related Topics*. New York: Wiley, 1982. But in a later article Lyons recognised that in 1967 Aldo Testa had devised the plural formulation. Aldo Testa: *La Struttura Dialogica del Linguaggio*. Bologna: Capelli, quoted in J. Lyons: 'La subjectivité dans le language et dans les langues', in Guy Serbat (ed.): *E. Beneveniste Aujourd'hui: International du C.R.N.S.* Paris: Société pour L'Information Grammaticale, 1984, p.131. It is at least arguable that Parmenides and Heidegger saw this point before and after the Cartesian definition. See George Joseph Seidel: *Martin Heidegger and the Pre-Socratics*. Lincoln: University of Nebraska Press, 1964, p.63.

16. H. Kung: *Does God Exist? An Answer for To-Day*. Garden City, New York. 1980. Wolfhart Pannenberg: *ATP., sup. cit.*

17. H.S. Sullivan: *The Interpersonal Theory of Psychiatry*. New York: W.W. Norton, 1953, p.44. Quoted in Felicity de Zulueta: *From Pain to Violence: The Traumatic Roots of Destructiveness*. London: Whurr, 1993, p.105.

18. Alistair MacIntyre: *After Virtue: A Study in Moral Theory*. London: Duckworth, 1981, p.213.

19. Karen Brison: *Just Talk: Gossip, Meetings and Power in a Papua New Guinea Village*. Berkeley, Calif.: California UP, 1992.

20. Fentress and Wickham: *op. cit.*, p.108.

Chapter 3

1. See, for instance, A. Bandura: *Social Learning Theory*. Englewood Cliffs, NJ: Prentice-Hall, 1977.

2. In saying that, I am not prejudging whether the institution is able to manage the conflict creatively, but I am rejecting the traditionalist view that conflict is a moral or social or institutional evil that has to be avoided. See S.P. Robbins: *Managing Organizational Conflict: A Non-traditional Approach*. Englewood Cliffs, NJ: Prentice-Hall, 1974.

3. S. Freud: *Totem and Taboo*. Standard Edition. London: Routledge & Kegan Paul, 1968. Vol. 13 cf. Rosalind Coward: *Patriarchal Precedents: Sexuality and Social Relations*. London: Routledge & Kegan Paul, 1983.

4. William Hamilton: 'Innate aptitudes of man', in R. Fox (ed): *Biosocial Anthropology*. London: Maltby, 1975.

5. John H. Crook: *The Evolution of Human Consciousness* Oxford: OUP, 1980, p.157.

6. R.I.M. Dunbar and P. Dunbar: 'Social dynamics of gelada baboons', in *Contributions to Primatology*, 6. Basle: Karger. See also H. Kummer: 'Rules of dyad and group formation among captive gelada baboons

(Thropithecus gelada)', in *Proceedings of the Symposium at the 5th Congress of the International Primatological Society of Japan*. Tokyo: Science Press, 1975.

7. C. Levi Strauss: *The Elementary Structures of Kinship*. Boston, Mass.: Beacon, 1969.

8. B.N. Aziz: *Tibetan Frontier Families: Reflections of Three Generations from D'Ing-ri*. New Delhi: Vikas, 1978. M.C. Goldstein: 'Fraternal polyandry and fertility in a high Himalayan village in Nepal', *Human Ecology*, 4. 1976.

9. John and S.J. Crook: 'Tibetan polyandry; problems of adaptation and fitness', in L.L. Betzig et al. (eds), *Human Reproductive Behaviour*. Cambridge: CUP, 1988; and cf. their essay on the same subject and reworking much of the same data in John Crook and Henry Osmaston (eds): *Environmental Resources, Society and Religious Life in Zangskar, Ladakh*. University of Bristol, 1994, pp.735–86.

10. M. Dickeman: 'The ecology of mating systems in hypergynous dowry societies', *Social Science Information*, 18. 1979, pp.163–94.

11. See Anthony Giddens: *New Rules of Sociological Method: A Positive Critique of Interpretative Sociologies*. 2nd rev. edn. Cambridge: Polity Press, 1993.

12. C. Rowland: *Radical Christianity*. Cambridge: Polity Press, 1988.

13. E. Bick: 'Experience of the skin in early object relations', *International Journal of Psychoanalysis*, Vol. 9. 1968, p.484. Cf. E. Bick: 'Further considerations on the function of the skin in early object relations: findings from infant observation integrated into child and adult analysis', *British Journal of Psychotherapy*, 2 (4), pp.292–9.

14. Paul Hoggett: *Partisans in an Uncertain World: The Psychoanalysis of Engagement*. London: Free Association Books, 1992, pp.11–115. The reference to Freud is to *The Ego and the Id*.

15. K. Benson: 'A framework for policy analysis', in D. Rogers and D. Whetter (eds): *Interorganizational Coordination*. Ames, Iowa: Iowa UP, pp.137ff, quoted in Hoggett, *op. cit.*, p.113.

16. Walter Wink: *Confronting the Powers*. Minneapolis: Fortress, 1991.

17. A. Etzioni: *A Comparative Analysis of Complex Organizations*. Glencoe, Illinois: Free Press, 1961.

18. That is not, of course, to deny that the institution may also, simultaneously, be experienced as alienating. We may be more familiar with alienation as a result of writers in the Marxian tradition (see Chapter 8), but that need not be the only emotional response of the employee.

19. Hoggett: *op. cit.*, p.124.

20. See Cohen: *op. cit.*, pp.151ff; and, there cited, A.C. Graesser and L.F. Clark: *Structures and Procedures of Implicit Knowledge*. Norwood, NJ: Ablex, 1985.

21. Laurence Kohlberg, Charles Levine, Alexandra Hewer: *Moral Stages: A Current Formulation and a Response to Critics*. Basel, London: Karger, 1983.

22. But it does not seem to interest Gillian Cohen, a surprising gap in an otherwise classic treatment.

23. David Hume: *Treatise of Human Nature*. Bk.1, pt.1, sec.3 p.9 of the OUP Selby-Bigge edition. Cf. Platinga: *op. cit.*, pp.19–20.

24. See Charles V. Brown: *Taxation and the Incentive to Work*. Oxford: OUP, 1983.

25. Edward Schillebeeckx: *Church: The Human Story of God* (trans. J. Bowden). London: SCM, 1990, p.17.

26. See Teun A. van Dijk: *Communicating Racism: Ethnic Prejudice in Thought and Talk*. London: Sage, 1988.

Chapter 4

1. See, for example, Christopher Bryant: *Jung and the Christian Way*. London: Darton, Lonjman & Todd, 1983. It is informative to notice the tentative and almost apologetic tone of Bryant's Introduction, and to recall that this book appeared only twelve years ago.

2. Ira Progoff: *Jung's Psychology and its Social Meaning. An Introductory Statement of C.G. Jung's Psychological Theories and a First Interpretation of their Significance for the Social Sciences*. London: Routledge & Kegan Paul, 1953.

3. Jung: *Collected Works*. Edited by H. Read, M. Fordham, G. Adler and W. McGuire. Trans. R. Hull. London: Routledge & Kegan Paul. Hereafter *CW.* Vol. 10, 275.

4. *CW.* 7, 268.

5. C. Jung and C. Kerenyi: *Introduction to a Science of Mythology*. Trans. R. Hull. London: Routledge & Kegan Paul, 1949, p.102. (Jung's contribution to this work was published in Vol. 9 of *CW.*)

6. *CW.* 8, 382. My emphasis.

7. Hobson has pointed to the complexity and multiplicity of the nature of this 'constellation' and has speculated whether some kind of mathematical representation was not appropriate. Recent developments in the mathematics of ordered randomness may well be suggestive in this connection. See R. Hobson: 'The archetypes of the collective unconscious', in M. Fordham et al. (eds): *Analytical Psychology: A Modern Science*. London: Heinemann, 1973.

8. A. Stevens: *On Jung*. London: Routledge & Kegan Paul, 1990, p.32.

9. C. Jung: *Contributions to Analytical Psychology*. London: Kegan Paul, 1928, p.46.

10. In his account of the development of personality, Jung portrays a flow of libido from the conscious 'down' into the unconscious. When the conscious and unconscious are brought into a more healthful relationship, the energy or libido thus released is, as it were, suspended between them, maintaining a dynamic equilibrium. See *CW.* 7, pp.245–53.

11,12. *CW.* 18, para. 1228.

13. Hobson: *op. cit.*, p.70.

14. Portmann has suggested a three-fold classification of archetypes: (1) those that are wholly determined by heredity, such as innate release

mechanisms in birds and animals; (2) those that are determined by heredity in a general way, but 'imprinted' by individual experience; (3) those that have a more social and environmental reference. See J. Jacobi: *Complex/Archetype Symbol in the Psychology of C.G. Jung*. Princeton, NJ: Princeton UP, 1959, p.40.

15.   Jung was heavily criticised for expounding the belief that the experience of archtypes was inherited. This was interpreted as subscription to the discredited theory of the inheritance of acquired characteristics (a theory about which some modern ethologists and psychologists would be less hostile than Jung's contemporaries). Jung therefore came to make the distinction between the archetype-as-such (inherited) and the archetypal image (not inherited but individually experienced).

16.   *CW.* 7. 151. Samuels draws an interesting parallel in this connection between inner psychological structures 'knowing' their destiny and the observed behaviour of quarks. A. Samuels: *Jung and the Post-Jungians*. London: Routledge & Kegan Paul, 1985, p.30.

17.   *CW.* 9, p.157.

18.   This has led some reductionist-minded critics to see archetypes as no more than 'instinctual drives and primordial reaction formation' enco-ded genetically; and to accuse Jung of pretentious mystification. One wonders whether such critics have any personal or clinical experience of the power of archetypal material, one of Jung's main points. See V. Brome: *Jung: Man and Myth*. London: Macmillan, 1978, pp.284–5. A. Plant's review of Lambert's *Analysis, Repair and Individuation* in *Journal of Analytical Psychology*. Vol. 27, No.3, 1982, pp.285–7. Cf. G. Atwood and R. Stolorow: 'Metapsychology, reification and the representational world of C.G. Jung', *International Review of Psychoanalysis*. Vol. 4, No.1, 1975.

19.   Compare A. Dry: *The Psychology of Jung: A Critical Interpretation*. London: Methuen, 1961, with D. Miller: *The New Polytheism*. Dallas: Spring, 1981, and J. Hillman: *Loose Ends*. Dallas: Spring, 1975.

20.   J. Hillman: *Revisioning Psychology*. New York: Harper and Row, 1975, p.213.

21.   Throughout this book, I use self in the sense of the selfhood of identity and Self as the core of the ego in Jungian theory.

22.   The late Revd Dr Roy Lee, personal communication.

23.   I shall from time to time in the rest of this book use this phrase in this typographical form to emphasise the ambiguity of the word: it repre-sents in the conventional sense, but it also re-presents in the sense of making present anew. In this latter sense it is close to the Hebrew idea, half-captured by the Greek 'anamnesis'.

24.   Samuels: *op. cit.*, p.212.

25.   *CW.* 9.ii, para.26.

26.   *CW.* 17, para 338.

27.   A. Guggenbuhl-Craig: *Marriage – Dead or Alive*. Zurich: Spring, 1977.

28.   H. Binswanger: 'Positive aspects of the animus', *Spring*, 1963, pp.82 ff.

29. Robert A. Johnson: *Understanding the Psychology of Romantic Love*. New York: Harper & Row, 1983.

30. N. Goldenberg: 'A feminist critique of Jung', *Signs: Journal of Women in Culture and Society*. 1976, pp.445 ff.

31. This does not represent an adequate summary of Jung's thought on marriage, however briefly stated. I have not, for instance, discussed his theory of containment and its dangers, an idea, reworked, that we shall encounter later. See *CW.* 17, 332.

32. Johnson: *op. cit.*, p.60.

33. Quoted in Johnson: *op. cit.*, p.163.

34. How alien this line of thought is to Jungian orthodoxy (a notion that he would anyway have rejected) is more difficult to say. Since Jung saw archetypes (at least in his later writing) as psychic processes rather than ideas, he acknowledged that each culture and historical period determines the substance of the archetype. 'They [the archetypes] draw the stuff of experience into their shape, presenting themselves in facts, rather than presenting facts. They clothe themselves in facts.' It is worth noting, however, that for him the 'contents of an archetypal character . . . do not refer to anything that is or has been conscious but to something essentially unconscious.' From this it follows that, if we are to be faithful to Jung, we need to see our 'deposit' to the collective unconscious as being an unconscious process; something over which we have no control and of which we remain unaware. Whether we need to follow Jung so far is, however, more problematic. We may, for example, want to at least hold open the possibility that some conscious material of great significance can be incorporated in the collective unconscious – and not only through a mechanism analogous to repression.

35. This is something that *social* memory cannot do by definition – since it is an imposed memory that does not chime with the real experiences of those required to adopt it.

36. J.G. Ballard: *Empire of the Sun*. London: Heinemann, 1989; and *The Kindness of Women*. London: Heinemann, 1991.

37. Edith Sitwell: *Fire of the Mind: An Anthology*. Compiled by E. Salter and Allanah Harper. London: Joseph, 1976.

38. D. Miller: *op. cit.*, and *Christs, Mediations on Archetypal Images in Christian Theology*. New York: Seabury Press; 1981. And J. Hillman with Laura Pozzo: *Egalitarian Typologies versus the Perception of the Unique*. Dallas: Spring, 1980 and *Inter Views*. New York: Spring, 1983.

39. Especially in *The Spiritual Problem of Modern Man*. 1938/31. *CW.* 10.

40. Hans-Gunter Heimbrock and Barbara Boudewijnse: *Current Studies on Rituals: Perspectives for the Psychology of Religion*. Amsterdam, Atlanta GA: Rodopi, 1990.

41. K. Helmut Reich: 'Rituals and social structure; the moral dimension', in Heimbrock and Boudewijnse: *op. cit.*

42. F. Nietzsche: 'Beyond good and evil', in *The Philosophy of Nietzsche*. New York: Random House, 1954, No. 289, p.606.

43. C. Jung: *Aion. CW.* 9ii, para 3. Jung seems to have thought that the whole of the unconscious could become – or certainly become – dominated by the Shadow. See Samuels: *op. cit.*, p.65.
44. *CW.* 9ii, 6.
45. *CW.* 11, para 8.
46. Anthony Stevens: *The Roots of War: A Jungian Perspective.* New York: Paragon House, 1989.
47. *ibid*, p.27.
48. *ibid*.
49. Walter Wink: *Engaging the Powers. Discernment and Resistance in a World of Domination.* Minneapolis: Fortress, 1992.
50. Lionel Tiger: *Men in Groups.* London: Panther, 1971.
51. N. Tinbergen: *The Study of Instinct.* Oxford: OUP, 1951. For summaries of parallel significant work by Mayer and Kohler, see Stevens: *op. cit.*, pp.47 ff.
52. Stevens: *op. cit.*, pp.55–6.
53. See A.F.C. Wallace: 'Psychological preparations for war', in M. Fried, M. Harris and R. Murphy (eds): *The Anthropology of Armed Conflict and Aggression.* Garden City, NY: Natural History Press, 1968.
54. Stevens: *op. cit.*, p.200.

Chapter 5
1. See A. Kuhn and A.M. Wolpe: *Feminism and Materialism.* London: Routledge & Kegan Paul, 1978. N. Chodorow: *op. cit.*
2. Joel Kovel: *White Racism: A Psychohistory.* London: Free Association. 1988 edn, with an introduction by Ivan Ward.
3. *ibid.*, p.66.
4. *ibid.*, p.67.
5. T.W. Adorno, Else Frenkel-Brunswick, Daniel J. Levinson, R. Nevitt Sanford et al. *The Authoritarian Personality.* New York: Free Press, 1950. But see too Richard Christie and Marie Jahoda (eds): *Studies in the Scope and Method of 'The Authoritarian Personality'.* Glencoe, III: 1954.
6. David R. Roediger: *The Wages of Whiteness. Race and the Making of the American Working Class.* London: Verso, 1991, p.14. It is surprising how the criticism of reductionism adheres to Kovel. Peter Loewenberg makes the same point in a personal communication. This is doubly surprising, as Kovel is anxious to stress the importance of intermediating structures, especially in the way in which racist societies actually change.
7. Brian Bird: 'A consideration of the etiology of prejudice', *Journal of the American Psychoanalytical Association*, 5, 1957, pp.490–513. See also Terry Rodgers: 'The evolution of an active anti-negro racist', *The Psychoanalytic Study of Society*, 1, 1960, pp.237–43.
8. Kovel: *op. cit.*, pp.67–8.
9. *ibid.*, p.74.
10. *ibid.*, p.75.
11. *ibid.*, p.71.
12. Talcott Parsons: *Social Structure and Personality.* Glencoe, III: Free Press,

964. F. Weinstein and Gerald Platt: *The Wish to be Free: Society, Psyche and Value Change*. Berkeley: California UP, 1969. Peter Loewenberg: *Decoding the Past: The Psychohistorical Approach*. Berkeley: California UP, 1969 (Knopf, 1985). See especially Loewenberg's discussion of some of the methodological problems of psychohistory: pp.3–34.

13. I. Dilman: quoted in *Freud and Human Nature*. Oxford: Blackwell, 1986, p.23.

14. See, for instance, Ian Craib: *Psychoanalysis and Social Theory: The Limits of Sociology*. London: Harvester Wheatsheaf, 1989, pp.87–92.

15. See his Introduction to the 1988 FAB edition of Kovel.

16. *ibid.*, p.1vi.

17. John Dollard: *Caste and Class in a Southern Town*. Garden City, New York: Anchor, 1957. Quoted in Kovel: *op. cit.*, p.71.

Chapter 6

1. See his trilogy: *Naming the Powers: The Language of Power in the New Testament*, and *Unmasking the Powers: The Invisible Forces that Determine Human Existence*. 1984 and 1986 respectively. Both Minneapolis: Fortress. The third of the trilogy was cited above.

2. See Frazer Watts and Mark Williams: *The Psychology of Religious Knowing*. Cambridge: CUP, 1988.

3. See K. Wynn: 'Addition and subtraction in human infants', *Nature*, 358, 1992, pp.749–50.

4. Republished in W.R.D. Fairbairn: *Psychoanalytic Studies of the Personality*. London: Routledge & Kegan Paul, 1952.

5. Published in R.E. Money-Kyrle (ed.): *The Writings of Melanie Klein*. New York: Free Press, 1946, Vol. 3, pp.1–24.

6. E. Spillius: 'Some developments from the work of Melanie Klein', *International Journal of Psychoanalysis*, 54, 1983, p.322.

7. See Hannah Segal: *Melanie Klein*. Harmondsworth: Penguin, 1981, p.117.

8. None of these explanations is wholly satisfactory and each poses further questions. None the less, it is probably true that most modern Kleinians would put most emphasis on the acquisition of cognitive skills, without necessarily denying the significance of either parenting or 'normal' development. The question remains, however: If the child is unable to cope adequately with its phantasy life, how can it learn adequately about procedures for reality testing?

9. M. Klein: 'Love, guilt and reparation', in M. Klein and J. Rivière: *Love, Hate and Reparation*. New York: Norton, 1964, p.65.

10. Hoggett, *sup. cit.*, p.23.

11. William Halton: 'Some unconscious aspects of organizational life; contributions from psychoanalysis', in Anton Obholzer and Vega Zagier Roberts (eds): *The Unconscious at Work: Individual and Organization Stress in the Human Services*. London: Routledge, 1994, pp.11–18

12. Walter Lowe: *Evil and the Unconscious*. American Academy of Religion: Studies in Religion, 30. Scholars Press, Chico, California, 1983.

13. J. Riviere: 'The unconscious phantasy of an inner world reflected in examples from literature', in Klein, Heimann and Money-Kyrle: *op. cit.*, pp. 360–1. Note that 'what we do with them [phantasies] inside ourselves' is heavily dependent upon the quality of containment that has accompanied the phantasies.

14. *ibid.*, pp.361–2.

15. But, for a new and potentially creative way into this area, see W. Gordon Lawrence: 'Won from the void and formless infinite: experiences of social dreaming', *Free Associations*, Vol. 2, Part 2, No. 22, 1991, pp. 259–94.

16. There is here the wider question of what size of group is amenable to this kind of approach. Bion confined himself almost wholly to small groups, so-called work groups. But, as I comment later, some of Klein's more enthusiastic followers have sought to apply her ideas to whole nation-states.

17. C. Fred Alford: *Melanie Klein* and *Critical Social Theory.* New Haven: Yale UP, 1989.

18. Wilfred Bion: *Experiences in Groups* and *Attention and Interpretation: A Scientific Approach to Insight in Psycho-Analysis and Groups.* New York: Basic Books, 1961 and 1970 respectively. Donald W. Winnicott: *Holding and Interpretation.* New York: Grove, 1986.

19. Winnicott: *op. cit.*, p.16.

20. Paul Hoggett: *Partisans in an Uncertain World: The Psychoanalysis of Engagement.* London: Free Association Books, 1992, p.66.

21. Bion's primary interest in time if not in theoretical depth, arising out of his work in the Army during the Second World War, was to analyse why groups ceased to function effectively at their 'work'. He argues that anxiety tended to force them into one of three 'basic assumptions' – dependency, fight/flight, or pairing. Later he looked at the way individuals can be helped to understand their own primitive sensations by examining how they operate in groups. It was in this latter connection that he most fruitfully used a Kleinian perspective. See Malcolm Pines (ed.): *Bion and Group Psychotherapy.* London: Routledge & Kegan Paul, 1985, and Robin Anderson (ed.): *Clinical Lectures on Klein and Bion.* Tavistock/Routledge, 1992, especially the lecture by Ronald Britton: 'Keeping things in mind', pp.102–13.

22. This line of argument quickly leads into the debate about the nature of functioning of bureaucracy that starts with Weber and stems into work on organizational development as researched by people like W.L. French and C.H. Bell. See their *Organization Development: Behavioural Science Interventions for Organization Improvement.* Englewood Cliffs, NJ: Prentice-Hall, 1984. And see Anton Obholzer: 'Managing social anxieties in public sector organizations', in Obholzer and Roberts (eds.): *sup. cit.*, pp.169–78.

23. Peter Speck: 'Working with dying people: on being good enough', in Obholzer and Roberts (eds): *sup. cit.*

24. R. Niebuhr: *Moral Man and Immoral Society.* New York: Scribner, 1932.

25. Otto Kernberg: *Internal World and External Reality: Object Relations Theory Applied.* Northvale, NJ: Jason Aronson, 1985.

26. Cf. Freud's account of the way the group seeks to substitute itself for the individual's ego in *Group Psychology and the Analysis of the Ego.* Trans. J. Strachey. New York: Norton, 1969.

27. See many of the essays, especially in Part 2, in Obholzer and Roberts (eds): *sup. cit.*

28. Britton: *sup. cit.*, p.105.

29. For a perceptive recent summary, see Jon Stokes: 'The unconscious at work in groups and teams; contributions from the work of Wilfred Bion', in Obholzer and Robers (eds): *sup. cit.*, pp.19–27. But see also what Stokes has to say about the sophisticated use of basic assumptions and the cultures to which they give rise, a neglected area of Bion's work.

30. R.E. Money-Kyrle: *Psycho-Analysis and Politics.* London: Duckworth, 1951.

31. M.J. Rustin: 'A socialist consideration of Kleinian psychoanalysis', *New Left Review,* 131, 1982, pp.71–96, reprinted as the opening chapter in his *The Good Society and the Inner World: Psychoanalysis, Politics and Culture.* London: Verso, 1992. Graham Little: *Political Ensembles: A Psychosocial Approach to Politics and Leadership.* Oxford: OUP, 1985. Money-Kyrle: *sup. cit.*

32. Rustin (1982): *sup. cit.*, p.96.

33. M.J. Rustin: 'Post-Kleinian psychoanalysis and the post modern'. Originally published in the pilot issue of *Free Associations,* 1984; and republished in *The Good Society: sup. cit.* In that edition, the quote is on p.149.

34. *ibid.*, 149–50.

35. I. Menzies (Lyth): 'A case study in the functioning of social systems as a defence against anxiety: a report on a study of the nursing service of a general hospital', *Human Relations,* 13, 1960, pp.95–121. See also her book of essays on the same theme: *Containing Anxieties in Institutions: Selected Essays,* Vol. 1. London: Free Association Books, 1988.

36. Menzies (1960): *sup. cit.*

37. *ibid.*

38. *ibid.* See also Anna Dartington: 'Where angels fear to tread: idealism, despondency and inhibition of thought in hospital nursing', in Obholzer and Robers (eds): *sup. cit.*, pp.101–9.

39. Obholzer: 'Managing social anxieties': *sup. cit,* p.171.

40. *ibid.*, p.177

41. Dartington: *sup. cit.*

42. For a more sociological account of the same phenomena, see J. Ehrenreich (ed.): *The Cultural Crisis of Modern Medicine.* London: Monthly Review Press, 1978. And cf. Hoggett: *sup. cit.*, p.72.

43. Elliot Jacques: 'Social systems as defence against persecutory and depressive anxiety', in M. Klein, P. Heimann and R.E. Money-Kyrle: *New Directions in Psycho-Analysis.* London: Tavistock, 1955

44. *ibid.*, p.492.
45. Speck: *sup. cit.*
46. Jacques: *sup. cit.*, p.482.

Chapter 7
1. Grace Stuart: *Narcissus*. London: Allen and Unwin, 1956.
2. There is here paradox within paradox; for, as Freud saw, the ego needs to love itself to develop, but the ego has nothing *to love* until it is developed. This issue was further explored by Heinz Kohut in *The Analysis of the Self: A systematic Approach to the Psychoanalytic Treatment of Narcissistic Personality Disorders*. New York: International UP, 1971; and by Otto Kernberg: *Borderline Conditions and Pathological Narcissism*. Northvale, NJ: Jacob Aronson, 1979. For a handy and not over-technical summary of their work, which complements mine, which tends to be based more on the British writers on the psychology of narcissism, see Donald Capps: *The Depleted Self: Sin in a Narcissistic Age*. Minneapolis: Fortress, 1993. Sadly, Capps's treatment is narrowly personal and therefore misses the social thrust of Lasch. He does, however, rightly and frequently bemoan the failure of theologians to take Lasch and the whole issue of narcissism sufficiently seriously (see, for example, p.4).
3. Christopher Lasch: *The Culture of Narcissism: American Life in an Age of Diminishing Expectations*. New York: Norton, 1979, p.81 (CoN hereafter.)
4. *ibid.*, cf. C. Lasch: *The Minimal Self: Psychic Survival in Troubled Times*. London: Pan, 1985. Many aspects of the arguments of this book run parallel to CoN, and for that reason the following analysis will concentrate on CoN almost exclusively.
5. Capps: *op. cit.*, pp. 51–69.
6. Lasch: *op. cit.*, p.41, quoting Kernberg. Bursten has sought to offer a typology of different forms of narcissism based on the presenting characterological symptoms, but this typology has been challenged as being over-defined and superficial. See Ben Bursten: 'Some narcissistic personality types', in Andrew P. Morrison (ed.): *Essential Papers on Narcissism*. New York: New York UP, 1988.
7. Lasch: *op. cit.*, p.84.
8. *ibid.*, p.85.
9. Kohut: *sup. cit.*
10. *ibid.*, pp.115–18. Obholzer, 'Managing social anxieties': *sup. cit.*, p.172.
11. Craib: *op. cit.*, pp.113–14.
12. See, for example, Erich Neumann: *The Origins and History of Consciousness*. New York: Pantheon, 1954, p.417. See also his *Art and the Creative Unconscious*. New York: Pantheon, 1959; George Steiner: *Language and Silence*. New York: Athenaeum, 1970; Theodore Roethke: *Collected Poems*. Garden City, NY: Doubleday, 1966. Quoted in Hopper: *op. cit.*, pp.234–6.
13. Lasch: *op. cit.*, p.48.

14. *ibid.*
15. Lasch: *op. cit.*, pp.72–3.
16. Frank Pinner: 'Ideas about time in psycho-dynamic theory', in Kirsch, Nijkamp and Zimmerman: *The Formulation of Time Preferences in Multidisciplinary Perspective: Their Consequences for Individual and Collective Decision-Making*. London: Gower, 1988.
17. *ibid.*, p.246.
18. Lasch: CoN, p.141.
19. *ibid.*, 141n.
20. *ibid.*, p.85.
21. *ibid.*, p.87.
22. Stephen Sales: 'Authoritarianism', *Psychology Today*, Nov. 1972, p.140. Quoted in Wink, Vol. 3, *op. cit.* See p.330 for additional references on changing destructiveness in American mass child media.
23. J.G. Ballard: *The Kindness of Women*. London: Harper Collins, 1991, pp.177 ff.
24. Wink: *op. cit.*, pp.11–12.
25. *ibid.*, p.13.

Chapter 8
1. Michael Lerner: *Surplus Powerlessness: The Psychodynamics of Everyday Life and the Psychology of Individual and Social Transformation*. San Francisco: Institute of Labor and Mental Health, 1986.
2. *ibid.*, p.123.
3. See below, p.162.
4. Lerner: *op. cit.*, p.12.
5. *ibid.*, p.43.
6. On the book jacket.
7. Ervin Staub: *The Roots of Evil: The Origins of Genocide and Other Group Violence*. Cambridge and New York: CUP, 1980.
8. See, for instance, H. Tajfel and J.C. Turner: 'An integrative theory of intergroup conflict', in W.G. Austin and S. Worchel (eds): *The Social Psychology of Intergroup Relations*. Monterrey, Ca: Brooks Cole, 1979.
9. H. Tajfel and A.L. Wilkes: 'Classification and quantitative judgement', *British Journal of Psychology*, 54, 1963, pp.101–14.
10. See C. Hovland and R. Sears: 'Minor studies in aggression VI: correlations of lynchings with economic indices', *Journal of Psychology*, 9, 1940, pp.301–10.
11. Staub: *op. cit.*, p.17.
12. See S.E. Asch: 'Effects of group pressure upon the modification and distortion of judgements', in H. Guertzkow (ed.): *Groups, Leadership and Men*. Pittsburgh: Carnegie, 1951. And M. Deutsch and H.B. Gerard: 'A study of normative and informational influences upon individual judgement', *Journal of Abnormal and Social Psychology*, 51, 1955, pp.629–36.
13. Staub: *op. cit.*, pp.17–18.
14. See Stanley Milgram: *Obedience to Authority: An Experimental View.*

New York: Harper & Row. 1974. But see, too, for a wider view of this experiment and the need to consider where power lies in such situations (as well as references to more up-to-date experimental research), Michael Hogg and Dominic Abrams: *Social Identification: A Social Psychology of Intergroup Relations and Group Processes*. London and New York: Routledge, 1989, p.61.

15. See S.H. Ng: 'Power and intergroup discrimination', in H. Tajfel (ed.): *Social Identity and Intergroup Relations*. Cambridge: CUP, 1982.

16. Staub: *op. cit.*, p.59. The resonances with both Jung and Klein should, I hope, be clear.

17. The quote is the title of an article by D.S. Holmes in *Psychological Bulletin*, 55, 1978, which was a reply to an article in the same number of the same journal by G.G. Sherwood which raised methodological questions about experimental data on which much projection theory is based.

18. Staub: *op. cit.*, p.64.

19. A. Bandura and R.H. Walters: *Adolescent Aggression: A Study of the Influence of Child Rearing Practices and Family Interrelationships*. New York: Ronald Press, 1959. L.D. Bron: 'Parent–child interaction, television violence and aggression of children', *American Psychologist*, 37, 1982, pp.197–211. R.D. Parke and R.G. Slaby: 'The development of aggression', in P. Mussen (ed.): *Manual of Child Psychology*, Vol. 4, 4th edn. New York: Wiley, 1983.

20. Alice Miller: *For Your Own Good: Hidden Cruelty in Child Rearing and the Roots of Violence*. New York: Farrar, Strauss Giroux, 1983.

21. P.G. Zimbardo, C. Haney, W.C. Banks and D. Jaffe: 'The psychology of imprisonment: privation, power and pathology', in Z. Rubin (ed.): *Doing Unto Others*. Englewood Cliffs, NJ: Prentice-Hall, 1974.

22. Staub: *op. cit.*, p.70.

23. Z. Bauman: *Modernity and Holocaust*. Cambridge and Oxford: Polity and Blackwell, 1989, p.167.

24. *ibid.*

25. M. Sherif, O.J. Harvey, B.J. White, W. Hood and C. Sherif: *Intergroup Conflict and Cooperation: The Robbers Cave Experiment*. University of Oklahoma, 1961.

26. Amitai Etzioni: 'A model of significant research', *International Journal of Psychiatry*, 6, 1968, pp.279–80.

27. John M. Steiner: 'The SS yesterday and to-day: a socio-psychological view', in Joel Dinsdale (ed.): *Survivors, Victims and Perpetrators: Essays in the Nazi Holocaust*. Washington DC: Hemisphere, 1980, p.431.

28. J.M. Rabbie and G. Wilkens: 'Ingroup competition and its effect on intergroup relations', *European Journal of Social Psychology*, 1, 1971, pp.215–34.

Chapter 9

1. The key texts are *Violence and the Sacred*. Baltimore: Johns Hopkins UP, 1977 (originally published in French in 1972). *Things Hidden since the*

Foundation of the World. Trans. Stephen Bann and Michael Metteer. London: Athlone, 1987. *To Double Business Bound: Essays on Literature, Myth, Mimesis, and Anthropology,* Baltimore: Johns Hopkins UP, 1978. *The Scapegoat.* Trans. Yvonne Freccero. Baltimore: Johns Hopkins UP, 1986. *Job: The Victim of his People.* Trans. Yvonne Freccero. London: Athlone, 1987.

2. A.J. McKenna: *Violence and Difference: Girard, Derrida and Deconstruction.* Urbana: Univ. of Illinois, 1992, p.95.

3. The relationship between Kleinian envy and Girard's desire has not, as far as I am aware, been properly explored. Note that Klein takes as definitive of envy the need to deny the enjoyment of the person envied and the destruction of whatever gives enjoyment and thereby arouses envy. This is not a significant theme in Girard.

4. See McKenna: *op. cit.,* p.95 and cf. Mark Juergensmeyer (ed.): *Violence and the Sacred in the Modern World.* London: Cass, 1992.

5. Burton L. Mack: 'The innocent transgressor: Jesus in early Christian myth and history', *Semeia* 33, 1985, pp.135–65.

6. *ibid.,* p.150.

7. *ibid.,* p.152.

8. Nancy Jay has recently given this argument a further twist by making the point that a sacrificial system demands a social and ecclesiastical hierarchy and an associated concentration of power in the hands of those who conduct the liturgy of sacrifice. Her argument is perhaps marginal to Pauline times, but becomes significant as soon as a liturgically separate priesthood is established. See her *Throughout your Generations Forever: Sacrifice, Religion and Paternity.* Univ. of Chicago Press, 1992. especially pp.112ff.

9. But Martin Bergmann has argued that, psychoanalytically, the sacrifice of Christ is a unique turning-point in that it is interpreted, against more primitive practices of (child) sacrifice, as evidence of a *loving,* rather than hating, father. See his *In the Shadow of Moloch: The Sacrifice of Children and its Impact on Western Religions.* New York: Columbia UP, 1992.

10. Nick Adams: *An Eschatological Reading of Jurgen Habermas' 'Ideal Speech Situation.'* Norrisian Prize Essay, University of Cambridge, 1995, p.2.

11. James Schmidt: 'Jurgen Habermas and the difficulties of enlightenment,' *Social Research,* 49, 1, 1982, pp.181–208.

12. J. Habermas: 'Reply to Critics', in J. Thompson and D. Held: *Habermas: Critical Debates.* Cambridge, Mass.: MIT Press, 1982, pp.227–8.

13. J. Habermas: *The Theory of Communicative Action.* Vol. 1: *Reason and the Rationalisation of Society.* Trans. Thomas McCarthy. Cambridge and Oxford: Polity and Blackwell, 1991, p.71. (Hereafter *TCA.*)

14. Habermas: *TCA.* p.335.

15. See, for instance, Fentress and Wickham: *op. cit.,* pp.91 ff.

16. Martin Buber, for instance, argued that Heraclitus' concept of logos as something common to all was an ancient precedent of Buber's own

claim that dialogue is the means of salvation from contemporary mistrust. See McFadyen: *op. cit.*, and Hopper: *op. cit.*, pp.167ff.

17. See Rick Roderick: *Habermas and the Foundations of Critical Theory.* London: Macmillan, 1986, pp.151 ff. Roderick criticises Habermas for his lack of emphasis on the Marxist prioritisation of production and suggests that Baudrillard, whose attempt to replace Marxist emphasis on production with a paradigm based on communication predates Habermas, falls even more squarely into the same trap and ends up by arguing in a circle (p.158).

18. See M. Foucault: *History of Sexuality* and especially Vol. 8: *The Care of the Self.* Harmondsworth: Allen Lane, Penguin Press, 1988.

19. P. Joutard: *Le Monde Alpin et Rhodanien.* 1982, pp.179–92, cited in Fentress and Wickham: *op. cit.*

20. W.B. Yeats: *Essays and Introductions.* London: Macmillian, 1961, p.11.

21. Adams: *op, cit.*

22. See N. Lash in W.G. Jeanroud and Jennifer L. Rike: *Radical Pluralism and Truth: David Tracy and the hermeneutics of religion.* New York: Crossroad, 1991, p.52

23. J. Habermas: *Towards a Rational Society: Student Protest, Science and Politics.* London: Heinemann, 1971.

24. R. Coles: *Self Power Other: Political Theory and Dialogical Ethics.* Ithaca, New York; London: Cornell UP, 1992, pp.156–7. But note that Merleau-Ponty's vision of a 'meeting at the cross-roads' becomes more and more a plea for the parliamentary system as his disenchantment with Marxism grows.

25. Lerner writes of his experience of 'destructive games' in the leftist movement with which he was identified in the United States in the 1960s and 1970s. See *Surplus Powerlessness, sup. cit.*

26. See Lash, *sup. cit.*

Chapter 10

1. Hans Urs von Balthasar: *Theodramatik III.* Einsiedeln: Johannes, 1980

2. Wolfhart Pannenberg: *Basic Questions in Theology: sup. cit.*; and Tupper: *sup. cit.*, pp.103, 104.

3. Colin E. Gunton: *The Actuality of the Atonement: A Study of Metaphor, Rationality and the Christian tradition.* Edinburgh: T. & T. Clark, 1988, pp.118ff.

4. T.F. Torrance: *The Mediation of Christ.* Edinburgh: T. & T. Clark, 1992 edition, p. 71; and cf. John McIntyre: *The Shape of Soteriology: Studies in the Doctrine of the Death of Christ.* Edinburgh: T. & T. Clark, 1992.

5. Albert Nolan: *Jesus before Christianity: Gospel of Liberation.* Cape Town: David Philip, 1976.

6. Torrance: *op. cit.*, p.86.

7. Donald L. Gelpi, SJ: *The Turn to Experience in Contemporary Theology.* New York: Paulist, 1994.

8. John Hick: *The Metaphor of God Incarnate.* London: SCM, 1993. It will become apparent that my account of the Atonement, at least in its

transformational/experiential form, can survive, though does not require, the abandonment of Chalcedonian orthodoxy, which cannot be said for most of the traditional accounts. I do not pursue this in the text because I believe Hick goes too far in his rejection of traditional Christology.

9. Hick: *op. cit.*, p.131.

10. Hick: *op. cit.*, p.130.

11. See above, Ch.6.

12. See Sheila McNamee: 'Reconstructing identity: the communal construction of crisis', in Sheila McNamee and Kenneth J. Gergen: *Therapy as Social Construction*. London: Sage, 1992, pp.186–99. See also, in the same volume, the essay by Harlene Anderson and Harold Goolishian: 'The client is the expert; a not-knowing approach to therapy'; and Gergen's own essay, with John Kaye: 'Beyond narrative in the negotiation of therapeutic meaning. See also Gergen's earlier collection of essays, edited with John Shotter: *Texts of Identity.* London: Sage, 1989; and especially the essays by Gergen, Shotter and Murray.

13. On Benjamin, see Robert Alter: *Necessary Angels: Tradition and Modernity in Kafka, Benjamin and Scholem.* Cambridge, Mass.; Harvard UP, 1991, p.105, where, quoting from Benjamin's *Moscow Diary,* he describes a painting of Cezanne 'thrusting itself forward . . . in corners and angles'. On Michel Foucault, see his *Language, Counter-Memory, Practice: Selected Essays and Interviews.* Edited with an introduction by Donald Bouchard and translated by Donal Bouchard and Sherry Simon. Oxford: Blackwell, 1977, p.162

14. *ibid.*, p.163

15. *ibid.*, p.161

16. See A. J. Raboteau, *Slave Religion.* New York: Oxford UP, 1978.

17. Foucault: *op cit.*, p.164.

18. See Pannenberg: *sup. cit.*

19. On exemplarist theories sometimes attributed to Abelard, see Olivier Quick: *The Gospel of the New World.* London: Nisbet, 1944; and Richard Weingart: *The Logic of Divine Love: A Critical Analysis of the Soteriology of Peter Abailard.* Oxford; Clarendon, 1970. On Balthasar's soteriology, see his *Theodramatik iii: sup. cit.*

20. Gunton: *op. cit.*, p.66 (his italics).

21. *ibid.*, p.67.

22. *ibid.*, p.70. The reference is to Rollo May: *Love and Will.* London: Collins, 1970.

23. *ibid.*, p.73.

24. *ibid.*, p.75.

25. Romans 12:14–21. This is, of course, close to Girard's primary emphasis – the quality of Jesus's love that leads him to accept his role as the scapegoat of Israel.

26. Gunton: *op. cit.*, pp. 80–1.

27. Anselm: *Cur Deus Homo?* 1, ii, c. 20, quoted by Balthasar. *op. cit.*, p.236.

28. P.T. Forsyth: *The Justification of God*. London: Duckworth, 1916. Quoted in Gunton: *op. cit.*, p.107.

29. Gunton: *op. cit.*, p.109.

30. K. Barth: *Church Dogmatics*. IV, I.G.W. Bromiley and T.F. Torrance (eds). Edinburgh: T. & T. Clark, 1953–6, pp.29–5. Quoted Gunton, p.11–112.

31. Gunton: *op. cit.*, pp.130ff.

32. J.B. Metz: *Faith in History and Society. Towards a Practical Fundamental Theology*. Trans D. Smith. London: Burns & Oates, 1980, p.132.

33. A recent good example is John Moses: *The sacrifice of God. A Holistic Theory of Atonement*. Norwich: Canterbury Press, 1992.

Chapter 11

1. See, for instance, Johann Auer and Joseph Ratzinger: *Dogmatic Theology*, Vol. 8, *The Church: The Universal Sacrament of Salvation*. Washington, DC: Catholic University of America Press. English edition, 1993, pp.82–3. Or for a Protestant example, see P. Lehmann: *Ethics in a Christian Context*. London, Lehmann, 1963.

2. Hans Kung: *The Church*. Tonbridge: Burns and Oates, 1968, pp.35–6.

3. Contrast Auer and Ratzinger: *op. cit.*, p.20, with Pannenberg, ATP, *sup. cit.*, p.295, the source of this quote.

4. Hoggett, *op. cit.*, p.149.

5. P.N. Trempelas: *Dogmatique de L'église Orthodoxe Catholique*. Trans. Pierre Dumont. 3 vols. Bruges: Chevetogne, 1966–8.

6. W.M. Abbott and Joseph Gallagher (eds): *The Documents of Vatican II: Introduction and Commentary by Catholic Bishops: Responses by Protestant and Other Scholars*. London and Dublin: Chapman, 1966.

7. See above, Ch.6.

8. Donald Winnicott: *Playing and Reality*. Harmondsworth: Penguin, 1974, pp.44–61.

9. *Adv. Haer.* 11, 24, 1.

10. See, for example, Gordon Molyneux: *African Theology: The Quest for Self-hood*. San Francisco and Lampeter: Mellen, 1993.

11. J.-M.R. Tillard: *Church of Churches: The Ecclesiology of Communion*. Minnesota: Michael Glazier, 1992, p.143.

12. For an interesting sidelight on the way Milton deals with this theme, see Regina M. Schwarz: *Remembering and Repeating: On Milton's Theology and Poetics*. Cambridge: CUP, 1988, and reissued with a new preface in which these questions are more fully discussed by University of Chicago Press, 1993. And for a very different but interestingly parallel treatment, see Pedro Casaldaliga and Jose Maria Vigil: *The Spirituality of Liberation*. Tunbridge Wells: Burns & Oates, 1994, especially the section on Contemplatives in Liberation.

13. And not only Jung and Berger. For an interesting essay on the way emotionality has crept back into Western self-expression but has remained unhooked from significant symbolic systems – and what that has done to both individuals and communities – see Daniele Hervieu-

Leger: 'Present-day emotional renewals: the end of secularization or the end of religion?', in William H. Swatos (ed.): *A Future for Religion? New Paradigms of Social Analysis*. London: Sage, 1993, pp.129–48.

14. For a revealingly Roman-authoritarian view of this process, see Tillard, *op. cit.*, p.144, where he makes it clear that the reception is by conciliar and synodal processes, which then pass down to the people what is to be received. This is, of course, entirely consistent with his high doctrine of the magisterium of the Church, but it is a view that many Anglicans and Protestants would find objectionably hierarchical. So would many women. See, on this whole theme, Letty M. Russell's wise and eirenic book: *Church in the Round: Feminist Interpretation of the Church*. Louisville, Ky: Westminster/John Knox, 1993. Especially chapters 2 and 3.

15. Edward Schillebeeckx: *Church: The Human Story of God*. London: SCM, p.214ff.

16. Hans Kung: *Infallible? An Enquiry*. Trans. E. Mosbacher. London: Collins, 1971. And see for a more extended and more recent discussion of this whole issue: P.J. Fitzpatrick: *In Breaking of Bread. The Eucharist and Ritual*. Cambridge: CUP, 1993.

17. David Selbourne: *The Spirit of the Age*. London: Sinclair-Stevenson, 1990.

18. See, for example, George Tavard: *The Church, Community of Salvation: An Ecumenical Ecclesiology*. Minnesota: Michael Glazier, 1992.

19. It is immediately obvious that I am putting the work of the Holy Spirit in a much wider context than that of much Roman Catholic and Orthodox teaching, which tends to link the Holy Spirit, yoke-like, to the magisterium. It is significant, for example, that Vatican II's Constitution on the Church comes near to arguing the case I am presenting but then, in a sleight of hand, inserts the word 'obey' for the people. 'The whole body of the faithful cannot err in matters of belief . . . By this appreciation of the faith, aroused and sustained by the Spirit of truth, the people of God, guided by the sacred teaching authority, *and obeying it*, receives not the mere word of men, but truly the word of God.' *Lumen Gentium*, 12.

20. Schillebeeckx: *op. cit.*, p.215. For the opposite view, see J. Ratzinger: 'The ecclesiology of the Second Vatican Council', in his *Church Ecumenism and Politics: New Essays in Ecclesiology*. Slough: St Paul, 1988.

21. See, for instance, a rather cautious statement of this emerging consensus in Auer and Ratzinger, *op. cit.*, pp.172–3.

22. Mary Grey: *The Wisdom of Fools: Seeking Revelation for Today*. London: SPCK, 1993.

23. See, for instance, the debates on the ordination of women in the Ecclesiastical Committee of the Houses of Parliament in London 1993.

24. Though there is, of course, a sense in which Orthodox (and perhaps especially Russian Orthodox) tradition has done just that. See Georges Florovsky, who seeks to write ecclesiology in the twentieth century based on the Christology of the fifth century: *Ways of Russian Theology*

Part I and *Creation and Redemption*, respectively vols 5 and 3 of the *Collected Works*. Belmont, Mass: Nordland, 1979, 1976.

25. See, for instance, Wink: *Engaging the Powers, sup. cit.*, p.300
26. Quoted in Helmut Peukert: 'Fundamental theology and communicative praxis as the ethics of universal solidarity', in A. James Reimer (ed.): *The Influence of the Frankfurt School on Contemporary Theology: Critical Theory and the Future of Religion*. Toronto Studies in Theology, vol. 64. Lampeter: Edward Mellen, 1992, p.233. Note that Johann Baptist Metz considers this exchange one of the most important theological debates in this century. It clearly affected his own thinking and writing on 'dangerous memories'.
27. *ibid.*, p.236.
28. A thought nicely but cautiously related in *Gaudium et Spes* in Vatican II.
29. J.B. Metz: *Faith in History and Society: Towards a Practical Fundamental Theology*. Trans. D. Smith. London: Burns & Oates. 1980.
30. Albert Nolan: *God in South Africa: The Challenge of the Gospel*. London: CIIR, 1988. Alan Falconer: *op. cit.*
31. For a history of '*extra ecclesiam nulla salus*', see Francis A. Sullivan, SJ: *Salvation Outside the Church: Tracing the History of the Catholic Response*. London: Chapman, 1992.
32. Gavin White: *The Church Your Mother Never Told You Of*. London: SCM, 1993.
33. Coles: *op. cit.*, p.102.
34. Cf. Harris: *op. cit.*, p.102.
35. See Valerie Raoul: *Distinctly Narcissistic: Diary Fiction in Quebec*. University of Toronto Press, 1993.
36. Th. Wurtenberger Jr: *Die Legitimitat Staatlicher Herrschaft: Eine Staatsrechtlich-Politische Begriftsgesichte*. 1973. Quoted by Pannenberg in *Anthropology in Theological Perspective*. pp.462, 468.
37. See P. Woodward: *Sudan 1899–1989: The Unstable State*. Colorado: Lynne Reiner, 1990.
38. A.D. Falconer: 'Remembering', *Studies*, 78, 310. Summer, 1989, pp.172–3. And of Schwarz, *sup. cit.*
39. See the speech by Richard von Weizsäcker in the Bundestag on 8 May 1985, forty years after the end of the Second World War; quoted in Brian Frost: *The Politics of Peace*. London: Darton, Longman & Todd, pp.31–2.
40. Hannah Arendt: *The Human Condition*. Chicago: Chicago UP, 1958, p.241.
41. See, for instance, D.W. Shriver Jr: 'Struggle for justice and reconciliation: forgiveness in the politics of the American civil rights movement, 1955–68', *Studies*, 78. Summer, 1989, p.310. And Victor de Waal: *The Politics of Reconciliation*. London: Hurst, 1990.
42. Frost: *op. cit.*, p.181.
43. *ibid.*, p.197.

Chapter 12

1. K. Wendt: *Pax Romana and the Peace of Jesus Christ.* Trans. John Bowden. London: SCM, 1987.
2. Rosemary Radford Ruether: *New Woman, New Earth: Sexist Ideologies and Human Liberation.* New York: Seabury, 1975.
3. Warren Carter: *Households and Discipleship: A Study of Matthew 19–20.* JSOT, 103. Sheffield, 1994.
4. Josephine Massyngberde Ford: *My Enemy is my Guest: Jesus and Violence in Luke.* Maryknoll, NY: Orbis, 1984. Cf. P. Esler: *Community and Gospel in Luke–Acts.* Cambridge: CUP, 1987. And J.C. Lentz: *Luke's Portrait of Paul.* Cambridge: CUP, 1993. William S. Kurz in *Reading Luke–Acts: Dynamics of Biblical Narratives,* Louisville, Ky: Westminster John Knox, 1993, uses reader-response theory to make some of the same points
5. Massyngberde Ford: *sup. cit.*
6. Terry Eagleton: *Criticism and Ideology.* London: Verso, 1976, p.90.
7. Itumeleng Mosala: *Biblical Hermeneutics and Black Theology in South Africa.* Michigan: Eerdmans, 1989, p.168.
8. Phyllis Trible: *God and the Rhetoric of Sexuality.* Philadelphia: Fortress, 1978, p.11.
9. J.P. Fokkelman: *Narrative Art in Genesis.* Amsterdam: Van Gorchum, Assen, 1975. Quoted Tribble: *op. cit.,* p.28. fn.57.
10. Edward Farley: *Ecclesial Reflection: An Anatomy of Theological Method.* Philadelphia: Fortress, 1982, p.324.
11. H. Gadamer: *Truth And Method,* 2nd revised edn. London: Sheed and Ward, 1989.
12. A.J. Raboteau: *Slave Religion.* New York: OUP, 1978.
13. See, for instance, Paul Ricouer: *Hermeneutics and the Human Sciences.* Ed. J.B. Thompson. Cambridge: CUP, 1981, p.93. For a recent discussion on this which relates precisely to the point about Luke made above, and to the approach of I. Mosala explored more extensively below, see Christopher Rowland: 'In dialogue with Itumeleng Mosala', *JSNT,* 50. 1993, pp.43–57.
14. See Christopher Rowland: *Radical Christianity, sup. cit.* And cf. Ilena Rashkow: *The Phallacy of Genesis: A Feminist Psychoanalytical Approach.* Louisville, Ky: Westminster/John Knox, 1993.
15. Jacques Ellul: *The Subversion of Christianity.* Trans Geoffrey Bromiley. Grand Rapids, Mich.: Eerdmans, 1986, p.59.
16. Mosala: *op. cit.* (see footnote 7 of this chapter).
17. For an account of the intellectual background on which Mosala is drawing, especially Norman Gottwald, see C. Rowland: *JSNT, sup. cit.*
18. See, for example, Jerome H. Neyrey (ed.): *The Social World of Luke–Acts: Models for Interpretation.* Peabody, Mass.: Hendrickson, 1991. And Halvor Moxnes: *The Economy of the Kingdom: Social Conflict and Economic Relations in Luke's Gospel.* Philadelphia: Fortress, 1988. And B.J. Malina and R.L. Rohrbaugh: *Social Science Commentary in the Synoptic Gospels.* Minneapolis: Fortress, 1992.

19. Fred R. Dallmayr: *Twilight of Subjectivity.* Amherst: University of Massachusetts Press, 1981, p.251. John Milbank: *Theology and Social Theory.* Oxford: Blackwell, 1990. And see also his book on Vico: *The Religious Dimension in the Thought of Giambattista Vico: 1668–1744. Part 1: The Early Metaphysics.* Lampeter: Mellen, 1991.

20. Mosala: *op. cit.,* p.32.

21. Hoggett: *op. cit.,* p.29.

22. D.W. Winnicott: *Through Paediatrics to Psycho-Analysis.* London: Hogarth, 1975.

23. M. Balint: *Thrills and Regressions.* London: Hogarth, 1959.

24. See R.S. Sugirtharajah (ed.): *Voices from the Margin: Interpreting the Bible in the Third World.* London: SPCK, 1991.

25. Cf. Paul Ricouer: 'Philosophical Hermeneutics and Theological Hermeneutics', in *The Centre for Hermeneutic Studies in Hellenistic and Modern Culture, 17th Colloquy.* Berkeley: California University Press, 1975, p.19. But see also the criticisms to this approach by Farley: *op. cit.,* p.324 n.1.

26. Stanley R. Hopper: *The Way of Transfiguration; Religious Imagination as Theopoesis.* Eds K. Keiser and A. Stoneburner. Louisville, Ky: Westminster/John Knox, 1992.

27. See, for example, Frazer Watts: *op. cit.*

28. P. Trible: *God and the Rhetoric of Sexuality.* Philadelphia: Fortress, 1978, pp.60–3.

29. See Margaret Ann Palliser: *Christ our Mother of Mercy: Divine Mercy and Compassion in the Theology of the 'Shewings' of Julian of Norwich.* Berlin: Walter de Gruyter, 1992, pp.68–72.

30. M. Milner: 'The role of illusion in symbol formation', in Klein, Heimann and Money-Kyrle: *op. cit.,* pp.82–108.

31. Hoggett: *op. cit.,* p.22.

32. D.W. Winnicott: *Playing and reality. sup. cit.,* p.76.

33. Hoggett: *op. cit.,* p.20. But note that I am not implying (and should not be taken to be implying) that the text has no power to demand obedience. There is always the danger of a kind of narcissistic withdrawal from the reality of the text when one moves in the direction of deconstructionism. I hope to guard against that and repeat the caveat here.

34. Stephen Moore: *Mark and Luke in Post-structuralist Perspectives: Jesus Begins to Write.* New Haven: Yale UP, 1992. See also his essay on the deconstructive criticism of Mark's Gospel in Janice Capel and Stephen D. Moore: *Mark and Method: New Approaches in Biblical Studies.* Minneapolis: Fortress, 1992.

35. Moore: *Mark and Luke. op. cit.,* pp.24, 25.

36. W. Bion: *Learning from Experience. sup. cit.,* pp.98–9.

37. Hoggett: *op. cit.,* p.46.

38. Gayatri Spivak, in translator's introduction to J. Derrida: *Of Grammatology.* Baltimore: Johns Hopkins UP, 1974, p.lxxvii.

39. Hoggett. pp.12, 15. But note his overall cautious and even negative

assessment of the value of fantasy. I hope I share the caution but not quite the same degree of negativity.

40. J.L. Borges: 'The mirror of enigmas', *Labyrinths*. New York: New Directions, 1964

41. Keiser and Stoneburner (eds): *sup. cit.* I owe much to Hopper in the following pages.

42. Hoggett: *op. cit.*, p.36, quoting Steve Lacy: *The Wire*, No. 1, 1982.

43. Farley: *op. cit.*, p.325.

44. Yeats, Kierkegaard and Jung all make this distinction in different ways. Perhaps at this stage it does not much matter whose 'paradigm' we follow. The point is to arrive, not to worry too much about the route taken.

45. This is Bion's definition of patience too. From a letter to George and Thomas Keats, 21 December 1817. Quoted in Hoggett: *op. cit.*, p.68.

46. Hopper: *op. cit.*, p.199.

47. *Ibid.*, p.221.

48. Herbert Marcuse: *One-Dimensional Man: Studies in the Ideology of Advanced Industrial Society.* London: Ark, 1986.

49. Metz: *op. cit.*, p.90.

50. C. Castoriadis: *Cross-Roads in the Labyrinth*. Brighton: Harvester, 1984. p.26. Quoted by Joe Harris: 'Reconciliation as Remembrance', in Alan D. Falconer (ed): *Reconciling Memories*. Dublin: Columba Press, 1988, p.49.

Select Bibliography

T.W. Adorno, Else Frenkel-Brunswick, Daniel J. Levinson, R. Nevitt Sanford et al: *The Authoritarian Personality*. New York: Harper, 1950.

C. Fred Alford: *Melanie Klein and Critical Social Theory*. New Haven: Yale UP, 1989.

Robin Anderson (ed.): *Clinical Lectures on Klein and Bion*. London: Tavistock/ Routledge, 1992.

Hannah Arendt: *The Human Condition*. Chicago UP, 1958.

Urs von Balthasar: *Mysterium Paschale: The Mystery of Easter*. Edinburgh: T. & T. Clark, 1990.

A. Bandura: *Social Learning Theory*. Englewood Cliffs, NJ: Prentice-Hall, 1977.

Karl Barth: *Church Dogmatics* III/1. E.T. edited by G.W. Bromiley and T.F. Torrance. Edinburgh: T. & T. Clark, 1945/1958.

Karl Barth: *Church Dogmatics* IV/1. 1953/1956.

Karl Barth: *Church Dogmatics* IV/3. 1959/1961.

Karl Barth: *The Christian Life. Church Dogmatics* IV/4 *Lecture Fragments*. E.T. by Geoffrey Bromiley. Grand Rapids: Eerdmans, 1976/1981.

Peter L. Berger: *Invitation to Sociology*. Harmondsworth: Penguin, 1971.

Martin Bergmann. *The Shadow of Moloch: The Sacrifice of Children and its Impact on Western Religions*. New York: Columbia UP, 1992.

Wilfred Bion: *Attention and Interpretation: A Scientific Approach to Insight in Psychoanalysis and Groups*. New York: Basic Books, 1970.

Dietrich Bonhoeffer: *The Cost of Discipleship*. London: SCM, 1959.

Dietrich Bonhoeffer: *Letters and Papers from Prison*. London: SCM, 1971.

J.T. Bridges: *Human Destiny and Resurrection in Pannenberg and Rahner*. New York: P. Lang, 1988. America University Studies, Series VII/7, Theology and Religion, Vol. 32.

Karen Brison: *Just Talk: Gossip, Meetings and Power in a Papua New Guinea Village*. Berkeley: California UP, 1992.

V. Brome: *Jung, Man and Myth*. London: Macmillan, 1978.

John Brookshire Thompson and David Held: *Habermas: Critical Debates*. London: Macmillan, 1982.

J.A.C. Brown: *Freud and the Post-Freudians*. Harmondsworth: Penguin, 1969.

Christopher Bryant: *Jung and the Christian Way.* London: Darton, Longman & Todd, 1984.

Ben Bursten: 'Some narcissistic personality types', in *Essential Papers on Narcissism*, ed. Andrew P. Morrison. New York: New York UP, 1986.

Thomas Butler: *Memory, History, Culture and the Mind.* Oxford: Blackwell, 1989.

Donald Capps: *The Depleted Self: Sin in a Narcissistic Age.* Minneapolis: Fortress, 1993.

E. Cassirer: *Language and Myth.* Translated by S. Langer, New York: Harper, 1946.

E. Cassirer *The Philosophy of Symbolic Forms.* Vol. II. New Haven: Yale UP, 1955.

Richard Christie and Marie Jahoda (eds): *Studies in the Scope and Method of 'The Authoritarian Personality'.* Glencoe, Illinois: Free Press, 1954.

Gillian Cohen: *Memory in the Real World.* Hove: Lawrence Erlbaum, 1989.

Paul Connerton: *How Societies Remember.* Cambridge: CUP, 1991.

Rosalind Coward: *Patriarchal Precedents: Sexuality and Social Relations.* London: Routledge & Kegan Paul, 1983.

Ian Craib: *Psychoanalysis and Social Theory: The Limits of Sociology.* London: Harvester Wheatsheaf, 1989.

John H. Crook: *The Evolution of Human Consciousness.* Oxford: OUP, 1980.

John Crook and Henry Osmaston (eds): *Environmental Resources, Social and Religious Life in Zangskar, Ladakh.* University of Bristol Press, 1994.

Teun A. van Dijk: *Communicating Racism: Ethnic Prejudice in Thought and Talk.* London: Sage, 1988.

F.W. Dillistone: *Myth and Symbol.* London: SPCK, 1966.

F.W. Dillistone: *The Christian Understanding of the Atonement.* London: SCM, 1984.

I. Dilman: *Freud and Human Nature.* Oxford: Blackwell, 1986.

Dom Gregory Dix: *The Shape of the Liturgy.* London: A. & C. Black, 1945.

Mary Douglas: *Purity and Danger: An Analysis of the Concepts of Pollution and Taboo.* London: Ark, 1984.

A. Etzioni: *A Comparative Analysis of Complex Organizations.* Glencoe, Illinois: Free Press, 1961.

W.R.D. Fairbairn: *Psychoanalytic Studies of the Personality.* London: Routledge & Kegan Paul, 1952.

E.R. Fairweather: 'Incarnation and Atonement: An Anselmian Response to Aulen's *Christus Victor*', *Canadian Journal of Theology* 7, 1961, pp.167–175.

Alan D. Falconer (ed): *Reconciling Memories.* Dublin: The Columba Press, 1988.

Alan D. Falconer: 'Remembering', *Studies*, 78, 310. Summer 1989, pp.172–3.

James Fentress and Christ Wickham: *Social memory. New Perspectives on the Past.* Oxford: Blackwell, 1992.

P.J. Fitzpatrick: *In Breaking of Bread: The Eucharist and Ritual*. Cambridge: CUP, 1992.

Georges Florovsky: *Creation and Redemption*. Vol. 3 of the *Collected Works*. Belmont, Mass.: Nordland, 1976.

Georges Florovsky: *Ways of Russian Theology, Part I*. Vol. 5 of the *Collected Works*. Belmont, Mass.: Nordland, 1979.

P.T. Forsyth: *The Justification of God*. London: Duckworth, 1916.

M. Foucault: *The History of Sexuality*. London: Allen Lane, 1978.

Hans Frei: *The Identity of Jesus Christ*. Philadelphia: Fortress, 1975.

W.L. French and C.H. Bell: *Organization Development: Behavioural Science Interventions for Organization Improvement*. Englewood Cliffs, NJ: Prentice-Hall, 1984.

S. Freud: *Group Psychology and the Analysis of the Ego*. Translated by J. Strachey. New York: Norton, 1959.

S. Freud: *Moses and Monotheism* (1937–39). London: Routledge & Kegan Paul, 1951.

S. Freud: *New Introductory Lectures* (1916–17). London: Routledge & Kegan Paul, 1962. Vol. ii, standard edition.

S. Freud: *Psychopathology of Everyday Life* (1901). London: Routledge & Kegan Paul, 1966. Vol. vi, 2nd standard edition.

S. Freud: *Totem and Taboo* (1912–14). London: Routledge & Kegan Paul, 1968, standard edition, vol. 13.

S. Freud: *Interpretation of Dreams* (1900). London: Routledge & Kegan Paul, 1971.

Erich Fromm: *Man for Himself*. New York: Macmillan, 1947.

Erich Fromm: 'The theory of mother right and its significance for social psychology', in *The Crisis of Psychoanalysis*. Harmondsworth: Penguin, 1973.

Brian Frost: *The Politics of Peace*. London: Darton, Longman & Todd, 1991.

H. Gadamer: *Truth and Method*. New York: 1975.

Kenneth Galbraith: *The Culture of Contentment*. London: Sinclair-Stevenson, 1992.

Anthony Giddens: *New Rules for Sociological Method: A Positive Critique of Interpretative Sociologies*. 2nd revised edition. Cambridge: Polity Press, 1992.

René Girard: *Violence and the Sacred*. Trans. by Patrick Gregory. Baltimore: Johns Hopkins UP, 1972.

Tim Gorringe: *Redeeming the Time: Atonement through Education*. London: Darton, Longman & Todd, 1986.

Mary Grey: *The Wisdom of Fools: Seeking Revelation for Today*. London: SPCK, 1993.

A. Grunbaum: *The Foundations of Psychoanalysis: A Philosophical Critique*. Berkeley: U of California Press, 1984.

Gustavo Gutierrez: *A Theology of Liberation*. London: SCM, 1974.

M. Halbachs: *The Collective Memory*. Translated by F.J. Ditter. San Francisco: Harper & Row, 1980.

J. Habermas: *Towards a Rational Society: Student Protest, Science and Politics*. London: Heinemann, 1971.

J. Habermas: *Legitimation Crisis*. London: Heinemann, 1976.

J. Habermas: *Knowledge and Human Interests*. Translated by Jeremy J. Shapiro. Cambridge and Oxford: Polity Press and Blackwell, 1987.

J. Habermas: *The Theory of Communicative Action*. Vol. 1 of *Reason and the Rationalisation of Society*. Translated by Thomas McCarthy. Cambridge and Oxford: Polity Press and Blackwell, 1991.

J. Habermas: 'A reply to my critics' in J.B. Thompson and D. Held (eds.), *Critical Debates*. Cambridge, Mass.: MIT Press, 1982.

F.C. Happold: *The Journey Inwards*. London: Darton, Longman & Todd, 1976.

Rom Harré: *Social Being: A Theory for Social Psychology*. Oxford: Blackwell, 1979.

Rom Harré: *Personal Being*. Oxford: Blackwell, 1983.

Rom Harré: *The Social Construction of Emotions*. Oxford: Blackwell, 1986.

Stanley Hauerwas: *A Community of Character. Towards a Constructive Christian Social Ethic*. Notre Dame: U of Notre Dame Press, 1981.

J. Hillman: *Loose Ends*. New York/Zurich: Spring 1975.

J. Hillman: *Re-Visioning Psychology*. New York: Harper & Row, 1975.

J. Hillman: *Egalitarian Typologies versus the Perception of the Unique*. Dallas: Spring, 1980.

J. Hillman: *Facing the Gods*. Dallas: Spring 1980.

J. Hillman: *Archetypal Psychology*. Dallas: 1983.

J. Hillman: *Inter Views*. New York: Spring 1983.

Michael Hogg and Dominic Abrams: *Social Identifications: A Social Psychology of Intergroup Relations and Group Processes*. New York and London: Routledge, 1988.

Paul Hoggett: *Partisans in an Uncertain World: The Psychoanalysis of Engagement*. London: Free Association, 1992.

Stanley Romaine Hopper: *The Way of Transfiguration: Religious Imagination as Theopoesis*. Edited by Kelvin Keiser and Tony Stoneburner. Louisville, Ky: 1992.

I.M.L. Hunter: *Memory*. Harmondsworth: Penguin, 1964.

Elliot Jacques: 'Social systems as defence against persecutory and depressive anxiety', in *New Directions in Psycho-Analysis* by M. Klein, P. Heimann and R.E. Money-Kyrle. London: Tavistock, 1955.

Nancy Jay: *Throughout your Generations Forever: Sacrifice, Religion and Paternity*. U of Chicago Press, 1992.

Mark Juergensmeyer (ed.): *Violence and the Sacred in the Modern World*. London: Cass, 1992.

Otto Kernberg: *Borderline Conditions and Pathological Narcissism*. Northvale, NJ: Jacob Aronson, 1979.

Otto Kernberg: *Internal World and External Reality: Object Relations Theory Applied*. Northvale, NJ: Jason Aronson, 1985.

Richard Kearney: 'Myth and critique of tradition', in *Reconciling Memories*, edited by A. Falconer. Dublin: Columba, 1988.

Russell Keat: *The Politics of Social Theory; Habermas, Freud and the Critique of Positivism*. Oxford: Blackwell, 1981.

Melanie Klein: 'Love, guilt and reparation', in *Love, Hate and Reparation* by M. Klein and J. Riviere. New York: Norton, 1964.

Melanie Klein: *The Writings of Melanie Klein*, 4 vols., edited by R.E. Money-Kyrle. New York: Free Press, 1964–75.

Laurence Kohlberg, Charles Levine, Alexandra Hewer: *Moral Stages: A Current formulation and a Response to Critics*. Basel/London: Karger, 1983.

Heinz Kohut: *The Analysis of the Self: A Systematic Approach to the Psychoanalytic Treatment of Narcissistic Personality Disorders*. New York: International UP, 1971.

Joel Kovel: *White Racism: A Psychohistory*. London: Free Association Books, edn 1988.

Hans Kung: *The Church*. Tonbridge: Burns & Oates, 1968.

Hans Kung: *Infallible? An Enquiry*. Translated by E. Mosbacher. London: Collins, 1971.

Hans Kung: *Does God Exist? An Answer for Today*. Translated by E. Quinn. London: Collins, 1980.

Paul Lakeland: *Theology and Critical Theory: The Discourse of the Church*. Nashville: Abingdon Press, 1990.

G.W.H. Lampe: *God as Spirit*. Oxford: Clarendon Press, 1977.

Christopher Lasch: *The Culture of Narcissism: American Life in an Age of Diminishing Expectations*. New York: Norton, 1979.

N. Lash: 'Conversation in Gethsemane', in *Radical Pluralism and Truth*. Edited by W.G. Jeanroud and Jennifer L. Rike. New York: Crossroad, 1991.

N. Lash. *A Matter of Hope*. London: Darton, Longman & Todd, 1981.

E. Thomas Lawson and Robert N. McCauley: *Rethinking Religion: Connecting Cognition and Culture*. Cambridge: CUP, 1990.

Michael Lerner: *Surplus Powerlessness: The Psychodynamics of Everyday Life and the Psychology of Individual and Social Transformation*. Oakland, Ca: Institute of Labour and Mental Health, 1986.

Walter Lowe: *Evil and the Unconscious*; American Academy of Religion; Studies in Religion 30. Chico, Ca.: Scholars Press, 1983.

Peter Loewenberg: *Decoding the Past: The Psychohistorical Approach*. Berkeley: UC Press, 1969.

E. Loftus: *Eyewitness Testimony*. Cambridge, Mass.: Harvard UP, 1979.

Vladimir Lossky: *In the Image and Likeness of God*. London: Mowbrays, 1974.

Ned Lukacher: *Primal Scenes: Literature, Philosophy, Psychoanalysi*. Ithaca: Cornell UP, 1986.

A.R. Luria: *The Neuropsychology of Memory*. Washington, DC: Winston, 1976.

Terence McCaughey: *Memory and Redemption: Church, Politics and Prophetic Theology in Ireland*. Dublin: Gill and Macmillan, 1993.

Alistair McFadyen: *The Call to Personhood: A Christian Theory of the Individual in Social Relationships*. Cambridge: CUP, 1990.

A. MacIntyre: *After Virtue: A Study in Moral Theory*. London: Duckworth, 1981.

John McIntyre: *St Anselm and his Critics: A Re-interpretation of the Cur Deus Homo*. Edinburgh and London: Oliver & Boyd, 1954.

John McIntyre: *The Shape of Soteriology. Studies in the Doctrine of the Death of Christ*. Edinburgh: T. & T. Clark, 1992.

A.J. McKenna: *Violence and Difference: Girard, Derrida and Deconstruction*. Urbana; Illinois UP, 1992.

Rollo May: *Love and Will*. London: Collins, 1970.

I. Menzies (Lyth): 'A case study in the functioning of social systems as a defence against anxiety: a report of a study of the nursing service of a general hospital', *Human Relations*, 13, 1960, pp. 95–121.

I. Menzies (Lyth): *Containing Anxieties in Institutions: Selected Essays*, Vol. 1. London: Free Association Books, 1988.

J.B. Metz: *Faith in History and Society: Towards a Practical Fundamental Theology*. Translated by D. Smith. London: Burns & Oates, 1980.

Jurgen Moltmann: *The Crucified God*. London: SCM, 1974.

R.E. Money-Kyrle: *Psycho-Analysis and Politics*. London: Duckworth, 1951.

John Moses: *The Sacrifice of God: A Hotislic Theory of Atonement*. Norwich: Canterbury Press, 1992.

R. Niebuhr: *Moral Man and Immoral Society*. New York: Scribner, 1932.

Albert Nolan: *God in South Africa: The Challenge of the Gospel*. London: CIIR, 1988.

Albert Nolan: *Jesus before Christianity: The Challenge of the Gospel*. Cape Town: David Philip, 1976.

Anton Obholzer and Vega Zagier Roberts (eds): *The Unconscious at Work*. London: Routledge, 1994.

W. Pannenberg: *Revelation as History*. London: Macmillan, 1968.

W. Pannenberg: *Jesus as God and Man*. London: SCM. 1968.

W. Pannenberg: *Theology and the Kingdom of God*. Edited by Richard Neuhaus. Louisville, Ky: Westminster Press, 1969.

W. Pannenberg: *Basic Questions in Theology*. Vol. 1. London: SCM. 1970.

W. Pannenberg: *Anthropology in Theological Perspective*, Edinburgh: T & T Clark, 1985.

Helmut Peukert: 'Fundamental theology and communicative praxis as the ethics of universal solidarity', in *The Influence of the Frankfurt School on Contemporary Theology, Critical Theory and the Future of Religion*. Edited by

A. James Reimer. Toronto Studies in Theology, Vol. 64. Lampeter: Edward Mellen, 1992.

Malcolm Pines (ed.): *Bion and Group Psychotherapy*, London: Routledge & Kegan Paul, 1985.

Theodore Platinga: *How Memory Shapes Narrative*. Lampeter: Mellen, 1992.

O.C. Quick: *The Gospel of the New World*. London: Nisbet, 1944.

Uta Ranke-Heinemann: *Eunuchs for Heaven: The Catholic Church and Sexuality*. London: Deutsch, 1990.

P. Ricouer: *The Conflict of Interpretation*. Edited by D. Ihde. Evanston: Northwestern UP, 1974.

David R. Roediger: *The Wages of Whiteness, Race and the Making of the American Working Class*. London: Verso, 1991.

C. Rowland: *Radical Christianity*. Cambridge: Polity Press, 1988.

Letty M. Russell: *Church in the Round: Feminist Interpretation of the Church*. Louisville, Westminster/John Knox, 1993.

M.J. Rustin: 'A socialist consideration of Kleinian psychoanalysis', *New Left Review,* 131, 1982, pp. 71–96.

M.J. Rustin: 'Post-Kleinian psychoanalysis and the post-modern', *Free Associations* 1, 1984.

M.J. Rustin: *The Good Society and the Inner World: Psychoanalysis, Politics and Culture*. London: Verso, 1992.

J. Sabini and M. Silver: *Moralities of Everyday Life*. Oxford: OUP, 1982.

Oliver Sacks: *The Man who Mistook His Wife for a Hat*. London: Pan/Picador edition, 1986.

A. Samuels: *Jung and the Post-Jungians*. London: Routledge, 1985.

E.P. Sanders: *The Historical Figure of Jesus*. London: Allen Lane, 1993.

Edward Schillebeeckx: *Church: The Human Story of God*. Translated by J. Bowden. London: SCM, 1990.

James Schmidt: 'Jurgen Habermas and the difficulties of enlightenment', *Social Research*, 49. 1, 1982, pp. 181–208.

Hanna Segal: *Melanie Klein*. Harmondsworth: Penguin, 1981.

R.J. Siebert: *The Critical Theory of Religion: the Frankfurt School from Universal Pragmatic to Political Theology*. Berlin: Mouton, 1985.

David Selbourne: *The Spirit of the Age*. London: Sinclair-Stevenson, 1993.

George Steiner: *Language and Silence*. New York: Athenaeum, 1970.

A. Stevens: *Archetype, A Natural History of the Self*. London: Routledge & Kegan Paul, 1982.

J. Storr: *Jung*. London: Fontana/Collins, 1973.

Grace Stuart: *Narcissus*. London: Allen and Unwin, 1956.

George Tavard: *The Church, Community of Salvation: An Ecumenical Ecclesiology*. Minnesota: Michael Glazier, 1992.

Ronald F. Thiemann: *Revelation and Theology: The Gospel as Narrated Promise*. Notre Dame: U of Notre Dame Press, 1985.

Niels Thomassen: *Communicative ethics in Theory and Practice*. Translated by John Irons. London: Macmillan, 1992.

J-M.R. Tillard: *Church of Churches: The Ecclesiology of Communion*. Minnesota: Michael Glazier, 1992.

Thomas F. Torrance: *The Mediation of Christ*. Edinburgh: T. & T. Clark, 1992.

Frank E. Tupper: *The Theology of Wolfhart Pannenberg*. London: SCM, 1974.

Victor de Waal: *The Politics of Reconciliation*. London: Hurst, 1990.

F. Watson (ed.): *The Open Text*. London: SCM, 1993.

Frazer Watts and Mark Williams: *The Psychology of Religious Knowing*. Cambridge: CUP, 1988.

R.E. Weingart: *The Logic of Divine Love: A Critical Analysis of the Soteriology of Peter Abailard*. Oxford: Clarendon Press, 1970.

J.S. Whale: *Victor and Victim: The Christian Doctrine of Redemption*. Cambridge: Cambridge UP, 1960.

Gavin White: *The Church Your Mother Never Told You Of*. London: SCM, 1993.

Walter Wink: *Confronting the Powers*. Minneapolis: Fortress, 1991.

Donald W. Winniccott: *Holding and Interpretation*. New York: Grove, 1986.

Donald W. Winniccott: *Playing and Reality*. Harmondsworth: Penguin, 1974.

Ludwig Wittgenstein: *Philosophical Investigations*. E.T. by G.E.M. Anscombe. Oxford: Blackwell, 1945–9/1958.

John Howard Yoder: *The Priestly Kingdom: Social Ethics as Gospel*. Notre Dame: U of Notre Dame Press, 1984.

Frances Young: *Sacrifice and the Death of Christ*. London: SCM, 1975.

Index of Names

Index of Key Words